Shepherding
OUTDOORS

– VOLUME 2 –

MORE SHORT STORIES
from a
SOUTHERN FATHER

by WALT MERRELL

83 Press
2323 2nd Avenue North
Birmingham, AL 35203
83press.com

ISBN: 978-0-9835984-3-5
Printed in U.S.A.

for my daughters,
BAY, CAPE, AND BANKS

During the pandemic quarantine of 2020, our family struggled to find balance. We struggled to balance our faith that God was truly sovereign with our desire to respect our neighbors and remain isolated. We did not want to disregard what doctors were suggesting, but we knew that God was still on the throne. We remained quarantined for several weeks, but at some point, the entire family yearned for something more. As it turned out, that something more was a remote stretch of mangrove forests and brackish water known as Florida's Nature Coast. A few days in the remote backcountry of the Crystal River and Homosassa River watershed did our family good. From swimming with manatees to airboat rides and beautiful sunsets, escaping to God's natural tapestry was not only good for rest and relaxation, but also good for us to simply break up the monotony of the quarantine.

FOREWORD

The worker bee.

I did not know Walt when he was a little boy, but my goodness, I've seen pictures! His light blond hair and long, lanky body that many little boys often have seem to take center stage in all the pictures from his youth.

The first time I laid eyes on Walt was when our daughter, Hannah, decided to bring him home from college to meet my last husband George and me. That, my friends, was more than 25 long years ago. He seemed like just a boy then—you know, the "young and in love" type. My first impression of him was impressive. He displayed good manners ("yes, ma'am" and "no, ma'am", "thank you" and "please"). Immediately, we knew he wasn't one of the run-of-the-mill boys. He had long, wavy brown hair, and he often wore it in a ponytail. Truth was, most girls his age would've given their life to have his hair! He wore "Jesus" sandals, and somehow, they fit with his hair and his personality perfectly. I'll never forget seeing him for the first time as he walked with Hannah through that lush green Alabama grass in our yard on that first visit.

Those days are long gone now, but they are not forgotten. The boy that once stood in my kitchen now sits at our supper table—a full-grown man with a beautiful family of his very own. The hair—well, it's salt-and-pepper-colored now. He doesn't have a ponytail, but he does keep a little length on it still because he knows that's how Hannah likes it.

Walt wasn't brought up around lots of girls, but honey, he has a full share of them now—Bay, Cape, Banks, Hannah, and me! No wonder he runs to get on his big red tractor every chance he gets. Seems like I can hear that big diesel engine coming through the woods right now!

There is a special, wonderful side of Walt that gives him his life's special drive. It's Jesus! Walt is a true people helper. That is his gift! He is a worker bee when it comes down to helping people. His virtues are being kind and helping people in need. Not only does he help with their physical needs, but he is always ready to help with spiritual advice, wayward children, marriage problems, financial burdens, sickness, and whatever else might be weighing heavy in the lives of others. He does these things by being an intensively good listener, and then, he's ready to do what seems impossible to help every person he knows who is in need.

I remember one time I stepped outside of my door and saw Walt climbing up in the bed of my old truck. He had pulled my very full garbage hobo next to the truck. Before I knew it, he was jumping up and down in my garbage hobo trying to pack it down as tight as possible. You see, he was trying to make room for the rest of my trash that was piled up in the bed of my truck. Now, how many sons-in-law would do that? Mine did!

Walt wears many hats—Jesus follower, husband, daddy, deacon, district attorney, child advocate, addiction counselor, tractor lover, chocolate eater, backyard mechanic, project planner, hunter, fisherman, woodsman, camper, kayaker, and son-in-law, just to name a few. But the most important hat he wears is the "helper hat."

As I think of Walt's life here in Andalusia, Alabama, I can easily see how he is growing stronger into the man he is today. He is just like the rest of us—in need of love, a tight hug, a strong handshake, true friendship, life purpose, and goals for the future. He constantly works on all these needs. The worker bee in him continues to grow stronger in his faith as well. He learns from his mistakes, listens to wise advice, leans on Jesus, studies scripture, and for sure, honors being married to a good woman, our Hannah.

They have both grown together as one through their years of marriage. Every trial and hardship that has come their way, they have conquered together. He leans on her, and she leans on him, and both of them lean on Jesus while climbing the steep mountain of life.

Ecclesiastes 4:12, NLT
"A person standing alone can be attacked and defeated, but two can stand back-to-back and conquer. Three are even better, for a triple braided cord is not easily broken."

I have seen Walt live by this. His strong cord is wound tightly together with Jesus, Hannah, and himself. I believe Walt will continue to grow and be a real helper to others. Why? Because I see his love for family continue to grow every day. His hugs get tighter to me and to others that are in need. His handshake is strong and real. Folks can count on him as a friend that will stick close, and most of all, this worker bee wants to work toward God's purpose and plan for his life.

I couldn't ask for a better "Walt." He is always ready to put down what he is doing to help me in my situation, and I'm always ready to offer him some hot biscuits and gravy. Truly, life is good.

I love you, Walt Merrell.

—BRENDA GANTT "BIG MAMA"—

To my left . . . our firstborn Bay, our middle princess Cape, my soulmate Hannah, our tiny dancer Banks, and our favorite biscuit maker, Brenda.

C O N T E N T S

Chapter
ONE

STILL IN THE EARLY YEARS

— T H E   T H I N G S   W E   D O —

Part One

Hannah and I lived in Centreville, Alabama, for a couple of years after we were married. I was still in law school, and she worked full-time at the Hale Empowerment and Revitalization Organization (HERO) Family Resource Center. She was a social worker by profession. After graduation from law school—several of my friends graduated summa cum laude while I merely graduated—we had a difficult choice to make.

Longtime Selma, Alabama, District Attorney Ed Greene offered me a job manning the Centreville office. There was some allure to the thought of staying in Bibb County, which we had fallen in love with.

"It will be yours to run, son," Mr. Greene offered. "I'll even give you a state car to drive."

"That's very generous of you, sir, but might I ask a few more questions?" I asked. "Who will handle the rape cases?"

"That would be you, son," he replied.

"The burglary cases and robbery cases?" I continued.

Again, he responded, "That will be you."

"The murder cases?" I asked, my voice cracking and quivering slightly.

He chuckled . . . "You, son. But don't worry. You'll do just fine."

I had also been offered a job by a prominent plaintiff's lawyer in Daphne, Alabama. He was a gentleman and full of Southern charm, and he made me a fair offer to say the least. He was a great lawyer, and learning from him would, no doubt, be a blessing. There was also the allure of being close to my family . . . all of them living in Mobile and Baldwin Counties. The same was true for the Andalusia, Alabama, firm that had also offered me a job. Managing senior partner Ab Powell was a lawyer's lawyer. A trial lawyer through and through . . . he had tried cases—and won—against the best of them. He, too, would be a great legal mentor, and, if I accepted this job, we would be close to Hannah's parents, George and Brenda, and the whole Gantt family.

Then, there was the status quo . . . I was clerking for Justice Janie Shores on the Alabama Supreme Court. She was the first woman elected to the state's highest court, and she was a brilliant and practical jurist. It had been such an honor to clerk for her, and I could stay on, should I so choose . . . but . . . I also felt the need to spread my wings a little and move on to the next stage of my career.

There was also the Coast Guard. I had applied to the U.S. Coast Guard's Judge Advocate General Corps. Serving as a JAG officer—lawyers for the military branches—was something I had always dreamed of doing. Twice denied admission into the Navy because I had surgery to correct my acid reflux, I sought out the Coast Guard hoping to find a more willing—and lenient—health screening.

Interestingly, the Coast Guard granted me a waiver for my reflux surgery and then denied my admission based on poor hearing in my right ear. Too many rock concerts, I suspected. A friend in the Coast Guard said he "knew a guy." I wondered to myself, "Who 'knows a guy' who can fix hearing problems?" But sure enough, he did. I don't remember the doctor's name now (and wouldn't offer it even if I did for fear he might suffer some reprisal), but my friend introduced us. He was an ear, nose, and throat doctor. He examined me on the seat of a golf cart at our first meeting . . . onlookers staring . . . I felt as if I was involved in some secret medical conspiracy as he quietly said, "Come see me at my office at 5 p.m. on Tuesday afternoon," and ushered me away. Surely, I was supposed to swear a blood oath of secrecy or something.

Tuesday came, and I found myself being led into an examination room where I sat in a chair that obviously had been stolen off the bridge of the Federation starship, USS *Enterprise* on *Star Trek*. Captain Kirk must be mighty upset that the good doctor stole his chair. Lights above me radiated bright heat which was a bit relaxing. I squinted my eyes to dim the glare, such that I struggled to see who the three figures were coming into the room. The chair molded my body into a relaxed and reclined position. "Don't fall asleep," I commanded myself. I had been up too late the night before . . . studying.

"How are we going to handle this, Mr. Merrell?" I recognized the doctor's voice.

"I don't know, Doc. What needs to be done?" I asked. Then, he went on to explain how my ear canal on the right side was closed, and I needed a tube put into my right ear. He suggested it was not from rock concerts, but instead was an anomaly that had likely been there my entire life. He added that he thought the things I would be able to "hear" after the procedure—things I may not have ever heard before—would be remarkable. No doubt, this procedure should improve my hearing dramatically. He also explained that the procedure needed to be done under anesthesia in an operating room. "I can't do that, Doc. I don't have any health insurance," I responded.

"And therein lies the problem," he said, and went on to explain how his dad was in the Navy, and so was he, in a former life. He explained that he always wanted to do whatever he could to help young men and women find their way into the military. "Not only did I feel [joining the military] was my duty as a good American, but it was my heart's desire to serve," he noted.

Now, I knew why I liked this guy . . . he got it . . . he understood why I wanted to serve. "Doc, let me pay you in cash, and we can do the surgery here . . . right now,"

I offered. He almost scoffed at the notion. "Can't you apply for Medicaid? Or, what about your parents' insurance?" he asked. I told him I didn't have time—my hearing retest was in a few days. "It will be excruciatingly painful to do it without general anesthesia," he warned. "And I'm not sure it isn't malpractice to not do the procedure at the hospital."

"But Doc . . ." I persisted. Fifteen minutes later, I had convinced him. He truly was my only hope. "Tell you what . . . you draw up a "Release from Liability" document and sign it, and I'll do it," he offered. It didn't take me long to draft the document to his satisfaction. He knew I wasn't going to sue him, and he knew I'd never tell a soul who he was or the favor he did for me.

He told the two nurses in the room what he needed. I heard him say something about some "topical" something or another, "syringes, gauze," . . . and all sorts of medical jargon that sounded like gibberish to me. I wasn't really listening. I was daydreaming about what was to be—Lt. Commander Merrell, U.S. Coast Guard.

A few minutes passed, and everyone returned to the room with their hands full of necessities and masks over their faces. The good doctor nodded to one of the nurses, and she walked around behind my captain's chair. She was standing directly behind me . . . over the top of me almost.

I remember how calming her eyes were.

Doc sat down on a stool to my right and wheeled up close. He articulated the overhead light such that I could feel the heat on the right side of my face as he pushed my nose and chin away from him ever so slightly. The heat was soothing . . .

The nurse sat behind me with both of her hands on my shoulders. I joked about a shoulder rub, and everyone chuckled a bit. Perhaps, we were all nervous. I knew I was, and her hands on my shoulders comforted me as the nervous anticipation coursed through my veins at a fever pitch. She leaned back ever so slightly, and I could no longer see her eyes. I could only see the Doc and the other nurse in my peripheral vision. Doc leaned in close . . .

"I'm going to apply some topical anesthetic to the exterior of your eardrum. It's going to burn a little, but it will help numb your eardrum up some before I inject the shots." I didn't respond. I could tell he wasn't waiting for me to give him the green light. Out of the corner of my eye, I saw his right hand holding something, the likes of which I could not identify. He nodded to the sweet-eyed nurse behind me. She placed her right arm below my right ear and firmly clasped my chin. She then positioned her left forearm flat across my forehead and pressed down with what surely was all her body weight . . . all of a sudden, she seemed to develop "man hands."

The vice of her hands and arms was inescapable . . . she was as strong as an ox . . . her fingers dug into my jawline, and her forearm pressed my eyebrows down over my eyes such that I struggled to see at all. My legs twisted and arched like a turtle lying on its back. The other nurse grabbed my right wrist, leaving only my left hand to aimlessly paw at Nurse Man Hands' Popeye-like forearms . . . I was pretty sure I could see an anchor tattoo. I was helpless . . . she had me pinned. I was so taken aback by it all that I never put two and two together. I did not understand why she was being so aggressive . . .

Then, the good doctor poured what surely had to be molten lava into my right ear. "Holy craaaappppp!" I yelped through the grit of my teeth. Now, the nurse wanted to talk . . . "Just relax. It's only going to burn for a few seconds," she said as she clutched even firmer against my chin and forehead. My eyes started to water as they bulged from their sockets. I felt heat come over my entire face. Sweat beaded up on my forehead. Inside my ear, I could hear popping and gurgling as the intensity of the burn slowly subsided. Nurse Man Hands released me from the headlock, and Doc said, "I knew it was going to be rough. Usually, we don't do that because our patients are already asleep. That was a topical . . . now, I have to inject you with another deadener, but that topical should numb the pain for the shots." Somehow, none of that comforted me . . .

I was tired, and my ear still sounded as if it had boiling water inside of it. Snap, crackle, pop! I had become a living Rice Krispies experiment. Nurse Man Hands was to my left, and her eyes had shifted from sweet and almost seductive to now sinister and angry. She flexed both of her hands, as if she had cramps, massaging one with the other, working each finger . . . it was as if she took joy in contemplating the pain she was about to exact upon me.

Doc and the other nurse readied a syringe. He drew the plunger back, sucking a precise amount of Liquid Hell back into the vial of the syringe. After pulling the needle out of the glass container, he pushed the plunger forward ever so slightly, until the smallest droplets of Liquid Hell sprayed forth. "Alright. Here we go . . ." he said. Nurse Man Hands was on me like Hulk Hogan or "Macho Man" Randy Savage. I could hear her breathing in my ear as she squeezed all the blood from my head, and then I saw Doc drawing closer with the syringe. I closed my eyes and prayed, "Father, I cannot do this of my own strength. I lean on Jesus to help me carry this cross. Amen."

In that moment, as if Charlie Daniels himself hid behind the doctor's mask, "*fire blew from his fingertips*" as he plunged the needle deep into my eardrum. My eyes rolled back into my head, and I could feel myself, if only for a moment, on the verge of passing out. I've had broken bones, a busted chin, concussions, injuries from car wrecks and motorcycle crashes . . . you name it, I've probably experienced it, but nothing could prepare me for the intensity of having a needle loaded with boiling hot molten lava pierced into my eardrum. Tears rolled down from the corner of my left eye, and the pain was so intense, all I could do was groan. Nurse Man Hands made sure I didn't move my head even slightly, and, despite my deepest desire to come out of that chair, she pinned me such that a crane could not have lifted my head. Budge an inch, I did not.

I was exhausted . . . every muscle in my body had just flexed with every ounce of tension it could muster. I breathed deep, trying to replenish whatever oxygen had just been exhausted. The Doc was talking, but I had no idea what he was saying. It might as well have been Charlie Brown's teacher. I was almost delirious as the pain slowly diminished, and as it did, Nurse Man Hands relaxed her choke hold.

"The things we do . . ." was all I could mutter.

"Thank you, Jesus, that is over," was all I could think.

Part Two

My face was flushed. Tears puddled in the corner of my right eye, captured by gravity and the confines of the dam my nose and cheek made at that angle. I wiped the tears, and, through the blur of my vision, I'm pretty sure I saw Nurse Man Hands grinning.

"I swear, I think she is enjoying this," I said to myself. I worked my chin in a circular motion, rubbing my forehead at the same time. "Hilga has pretty strong hands, doesn't she?" the Doc asked. "Hilga?" I considered silently. "Who hires a nurse named Hilga? I'm pretty sure that is German for 'circus performer.'"

"Ummm, yeah. I guess so. I mean, for a girl," I said reluctantly. No way Hilga was going to get any shred of satisfaction from the hurt she had just put on me. And besides, the entire right side of my head was numb, so I was quite sure the headlocks were behind me. Hilga glared at me after the "for a girl" comment. If the Doc left the room, I was sure she would turn me into a human pretzel. The Doc chuckled, and I prayed he wouldn't leave the room.

"Okay, let's get this done before the numbing agent wears off," the Doc suggested.

"No argument from me," I replied.

He maneuvered my head back into its previous position, less Hilga Man Hands. She stood in the corner and watched . . . much like a buzzard waiting for the coyote to leave the carcass. Doc cautioned me, "In the next few minutes, you absolutely cannot move. No matter what. Don't move."

"What if it hurts?" I asked.

"You won't feel a thing," he assured me. "You will hear plenty. But you won't feel a thing."

A moment later, I could hear the Doc fumbling around in my ear. I couldn't feel his fingers, but I could hear them. The sound reminded me of something encased in a barrel full of water and thumping its way around inside. It was, at first, a dull, bass drum type of sound. Bum-bum, dome-doom, dut-brub. Then, the pitch changed altogether, and I heard him squeeze a rag empty of its water inside my ear . . . squeeezzzzeeee. I was tempted to recoil. The noises were unnerving—a "snitch" here and a "snip" there. Next came the friction of sandpaper grinding upon itself, followed by what could only be described as the sound cotton balls must make when drug over the stubble of an unshaven chin.

The noises echoed in my head, much like how the world sounds just before your ears pop when taking off or landing in an airplane. The echo intensified the sound and made everything in the room seem smaller. These noises were so big; I knew the tube he was inserting surely must be the size of a drainpipe. But, through it all, I never felt a thing. After a few minutes, it was done, and Doc stripped his latex gloves off, throwing a hook shot into the trash can on the other side of the room. He missed.

"I want you to sit here for a few minutes so I can monitor you as the Novocain wears off," the Doc directed. "If everything checks out, you'll be good to go." Twenty minutes later, the nurse was helping me up and steadying me as I stood for the first time in an hour or so. With her arm at the small of my back, she asked, "Can you tell a difference in your hearing?"

"I don't think so," I responded, the concern notable in my voice.

"Don't worry," she offered. "Usually, it's pitches that you will hear for the first time. Give it time." She smiled as she held my arm, walking me to the door. Hilga Man Hands was nowhere to be seen. I was beginning to understand the "good cop/bad cop" thing the nurses had going.

The Doc met me in the hall . . . his voice boomed. "It must be the tile floors," I reasoned.

"You're going to hear things you have not heard in a very long time — mostly different pitches," Doc said. "You'll hear the same voices you've always heard — they just might sound different. You'll hear new sounds, too, but mostly you'll just hear more than you remember ever hearing." Grateful, I paid the man what we agreed on: $50.

Doc lost money on me that day, but he was a man of principle and faith. He told me earlier in the day that he knew he was blessed, and he tried to pass the blessing along whenever he had the chance. That's what he did for me, too . . . and I, too, have been blessed . . . and learned from him to try to do the same thing as often as I can. Ever since, I've always tried to help folks when I could, and I am still waiting for the chance to put tubes in someone's ears! Guess the good Lord doesn't have that in the plans . . .

I walked out the front door of the doctor's office, and the world was abuzz. Birds! I could hear the birds like never before! Finches fluttered in the grass to the right of the front door, and when I came out, they all lifted in unison, and I heard the flutter of their wings before I saw them. Red birds tweeted back and forth across the parking lot, and a rather irate mockingbird yelled at me from atop a nearby tree.

I stood in the middle of the parking lot, the world spinning around me . . . it was almost too much to comprehend. Sure, I had heard birds before, but never like this. I was speechless . . . overwhelmed with appreciation for the gift that Doc just gave me. This time, a true tear did roll down my cheek. I was overcome with the beauty of it all. I never realized how beautiful the birds were until that moment . . . when I could hear how beautiful they sounded.

"It's a beautiful thing, isn't it?"

Surprised, I turned to identify the familiar voice behind me. Hilga stood a few feet from me, smiling from ear to ear. For the second time in our relationship, I wiped a tear away from my face so she would not think me weak. She grinned and told me it was okay to be emotional. "I was, too," she offered. Hilga then told me she had been nearly deaf as a child in a mountaintop village in Sweden. Her parents sent her to the U.S. when she was a middle-school-aged child to live with relatives, and, with the hope that she would find suitable treatment to correct her hearing deficiencies.

A young doctor fresh out of medical school did the surgery. "He gave me the greatest gift anyone has ever given me, other than the good Lord," Hilga said with a crack in her voice. "And I've been with him ever since." Hilga beamed with love, admiration, appreciation, and gratitude as she spent a few minutes telling me how she found her calling and how the Doc had changed her life. Nearly in tears once again, I knew the Lord was working all around me. I gave Hilga a hug and retreated to my car.

"Father, thank you, for the Doc and for Hilga . . . and for restoring sound into my life," I sobbed. "I don't know what Your plan is for me, but I know You can do great things through Your servants. I pray I am always humble enough and grateful enough for You to use me how You see fit." Imagining Jesus on the cross in that moment was overwhelming for me. "Most of all, Lord, thank You for Your Son and His sacrifice. Amen."

I drove home that afternoon oblivious to my career path, but intently focused on my life path. More than one thing changed for me that day . . . truly, the Lord does work in mysterious ways. I couldn't wait to tell Hannah of the day's events. I wanted her to feel the gratitude I felt, and I knew she would.

Three days later, I passed my Coast Guard hearing test with flying colors. "Mission accomplished!" I celebrated. I passed the first hurdle—something I was never able to accomplish with the Navy. Now on to the next . . . the interviews.

The Coast Guard told me they would hire 16 JAG officers that year. Most would be stationed in New Orleans and somewhere on the West Coast. New Orleans was so close to home. "Surely, this is a God thing," Hannah and I speculated. They narrowed the field to a list of candidates to be interviewed, and I made the cut. We drove to New Orleans for the interviews. Hannah was nervous the entire time. She had never been to the Big Easy. Growing up only a few hours away, I had been often, and while I wasn't entirely comfortable there either, I wasn't intimidated.

Growing up on and around Gulf Coast tugboats, I was quite comfortable with the Cajun culture of the waterworkers . . . their hard lines and leathered faces were usually just a façade, hiding a joy-filled spirit unlike most other cultures I had encountered. My Cajun friends always had a smile and always knew what they were going to eat for their next spicy, crustacean-filled meal, and they always, always, always had a song in their hearts. We should all be so lucky . . .

I interviewed with the Coast Guard three times over two days. Hannah wandered around New Orleans' more touristy locations to occupy her time. I never told any of the men or women who interviewed me about the Doc or Hilga or about what all I had gone through to get to this point, for I feared that my hearing issue might still be prohibitive, so I avoided ever mentioning it.

Perhaps I should have told them of my struggle and determination . . . perhaps it would have made the difference . . . perhaps . . . but it did not. I was number 17 of 32 after the interviews.

"Remember your prayer," Hannah reminded me. "You asked God to help you to be humble enough that He could use you however He wanted. He answered your prayer, just not in the way you wanted." Her words still resonate with me today.

Part Three

"Number 17 out of 32," I thought to myself. Tempted to adopt a posture of pity for being the first runner-up to the Coast Guard's selection process, I opted to keep busy instead. "Self-pity won't find you a job. This just wasn't meant to be," I told myself.

It was hard to argue with the latter. I had twice tried to enlist in the Navy as a route to the JAG Corps. Both times, I was turned away because I had reflux surgery when I was younger. Now, after an intense, in-office ear surgery and what was sure to be God opening doors through the Coast Guard, I didn't survive the interviews and was once again denied. Surely, God must open doors that create the illusion of our heart's desire just so He can close them again to help us focus on what we need instead of what we want? And so . . . I did. Or at least, I tried. Admittedly, I was frustrated. I wanted what I wanted and wasn't really sure why God didn't "make" that happen. After all, He is here to serve us, right? Oh, wait . . .

Hannah and I labored over the choice of homesteads.

The plaintiff's lawyer near my hometown was still very much interested. And it felt good to be recruited after the dejection I felt after the Coast Guard interviews. The pay was meager, but there was ample room to advance and grow. I'd be near my family, and that was a plus. But housing was an issue . . . a two-bedroom house would cost somewhere around $200,000 . . . did I mention the pay was meager?

Ed Greene was still interested in my taking over the Bibb County District Attorney's office. The pay was less than meager, though . . .

"I can pay you $19,000 a year plus that car I told you I'd get for you," he said.

"Mr. Greene, begging your pardon, sir, but my student loans are $800 per month, and what you're offering to pay me is barely enough to make that note," I responded.

"I know it will be tough, son," he offered. "But I'll get you a raise when I can. And don't overlook the value of the experience. None of your classmates will be trying murder cases their first year out of law school." When he said that, I felt a shiver run down my spine. I wanted that experience, and I wanted to be a trial lawyer, but trying murder cases on my own, my first year out of law school?

There is a reason why the biggest climb on the roller coaster is always first. You know the one—where the chain and gears "clack-clack-clack" all the way to the top. You check your pockets as you near the peak to make sure nothing slid out and into the seat. By the time you're to the top, your neck hurts ever so slightly because you've been craning it forward to offset the incline of your seat. Gravity pushes you back against the seat, and you strain to lean forward out of instinct. As you hear the last "clack" of the gears pulling the coaster up the slope, you lose sight of the rails in front of you—because they dive off into an unknown oblivion—and your heart sinks in mystery and fear right before your stomach does.

That sinking feeling in your heart . . . the one brought on by the mysteries of the unknown . . . how bad the slope is on the other side of the peak. That is the feeling I had when Mr. Greene told me I would man the Bibb County office alone . . . that sinking feeling in your stomach . . . the one where the coaster finally summits the climb and dives off the other side into a vat of terror that no sane person ever ought to subject themselves to . . . twisting right and darting left on the way down, accelerating well beyond what must be safe for such a contraption. The wind pulls at your hair and blows your mouth open. You look like a wide-eyed guppy coming down the side of a mountain. Yes, you know that sinking feeling in your stomach? Well, that's the feeling I had when he told me I'd be trying murder cases all by myself, as a lawyer fresh out of law school.

I loathe roller coasters. I'm nauseous right now . . .

Hannah and I both wanted to be "home." We were not sure Centreville was it, and though we loved it, we didn't have family there. So, staying on and continuing to clerk for the Alabama Supreme Court did not intimidate me nearly as much as working for the District Attorney in Bibb County, but it offered no more semblance of "home" than Bibb County did, either. "Home" is a funny thing, especially for Hannah and me. George and Brenda Gantt had two children, Dallas and Hannah. The Gantts lived in a modest, one-story ranch-style home throughout the entirety of Hannah's life. In fact, Brenda still lives in that same house today. They ate breakfast and dinner together every time circumstances allowed. Brenda cooked every meal, and George and Dallas shared a special father-son bond. They had the typical American family, and the life they lived was what most would call "The American Dream." That was her "home."

My parents divorced when I was in the third grade. It was not an easy time in my life, and curiously, it never really got any easier. Why, once, in a speech at my undergraduate graduation ceremony, I opined that even though "they" said Generation X didn't know sacrifice because we had never fought for our country, that "they" were wrong, because "we" survived the divorce wars of the 1980s. I had two brothers—both half-brothers—who were considerably older than me. There are 12 years separating my brother, Kenny, and me. My oldest brother, Trey, is 14 years older than me. For all intents and purposes, I was an only child, as they had moved out of a tumultuous household long before they ever graduated from high school. My mother raised me. She was, and still is, a strong and driven woman. Maternity is not her strong point, though I credit her with most all the drive and determination that I exhibit. She molded me for the better.

The definition of "home" meant two different things for Hannah and me. I wanted a place to live and things to do. Hannah wanted a house within which our "home" would exist. If y'all don't already know it . . . I am one lucky man.

Even though we had several discussions and prayed often about making the right decision, I knew all along what it would be. Like *The Beverly Hillbillies*, "Andalusia is the place you ought to be." Ab Powell was a brilliant trial lawyer, so the experience would be invaluable. The pay was similar to what the plaintiff's lawyer in Baldwin County had offered. Housing was reasonably priced. The schools were very good. Best of all, though, it seemed we would definitely find our "home" there.

It was settled, then . . . our "home" would be in Covington County, Alabama. I shared my sentiments with Hannah one Tuesday evening. Her beautiful Southern smile drew like an upside-down rainbow across her face—her teeth as white as snow—and a tear dripped out of the corner of her eye. I grabbed her close and held her tight. She wrapped her arms around me and squeezed at my rib cage. "Why didn't you tell me it would mean that much to you to go home?" I asked.

"I wanted you to go where God led you," she answered. I was at peace, and she was ecstatic.

A few minutes later, I phoned The Powell Law Firm and joyfully accepted their offer. We discussed a few details and hung up. Hannah and I hugged again after the conversation was over. I think it made it "official" to her, and it was a relief to me. I was excited to have a plan and a sense of direction. Next, she called her parents. Brenda's octave rose significantly in celebration of the news. She had dreaded the idea of us moving to New Orleans for a Coast Guard tour, so for Brenda, it was an answered prayer. Hannah and Brenda talked about neighborhoods and living arrangements and such and then melted into the "homey" conversations they have had all their lives. Listening to them talk about what the preacher preached on and about Uncle Pickens and Aunt Evelynn . . . listening to them talk with such love and joy about life—for the first time—gave me a glimpse of what "home" would look like in Andalusia. I was excited, too.

The next day, Wednesday, was business as usual. I attended class that morning, clerked for the court that afternoon, and went and worked at my second job as a farmhand that evening. I got home after dark. Hannah had been at work all day, too, and she had a couple of hamburger steaks sizzling in the pan. The meaty aroma filled the house. Rice and English peas simmered on the stove. She always greeted me when

I came in the door. She still does to this day . . . her greeting, her hug, her embrace are part of what makes our house a welcoming "home."

We hugged and kissed, and just as she pulled away to flip the hamburger steaks, the phone rang. It was an old, yellow push-button wall phone. It hung next to the doorway between the kitchen and the dining room. The cord was long enough to wrap around the house at least twice, and it was always balled up in a knot which drove me nuts. "Hello?" I answered.

"Mr. Merrell?" a voice asked.

"Yes, sir, this is he," I replied.

"This is Commander ___ of the United States Coast Guard. I'm calling to tell you that one of the other candidates has said that he no longer wishes to be a JAG officer in the United States Coast Guard. You're next on the list, young man. Welcome aboard!"

Hannah stirred the peas and tended to the rice. In that moment, she was one of the most beautiful creatures I had ever laid my eyes on. She had no idea what had just been offered.

For a moment, I was on a roller coaster . . . and, while my stomach did sink, my heart did not.

"Well, sir, I very much appreciate that, but I must decline. I know where my home is," I said.

The things we do for the people we love . . .

And with that, I never looked back. God is good in every circumstance. Trust Him. He has it all figured out for our benefit. And most times, what we want is rarely what we need. He knew exactly what our family needed in that season, and He led us down that precise path.

BAY WAS A CHUNKY BABY

Bay was a chunky baby . . . it wasn't her fault, though. We were new to parenting, and we fell headfirst into calamity over common sense.

A few weeks after Bay was born, the doctor suggested to us that she was underweight. He advised that we needed to wake her up every four hours and feed her, 24 hours a day. Every four hours . . . 24 hours a day. So, we did, for a couple of months, until exhaustion and common sense set it.

No doubt, it was grueling for Hannah because she was breastfeeding. The alarm would go off like the Grim Reaper announcing his presence, but without fail, Hannah would slip out from underneath the covers into the darkness of the room. I would hear the thumpity-thump of her feet walking out of the bedroom . . . the pine-planked floor betraying her presence. Sometimes, I would wake with her with no plan other than to try and comfort her. Other times, I would not wake. And sometimes, I would get up and try to get Bay up in advance or do other things to show sympathy and support for Hannah, but the fact of the matter was, she lost a couple of months' worth of sleep during that time.

There was little I could do to ease her burden.

Bay didn't necessarily want to eat all those times either. Not unlike Hannah or myself, what Bay preferred to do was sleep most of the night. Ironic, wasn't it? We had a baby who would sleep from 8:30 p.m. or so every night until dawn the next morning. What a blessing that was, but we had to wake her every four hours. Sometimes, she would wake up happy and eager to eat . . . it seemed to me that the longer our saga wore on, the more we trained her to eat when we woke her, and it was almost as if she came to understand that, "We are waking you up, and now, you should eat." But, sometimes, she was cranky, had no interest in eating, and all she wanted to do was be left alone.

So, as a special sort of torment, we'd put cold rags on her belly to wake her up back up if she fell sleep. On colder nights (we lived in an old house that didn't hold heat well) we'd put our cold hands on her cheeks. Other times, we found that tickling her ears worked well. We pulled her toes and poked her belly, too. We discovered and employed all sorts of tricks to get her to wake up and stay awake. The CIA should read some of our notes if they want to learn a few tricks for tormenting prisoners of war. Lord knows, we tormented poor Bay.

But, per the doctor's orders, we made certain that she kept eating. Poor child just wanted to sleep, and we were force-feeding her . . . baby waterboarding, if you will. Let's hope that Child Protective Services doesn't use this body of work as evidence against us. What might be worse, though, would be if Bay re-reads this story while she contemplates whether to put Hannah or me in a nursing home.

Nonetheless, and slowly but surely, Bay blossomed from a slightly underweight baby to a portly little chunk. She was cute as a button, and her appearance only complemented her very pleasant personality. She smiled a lot and laughed and wanted to touch and snuggle and coo. She was sweet back then, but that was long before she became a teenager.

After she gained a little weight and a few little fat rolls, Hannah kept feeding her on demand, but we relaxed the grueling schedule that deprived everyone of sleep. Thankful for a healthy baby and content that the grueling demands of the all-night buffet were unnecessary, the doctor gave us a reprieve. "But if she starts losing weight, you'll have to get back on the schedule," he admonished. We both nodded our heads with understanding.

A month passed, and all was well. Bay, portlier than ever, ate like a champ. So well-trained was she that no longer would she sleep all night long. Instead, we had conditioned her to wake up several times a night with an expectation that the all-night diner was "OPEN." Still, I was supportive of Hannah, but I clearly could only offer moral support. Much to her chagrin, Hannah found little reprieve from the sleepless nights. Bay had become an eating machine.

And then it started . . .

"Come here," Hannah said with an expression of exasperation and befuddlement. As I walked toward her, she asked me, "Do you smell anything funny?" I paused, trying to recollect if I had been the cause of any odoriferous illuminations in the past few minutes. Content, though, that I had not expelled anything that might cause alarm or offense, I simply shrugged my shoulders and said, "Nope." She looked at me disapprovingly, as if she had gleaned what my hesitation was for, and then turned away with a look of frustration and disapproval on her face. "What?" I asked in self-defense. She looked over her shoulder and glared at me. I sensed that this time, discretion would be wisest, so I just smiled and told her, "I love you." She snorted like a sow grizzly mama with cubs and stomped off.

A few hours later, though, she posed the same question to me. "Do you smell anything funny?" I paused mid-step as my head pivoted in an almost owl-like manner, from right shoulder to left, and then back again. I felt like a deer that had just emerged from the wood line, standing at the edge of a green field, trying to ascertain whether a trap lay somewhere in the midst of all of the lush green grass. Much like the

"God made dirt. Dirt don't hurt. Put it in your mouth, and let it work!"

As a kid, I bet us boys exchanged that saying a thousand times as we rough and tumbled through our childhood. So, when Bay came along, Hannah and I knew that as parents, we wanted our children outside and not in front of a television. From the earliest of ages, the girls were helping plant flowers and doing plenty of other things in God's dirt!

Few things are more soothing to the stresses of life than a good dog, the smile of a child, and cold, squishy mud between your toes.

apprehensive deer, I was reluctant to move and scared to answer.

"Is this a trick?" I considered in my own mind. "Why do you keep asking me this?" I answered her question with a question. She did not respond. So, intimidated by her silence and fearful that maybe I was suffering from gas without realizing it, I gave her the same answer as before. "Nope." Still, silence from her. It was unnerving. So, to break the tension of the silence, I suggested Bay had gas or maybe had burped, hoping that if I had been oblivious to any expulsions I might have made, I could "blame the kid." Still, with no comment in response, I went on about my business.

The next day, the interrogation continued. "Do you smell that?" Frustrated with the inquisition, I exclaimed, "I don't smell anything!" Hannah silently searched around the room with her eyes, and then her gaze fell on Bay. She was lying on a pallet on the floor. Swaddled in a cocoon, Bay's eyes tracked Hannah's movements as she folded clothes next to Bay. Bringing her eyes back to mine, Hannah matter-of-factly declared, "It's Bay. She stinks."

She then leaned over the top of Bay. Hannah crouched on her knees and hovered over Bay like a protective mother bear sheltering her cub from a threat. Bay wiggled slightly in her cocoon as she seemed to think, "Maybe it's time to eat again." Much to Bay's chagrin, though, Hannah began unwrapping Bay's swaddle and unbuttoning her onesie. Bay protested the intrusion of the cold air with a cough-like cry and a scowl on her face. Hannah then systematically searched Bay's body. I could see Hannah going through some sort of mental checklist. She pulled out the waistband of Bay's diaper . . . clean. She lifted Bay's underarms and took a big whiff. "Okay, there," she reported. "Is it her breath?" she asked rhetorically before answering her own question. "No, it's not her breath." (She did pause at this point to reflect on how sweet a baby's breath always smells, and she was right.) She then pulled Bay's socks off. Bay certainly took exception to such brutality and began to whimper louder. "It's not her feet either. What is it?" Hannah was exasperated as she continued to sniff the air like a bloodhound tracking an escaped convict.

In a scene reminiscent of *The Twilight Zone*, Hannah stuck her nose to Bay's toes, and like an anteater working the ground near an anthill, Hannah sniffed every inch of Bay's tiny little body. "I don't remember reading this in the *Parenting for Dummies* book," I quipped. "Shut up and get over here and help me, you dummy," Hannah said in a quick-witted reply. So, as any good father would do, I, too, bent over and started sniffing.

"You know, they will put us in the asylum if someone walks in right now?" Hannah didn't stop . . . sniff, sniff, sniff—she persisted. I followed suit. Like a beagle tracking a rabbit, she tracked up Bay's leg and into her belly button. Bay stopped crying and soon began giggling at all the attention. She smiled a smile that was as wide as the mouth of the Mississippi River, and I couldn't help but pause and soak it up. Bay has always had a beautiful smile. Even today, it is one of the things that draws people to her.

Hannah made her way across Bay's belly. Meanwhile, I was still sniffing her other leg reluctantly. Moms somehow overcome the feeling of "stupid" that attaches itself to acts of parenting much faster than dads do. Unwise to the benefit of selective silence, I declared, "This is stupid." My facial expression suggested that Hannah would be delusional to disagree with me. With her nose stuck in Bay's armpit, Hannah lifted her forehead, made eye contact with me in a sinister way, and, without saying a word, she let me know that I could sniff—or die.

Sniff, sniff, sniff. I made my choice, but make no mistake about it, I am my own man. "I'm doing this for her . . . not you." Hannah chuckled.

Then, like our dog, Lincoln, when he finally finds the scent of a deer we're trailing . . . Hannah's sniff intensified, and I could sense her weight shifting on the pallet.

Sniff, sniff, sniff, sniff . . . she was onto something. I sat up and watched. She was in the fat rolls on Bay's neck. She drew a deep, long sniff and then she lurched away from Bay in a convulsing motion. I thought she was going to throw up. Catching her breath, she placed her hands on Bay's neck and began to spread the fat rolls apart. The first one had no obvious signs of funk. Neither did the second fat roll that she peeled apart. But the third one . . . "Oh, gracious! That smells horrible!" The odor perforated my sinuses, and all at once, my gag reflex kicked in. Hannah leaned in and sniffed a little, again, convulsing away.

"Breast milk! It's where breast milk has settled into her fat rolls and soured!" Hannah exclaimed. By now, I'd stood up from the floor.

"I think I'm going to throw up!" I said. "I'm France! I surrender! I surrender!" I ran out of the bedroom. Hannah muttered something as I fled . . . I'm sure it was something about what a strong and courageous man I was.

Hannah then began a full spa treatment on Bay—soap and warm water—and Bay was in hog heaven. Hannah searched every fat roll on her tiny body, fleshed out every stray piece of lint she could find, and cleaned that baby like a new dime. And, as embarrassing it is to admit that we somehow let milk sour in our baby's fat rolls, it makes for a great illustration. For you see, no matter how bad Bay stunk, we loved her. No matter how dirty she was, we weren't giving up on her. And even though I retreated . . . I knew she was in good hands . . . unfailing hands . . . the best hands.

A mother's love should be unconditional. So should a father's. Hannah's love is, and mine is, too. So is His. And that's the illustration . . . all we have to do is confess, repent, and call Him Father. God loves His children so much that He sees past all the dirt and the sourness of bad decisions, and He sees the sparkling clean new baby that we all are. Trust Him . . . He won't ever leave us or forsake us. He loves us too much . . . even when we stink.

Bay was the family's first grandchild, so her feet rarely hit the ground. She was a snuggler too . . . she loved to lie on my or Big Daddy's chest and snuggle into the folds of our necks for long naps. Of course, what dad or granddad is going to turn that down? Most curious, though, was Bay's preferred method of nighttime sleeping. As first-time parents, Hannah and I struggled to make her sleep in her own bed, and most nights, she would crawl out from between us and climb up onto one of our pillows, where she would wrap her arms and legs around our heads . . . like she was the crown.

Deuteronomy 31:6, NIV

"Be strong and courageous. Do not be afraid or terrified because of them, for the Lord your God goes with you; He will never leave you nor forsake you."

John 3:16, KJV

"For God so loved the world, that He gave His only begotten Son, that whosoever believeth in Him should not perish, but have everlasting life."

I hope you have a blessed day . . . and I hope you smile when He brushes your cheek today.

CAPE LIKED THE NINNIE

Part One

That's what we called it . . . "ninnie." I have no idea where that name came from, but it sounded much less anatomical than "breast." "Nursing" and "breastfeeding" also occasionally worked their way into the dialogue, but still, though, ninnie was the preferred descriptive noun. The others sounded too clinical. Breastfeeding is intimate . . . personal. Not clinical. Ninnie it was.

Though, now, Cape is anything but a "titty" baby. Ninnie was much preferred to titty as well. Hannah and I quickly agreed that titties were only appropriate to discuss in connection with twisters and Texas tornadoes. Back to Cape . . . she stands 5 feet 10 inches and is as fit as a cheetah stalking the Serengeti Plains. She is lean and strong . . . quick and stealthy. She is a specimen of feminine athleticism. One has to wonder if those extra few months of the ninnie had anything to do with the specimen she is today.

Cape will, no doubt, kill me for writing this story. I don't do it to embarrass her, though. I wanted to write about her birth, but honestly, her birth itself is not story that I want to tell. The story I want to tell is about the ninnie. And, literally, when the doctor cleaned Cape off after delivery . . . all 9 pounds and 6 ounces of her . . . some 22 inches long . . . and laid her on Hannah for that crucial birth-bonding experience, Cape immediately started craning her neck for the ninnie. Hannah shuffled her up once or twice to nestle her in her bosom or in the crease of her neck. Cape kept craning for the ninnie.

And she didn't let go for nearly nine months. And on those rare occasions when she did let go, she was an irritable baby. Fact of the matter was, Cape only did three things for months: sleep, eat, and cry. It was one of the most trying seasons of our marriage. Hannah had almost exhausted herself with the routine . . .

"Whaaaaannnn! Whaaaaaaannnnn! Whannn! Whaaannn! Whaaaaaaannnnnn!" Cape cried as I held her. She twisted and lurched, trying to get out of my arms. At four months old, she was strong. She could easily hold her head up and had good use of her arms. She pushed hard with the palms of her hands against my chest . . . she meant she didn't want me to hold her. I resisted . . . Hannah needed this to work. I wanted this to work.

I often tried singing to her. Holding her close to my chest, wrapped in swaddling clothes where she couldn't flail about, we would rock in an old platform rocker that we had reupholstered when Hannah was pregnant with Bay. An old farmer's lullaby is still one of my favorites:

"Go to sleep you little baby.
Go to sleep you little baby.
Your mama's gone away, and your daddy's gone to stay.
Didn't leave nobody but the baby."

Sometimes, the lullaby would lull her bye-bye, and she would sleep . . . as long as I held her. Most times, it would not satisfy her. She truly only found comfort in two people's arms . . . her mama's and George's. I would try. Some nights, for hours on end, I would rock her and sing to her, offer her a bottle . . . gas drops . . . Orajel . . . sugar on the tip of my finger . . . lights on, lights off . . . television . . . cartoons . . . this room, now, that one . . . rock faster, now slower . . . and she would never stop crying. Eventually, Hannah would come find me and take Cape from me. Within 10 seconds in Hannah's arms, Cape would be sound asleep. I would stumble back to the bed, dejected.

And Cape didn't much care for sleeping by herself. She wanted you to hold her. Some nights, Hannah would sit nearly upright in the platform rocker and rest her arm on the armrest. I'd tuck pillows around her to prop up her arm and nestle her body where she could sleep, too. Other nights, she'd get in the bed and cradle Cape in her arms as they both slept on their sides, facing each other. We tried not to let Cape sleep in the bed with us . . . but some nights, it was the only way to find relief.

I was of almost no use to Hannah. I offered moral support, but truth was, there was very little I could do to console Cape. That being the case, slowly but surely, Hannah was exhausting herself.

But God has a way of working things out, doesn't He? One Sunday morning was exceptionally rough. It's long been a belief in this family that the devil makes himself known on Sunday mornings . . . he doesn't want a family to worship together. Cape was—sarcastically—demon-possessed this particular morning. She wouldn't stop crying for anyone or anything. She woke up screaming at about 5 a.m., and by 9 a.m., not much had changed. We both knew the "easy" thing to do would be to skip church, but I reminded Hannah that skipping church wouldn't get Cape to stop screaming. I scooped Cape up and carried her out into the backyard so Hannah could get dressed.

This was my shepherding outdoors moment . . . I pointed to the cows in the field next to the house and made "moooooo" sounds. She silenced herself for a moment. As soon as she lost interest in the cows and my impersonations, I spied a redbird sitting proudly atop a nearby fence post. Its bright red coat was offset by the early spring green leaves of the pecan trees glistening in the morning sun. The redbird captured Cape's attention . . . her arm stretched outward . . . her fingers crumpled up still, as she tried to grab for the redbird. When it flew off, Cape began to whimper again. Just in time, the chickens strutted across the yard hoping for breakfast . . . I directed Cape's attention to them, squatting down as the hens came nearer. They, too, captivated her . . . but when the rooster came through and ran all the ladies off, Cape became frustrated. "Haannn. Ahhaaannn!" She wanted to cry . . . Cape sputtered like an old diesel engine trying to crank for the first time after a long nap. I frantically search the yard for something else to distract her.

My old red Massey Ferguson tractor sat idle in the backyard. I had been plowing in the garden patch the day before. "Look at the red tractor, Cape," I offered in my softest voice, pointing to it and walking towards it at the same time. She noticed the redness and stopped trying to crank her crying engine. With Cape wrapped in one arm, I held firmly to the grab bar on the 100-horsepower behemoth and pulled us both up into the cab. The tractor seat was wet from the morning dew, but I sat down anyway. Demanding times require sacrifices. Wet butt and all, I talked to Cape about everything she could see from our high perch. The view was certainly different from "up here." She curiously studied her surroundings, for this new vantage point offered a different perspective . . . such is true in life, too. So much in life is simply a matter of perspective. One man's trash truly is another man's treasure, because their perspectives are from different places. Sometimes when I find myself frustrated by life, when I lack contentment, I don't seek to change my place in life. Instead, I work to change my perspective.

After all, the Apostle Paul's point was well taken when he said, "I know how to be abased, and I know how to abound. Everywhere, and in all things, I have learned both to be full and to be hungry, both to abound and to suffer need," Philippians 4:12, NKJV. Paul taught us to change our perspective to find contentment . . . and Cape's new perspective—or at least her view—brought her some momentary contentment. But I knew it wouldn't last as she whimpered again. I pushed the clutch down on the tractor and turned the key, and the beast roared to life. The combustion of the engine startled Cape initially. I held her close and talked softly into her ear to offer her some measure of comfort . . . not that I was much comfort to her . . . but I hoped the ring of my soft voice in her ear might give her the assurance that "I am here." Still clutching her in one arm, I shifted the tractor into a low gear and eased off the clutch. Slowly, we rumbled forward.

Like so many master plans in my life, the genius of the plan is often undone by the shortcomings of my own execution. I felt the tractor tug and jerk slightly under my seat. Curious as to what might cause such a reaction, I looked back over my shoulder to find that I had left the three-row bottom plow "down." I quickly grabbed the lever and pulled sharply upwards . . . the hydraulics lifted the plows slowly out of the ground. But by then . . . the damage was done. Looking back behind me, I had plowed three rows straight through the middle of the backyard. And if you don't know what a bottom plow is . . . it plows deep. A bottom plow reaches down a foot or so into the depths and turns the bottom dirt up to the surface. "What a mess," I thought to myself as I shook my head. "Hannah is going to kill me."

I throttled up and eased out into the pasture. Cape was riding nicely, enjoying the world as it went by. She watched the row of popcorn trees tangle in the fencerow . . . their yellowish green leaves popping open like their namesake. Then, she turned her attention to the huge live oak that cast its net wide and broad across the edge of the pasture . . . sweeping out well into the green field. I turned the tractor to avoid dragging the massive oak's low-hanging limbs over the canopy of the tractor. A few of last year's acorns still littered the ground nearby. Soon enough, we rounded the end of the pasture, and I tried to divert her attention to the rows of planted pine trees.

The tractor grumbled through the silence of the morning air . . . the seat jostled and vibrated under my posterior as we moved over the earthen terrain . . . nothing about this would conjure images of tranquility. Yet, as I pointed towards the perfectly straight rows of pine trees, I looked down at a soundly sleeping baby in my arms.

For, perhaps, the first time in her short life, Cape had fallen asleep in my arms without me putting on a full-blown circus spectacle. Either way, I was content.

Part Two

But alas, the tractor could not be the "answer" to our problems. In fact, the victory was short lived . . . have you ever tried to climb down off of a 100-horsepower Massey Ferguson tractor without waking the sleeping baby in your arms? My big ole butt! I was lucky I didn't drop her . . . much less, not wake her up. Of course, by the time I climbed down those two steps to solid ground, the silence of the morning disturbed her just enough. "Wha-haaaaannnnn!" Cape cried. And I groaned in failure.

Hannah was standing at the back door of our small farmhouse. She had the screened door pushed open with her left hand while the right hand held the back door . . . it was prone to swing harshly and slam against the wall. The old farmhouse has settled considerably through the years, and the uneven floor persuaded that back door to headbutt the wall every time anyone let it go. The look on her face was unforgettable.

Hannah has a way of speaking without ever opening her mouth. I rarely have to ask how her day was . . . sad eyes tell me of a hard day; clenched jowls tell me of a rough day; bright eyes and a big smile . . . well, that is obvious. As I passed Cape to Hannah in the threshold of the door, I could see despair in her eyes. I know she saw a glimmer of hope as she saw me make a few laps around the pasture. I'm sure she wondered, "How on earth did he get that baby to sleep on the tractor?" I wondered the same myself . . . and I am certain that she watched with excitement as though, perhaps . . . just perhaps . . . I had finally found a way to relieve her of some of the struggle she had suffered with Cape's colic. But now . . . the deep and desperate eyes told me that the hope was dashed . . . and that to have had the glimmer of hope and watch it disappear was far worse than never having had hope at all.

I tried to comfort her as she turned and walked back into the house with Cape.

Cape didn't sleep for the first six months of her life unless Hannah or George was holding her. As a dad, I struggled with that. I wanted to be "enough" for her, and I still do today. Now, she is a teenager, and though I still feel like I compete for her time, it's for entirely different reasons. All I really have ever known to do is always be here when she needs me.

"Maybe she will fall back to sleep quickly," I offered with earnest desire. Hannah sunk into the platform rocker—now in its second tour of duty—and began to rock and sing simultaneously.

> *"Ole Stewball was a racehorse,*
> *And I wish he were mine.*
> *He never drank water,*
> *He always drank wine.*
> *His bridle was silver,*
> *His mane was gold,*
> *But the worth of Ole Stewball,*
> *Has never been told.*
> *Went to the races,*
> *Ole Stewball was there.*
> *The betting was heavy,*
> *On the bay and the mare.*
> *But way up yonder,*
> *Ahead of them all,*
> *Came a dancin' and prancin'*
> *My noble Stewball…."*

Hannah learned that song from Brenda. I don't know from whence it came . . . but the slow and methodical melody, coupled with Hannah's long Southern drawl always seemed to be the perfect anecdote for an ill-tempered baby. Frankly, there was many a night in that time of our marriage where I would sit outside the baby's room in darkness and just soak up Hannah's voice. It echoed through the house . . . and it was beautiful.

Hannah is often told that she sounds just like Reba McEntire. I don't hear her drawl like I use to, so I am not entirely sure. That said, I'm not sure if Hannah can "sing" or if I just find comfort in her voice. No matter . . . I believe one thing to be most certainly true—a baby will always find comfort in the beauty of its mama's voice. Our children always did.

Hannah's hair was still in rollers. My diversion on the tractor had given her enough time to get halfway dressed for church. A big loop of bangs hung down in her eyes as she rocked Cape. The rest of her hair was tucked tightly underneath the small, pink, plastic coils. Her makeup was aptly applied, although I've always told Hannah that the thing I find most beautiful about her is her natural elegance. She never needs makeup. Cape resisted at first, but within half of the chorus of "Ole Stewball" and after about six swift rocks in the chair, Cape was sound asleep. Hannah continued to sing . . . her eyes were closed, and I could see the sense of despair on her face.

We both knew that if she got up, Cape would most likely start to cry . . . and short of cranking the tractor, there was very little I could do.

A few minutes later, Hannah was easing down the hall, still mimicking the action of the platform rocker . . . rocking to and fro as she walked, bending at the waist . . . humming the tune to "Ole Stewball." She clutched Cape tightly to her bosom. Despite the gyrations and jostles, Cape was so swaddled to Hannah's chest that she never moved. Instead, she felt the movement . . . and she slept soundly. Slipping down the hall to Cape's bedroom, Hannah bent over the baby bed, still clutching her close, until she could lay Cape straight away onto the bed. Quickly, she surrounded Cape with blankets . . . the pressure of which, she hoped, would mimic her mother's warmth and presence.

Hannah emerged from the bedroom on her tiptoes. Our old farmhouse had oak floors. Any poorly placed step would surely set off a pop or a crackle that would otherwise be the buzzer of an alarm clock for our precious Middle Princess. I dared not speak a word. I told Hannah with my eyes that I was sorry . . . and that I loved her. She told me with hers that she was close to her wit's end. As Hannah came near to me, I clutched her in my arms and pulled her tight to my chest. I didn't know what else to do.

We stood, right there, in the edge of the kitchen for what seemed like hours. Over the course of a few minutes, I felt the tension from Hannah's muscles release. Her shoulders relaxed. She laid her head on my chest. I couldn't see them, but I felt certain she had her eyes closed. I kept constant pressure on her with my arms . . . assuring her that I wasn't going to let go.

We missed Sunday School that morning. The devil won Round One. We made it to "Big Church," though . . . so he lost the rest of the rounds. Cape cried most of the way to church. We always felt guilt for taking her to the nursery, but that's where the Lord worked valiantly. As we walked through the nursery door that morning, Cape was in rare form. Tension had crept back into Hannah's spirit, and mine, too. Few things are more grueling than riding 20 minutes in a car with a baby who will only stop screaming to catch her breath. Handing her to the nursery worker—a man I hardly knew—I apologized and assured him we would come back at a moment's notice. "It's alright. I've got her," he assured me. His eyes told me not to worry. So, we turned and walked away, and they never summoned us.

Sunday after Sunday, the same sequence unfolded. And, every Sunday, that same nursery worker assured us he had everything under control. And he never called for us. I didn't know then how important that hour of rest and worship was for Hannah. But it was . . . the Lord used that nursery worker to help Hannah find refuge in Him. And she did.

By the way, that nursery worker's name is Claude Summerlin, and today, he is one of my dearest friends. Cape loves him dearly, also. For as much as God knew then that Hannah needed Claude, God also knew Cape and I would need Claude later.

God is good. All the time. Even in the storm.

Cape always had her tongue poked out. We used to poke it with
our index fingers . . . she would pull it back into her mouth and
then cackle in the way only a baby can do. Over time, she slowly
changed her posture, and now, she only shows us her tongue when
she sticks it out at us! Of course, sometimes, we all laugh at that, too.

Part Three

For the first nine months of Cape's life, there were only two things that brought her some measure of peace: the ninnie, and being held by George. Sure, she would sleep if I drove her around the pasture on the tractor or if we sat her in her car seat on top of the running clothes dryer, but less the extreme . . . she was ill-tempered and wanted to cry. But she couldn't stay on the ninnie all of the time, nor could George come live with us.

A crying baby is a test of the strength of a marriage. To complicate our marriage even more, I worked beyond a nine-to-five . . . and Dolly Parton was right to be sarcastic . . . "*What a way to make a living*." We were, in fact, "*barely getting by*." I was a young prosecutor assigned to our circuit's Drug Task Force. A few years earlier, Covington County was identified as one of the top 10 counties in the nation for methamphetamine use and production. Red phosphorous methamphetamine labs were commonplace at the time, and getting called out three or four nights a week would not have been out of the ordinary for me.

Those working nights would all unfold in similar fashion.

"Cha-chiiirrrp. Cha-chiiirrp." My Southern Linc long-range communication device would "chirp" when someone from law enforcement called. Startled by the abrupt chirp in the silent night, I fumbled around on the bedside table, searching for the device. I'd press the push-to-talk button . . . the Southern Linc was nothing more than a two-way radio or walkie-talkie for adults . . . "Go ahead," I'd whisper, as I slid out of the bed and into the living room. The voice on the other end would then detail some tale of informants and snitches and discuss search warrants and charges. Sometimes, I could navigate the issues through the course of the conversation . . . sliding back into the bed a short while later. Other times, the voice would direct, "We think you need to come out here."

Rarely did I refuse.

I felt some burden of loyalty to the officers, and when they asked for my attendance, I felt obliged. More than that, too, I liked field work and enjoyed the fellowship of those men. So, the burden of the 2 a.m. sleep interruption was oftentimes alleviated by the mystery of the crime and the fellowship of the investigating team. Truth was . . . I was still young enough and dumb enough to think that I could somehow balance leaving and being at work all the time with the sometimes desperate needs of my family.

And sometimes, the chirp of the radio or the squeak of the door as I left to go draft a midnight search warrant made the night even more desperate.

"Wha-waaaaannnn," Cape sounded out, startled by the alarm of the radio signal resonating through the house in the midnight dreary. I stumbled over to her crib and scooped her up . . . slipping out into the kitchen where the platform rocker was. Hoping I could instantaneously rock her back to sleep, hoping to spare Hannah the disturbance, I delayed answering the call. But this was a delicate game of Russian roulette . . . for, you see, not answering the radio call right away would surely invite another chirp. But answering the call now—and thus starting a conversation—would surely provoke Cape to become fully awake . . . and create chaos in the house. Either way was a losing proposition . . . this dance required precise execution . . .

I rocked and hummed . . . "*Go to sleep, you little baby . . . Go to sleep, you little baby*," wagering that I could get her back to a sound slumber before the next chirp rang through the night . . . and then I could slip into the living room away from everyone before I answered. "*Go to sleep, you little baby . . .* " It was working . . . she was back asleep, for she was never truly awake. Laying her gently back into the crib, I eased out into the darkness . . . "Go ahead," I whispered to the incoming caller, and the cycle repeated itself.

I was not always so lucky, though. There were plenty of nights when that second chirp would come far too soon, and Cape would be startled to life in my arms. There are few things more abrupt than the blast of a two-way radio just as you try to rock your infant back to sleep. It might as well have been a shotgun blast in the middle of the second stanza of "Amazing Grace" during the invitation at Sunday morning church service. Of course, once she was fully awake and realized I was not George and that I did not have a ninnie, there was no consoling her. Reluctantly . . . regrettably . . . I would carry her into the bedroom to Hannah. Dutifully and faithfully, Hannah would rise and take care of her.

I still remember the anguish I felt over work causing such calamity in my home. I'd answer the call, conversing long enough to assess whatever the situation might be. Then, I would slip into some appropriate clothing, kiss Hannah on the forehead as she rocked Cape, and head into the darkness of the night and of the world. "Be careful and come home to me," Hannah would always whisper. Pulling the door shut and locking it as I left, I always regretted waking the baby up and leaving the mess for Hannah to clean up.

Like I said . . .

The burden of a crying baby is stressful on a marriage. But the burden of torn allegiances and misplaced priorities can wreak havoc. And it was . . . something had to give, or something else would break.

And then the Lord shook us.

Jeff and Jennifer Sellers were, and still are, some of our best friends. Ours is an odd friendship, too, that followed an uncommon path. When we first moved back to Andalusia, Alabama, a man by the name of Jon Sellers took me under his wing. A local New York Life insurance agent, Jon was a man's man, and he went well beyond trying to sell me insurance. Soon enough, we were fishing on occasion, meeting for coffee regularly, and building a great friendship. Jon was twice my age, at least, yet we bonded as if we were childhood friends.

Soon enough, Jon introduced me to his son, Jeff. Through the years, Jeff and I built a friendship of fortitude . . . the kind of friendship that stands the test of time and withstands the toughest of tests—including the death of his father. Our friendship was odd in its origins . . . odd, I say, because I befriended a man twice my age to find another great friend in his son. And our friendship has seen turmoil and storms untold . . . and weathered them all.

One such storm was a tragedy layered in God's plan for Hannah and me.

Jennifer was pregnant with their second child—a boy, Jonathan, named after Jeff's father and my dear friend, Jon. She was due any day . . . we had done the baby showers and all the hoopla, and now, it was time to get down to business. Jonathan would complete their family plan. Having a daughter, a strawberry redhead named Hannah, the addition of one boy to complement the one girl would fulfill all of Jeff and Jennifer's hopes.

Jennifer is one of those moms who you suspect only exist on television. Like Clair Huxtable, Jennifer always has a resolution for any problem her kids encounter. But like Aunt Bee, Jennifer always guides her children while they do the heavy lifting . . . careful to make sure they experience life and don't simply ride on the coattails of parental enabling. Also, like Carol Brady, Jennifer always has a smile on her face . . . no doubt, she has always been a source of warmth and comfort for her children. Point is . . . Jennifer is one of those kind of moms who gives joy to her kids, and it is joyful to watch her interact with her children.

Likewise, Jeff is a proud father. He carries a grin most times, as the reflection of adoration for his children glimmers in his eyes. Jeff is a jolly sort . . . skinny though, not portly at all . . . always quick with a good joke or a funny anecdote, Jeff is quick to lift the mood in a room. More than that, though, Jeff knows how to discipline his kids, prompting them to "do better next time" while carrying a smile and a twinkle in his eye. Like his dad, Jeff has a way about him . . . he motivates everyone around him.

They were so excited about Jonathan. It had been a busy nine months. Hannah and Bay are nearly the same age, so we tried to give Jennifer a reprieve from time to time, inviting Hannah to stay with us for an afternoon. Jeff and Jon busied themselves with preparing for the baby boy. They regaled each other with fanciful conjecture about big game hunts and first dates for Jonathan, as they skipped reading the "some assembly required" directions for anything that was bought for the young buck's nursery.

Jonathan would be king . . . and he would be here in just a few days.

I confess that all the baby activity was alluring to Hannah and me. We had been deliberate with our children. We planned to have Bay. We planned to have Cape. Now, we were discussing adding a third to the mix . . . something we had never considered before. Two had always been our perfect number. We wrestled, though . . . Cape was a beautiful baby girl, and we loved her desperately . . . but we were sure we were not at all ready for another protracted visit from Old Man Colic. Nestled in each other's arms as Cape slept, we lay in bed one night contemplating the pros and cons of another new baby when the peacefulness of the night was interrupted by the "chirp" of the two-way radio.

Hannah rolled her eyes and pulled away. One need not be an FBI agent to recognize that she had grown weary of work obligations tearing me away from the family. "Oh, sure . . . go deal with the drug dealers," she quipped with a tinge of resentment in her voice. Scurrying to get to the radio before it sounded off again and woke Cape, "Go ahead," I answered, without looking at the small screen to see who was calling. The voice on the other end caught me off guard . . . it was Jeff. His voice broke ever so slightly, and I could hear panic in his words. "Something is wrong with Jonathan," he said.

Part Four

Jennifer's baby was due in just a few days. This being her second pregnancy, she was no stranger to those last few days . . . and she sensed something was not quite right. "She felt like Jonathan had quit moving . . . she had not felt him kick. Something was off," Jeff described over the radio. I climbed out of the bed, turning the radio outward to project the conversation towards Hannah. She listened intently as I began to get dressed with one hand while the other one held the radio. "We are at the hospital now," Jeff said. "They are about to do an ultrasound."

"I'll be there shortly," I responded, and with that, Hannah and I both got dressed.

"What about the girls?" I asked. Hannah's mom was out of town, and I was curious as to whether we were taking them to the hospital with us or if Hannah had thoughts of a different arrangement. "I'll call Daddy and see if he will keep them," she suggested. "Sounds good," I offered, walking down the hall to round the rug rats up and get them ready to go. Bay was playing in her room. She was three years old . . . maybe four. Cape was an arm baby.

Reflecting, I find irony in the situation. Bay was so quiet as a toddler, playing carefully in her room so as not to disturb the sleeping hyena in the next room. Perhaps, she, too, was sensitive to Cape's demands . . . and, for such a young child, she was mindful not to "clang" or "clack" toys, fearful that the disruptive serenade would wake up her little sister. I found Bay standing in front of the mirror in her room . . . in full princess attire. The pink Halloween princess costume fell past her ankles and jumbled on the floor. It was still a "year or two too big," but the oversized dress only complemented her oversized imagination. She cocked her hip out to the side as she swirled the dress round and round . . . when she saw me standing in the doorway, she stopped and grinned. She was sheepishly embarrassed that I had caught her admiring herself, but I knew it was not vain conceit that drew her attention. Instead, she was consumed by the colorful creativity that children feast on. "You look beautiful," I offered as I crouched down beside her. "Thank you, Daddy. Look at my crown," she said, pointing to the tiara on her head. I adjusted it slightly . . . "Oh, it is so beautiful,

I don't know that I have even seen a bond like these two have.
Bay always looked after Cape, and still does today. In their own
way, they both look after Banks now. Bay is three years older than
Cape . . . just old enough to be a big sister, and close enough
in age to be a best friend. As their dad, I always knew that if I
made one of them mad at me, the other one would be mad, too.
That was one of the more difficult dad things I had to parent
through . . . knowing they were both mad but only disciplining
one of them. No matter though, the strength of their bond has
always been a joy to watch.

too! But you know what makes all of it the prettiest?" I prompted.

"What, Daddy?" she asked.

"You do. You are what makes it pretty." I was down at eye level with her trying to speak truth into her . . . not just talk at her.

"I know, Daddy. Don't I look pretty with my princess dress?" she asked with the innocence of a child. She heard me . . . but didn't understand what I was trying to teach. So, I tried again.

"You look beyond pretty, Butterbean," I said. "You look beautiful. But what I want you to understand is that it's not the dress that makes you look pretty. Instead, it's you that makes the dress look pretty. Does that make sense? You are what makes it all look pretty." She nodded her head in agreement, but I was confident that she wasn't entirely ready for this life lesson. That was okay. I would offer the same sentiment time and again in the coming years. It was important to me that the girls knew that their beauty did not come from what they put on their bodies.

A few minutes later, and we were on our way. Cape cried the entire ride to George and Brenda's house—the bouncing of the truck in motion did nothing to soothe her. Bay tried, from the adjacent booster seat, to comfort her . . . tickling under her chin and holding her hand . . . but Cape wasn't interested. Ten long and ear-piercing minutes later, we pulled into George and Brenda's driveway.

Brenda was out of town. I don't remember where she had gone; though, it was unusual for her to be somewhere without George. I just remember George was by himself. "Daddy, I'm sorry she is so fussy," Hannah apologized as she handed Cape to him. Like the big teddy bear that he was, he wrapped Cape in his big arms and swallowed her up in his love. "It is alright sugar-puss," he cooed. I wasn't sure if he was consoling Hannah or Cape or both. Either way, I am sure both were comforted . . . for Cape rested quietly in his arms after just a few minutes. Her silence clearly meant she was at peace . . . and for Cape to be at peace meant Hannah, too, would be at peace. Both of those things gave me peace.

"Daddy, I don't know how we are going to do this," Hannah said. "She still won't take a bottle, and I don't know when I'll be able to come back and nurse." Hannah was worried. George was not. "Did you bring me some bottles? And formula?" he asked.

"Yes, sir," Hannah said sheepishly.

"Good, then. Y'all go ahead," George urged. "Don't worry about coming back to get the girls tonight. Y'all go the hospital and be with your friends. I'll take care of the girls." His words were confident and reassuring, but Hannah still had reservations. "Well, if it gets to be too much, you call me," she responded. George laughed in a way that only he did—a deep, bellowing laugh—and then he kissed Hannah on the forehead and reminded her that he did raise two of his own. She grinned with uncertainty and walked out the door.

There was already a very special bond between George and Cape. He never acknowledged that he had a favorite of the three girls . . . but if I were a betting man, I'd wager that bond between them was unlike any other. I never understood why she found comfort in his arms, almost exclusively. Not that she shouldn't, but the exclusivity of her comfort was both confounding and disheartening. Admittedly, I was envious at times. I was her daddy. I didn't understand why I couldn't give her the same comfort that George did. But, as much as I struggled with the emotions that flowed from that circumstance, I also found joy in knowing that they had such a special bond . . . and over the next few days, it would only get stronger.

Andalusia Health's maternity ward is a diamond hidden in a rural forest. All three of our girls were born there. Each time, the care was beyond professional, but the love we felt from perfect strangers was immeasurably more. Walking through the double doors of the maternity ward, Hannah and I saw the warm and familiar faces of nurses we now called friends. They all were there with Cape, and some of them with Bay, too. Some of them helped deliver Banks, and some still work there today. Those nurses are truly a blessing. Not only are they experts in their craft, but they are so much more . . . they care.

"Hey, Tracey," Hannah greeted an old friend who had been there for some part of both Bay and Cape's deliveries. Tracey feigned a smile and offered a hospitable, "Hey, y'all," but I immediately knew she was distracted and tormented. Tracey's eyes look tired as she passed us by and eased down the hallway. The next nurse we met coming out of Jennifer's room was even less engaging . . . she didn't make eye contact at all. The air was thick in the hall. For the first time in my experience, the maternity ward felt sterile and flat. I didn't understand it all . . . at least I didn't understand it in the moment. Just as I went to knock, Jeff pulled the door open. His slender face was flush, and his eyes were strained. Hannah instinctively gave him a hug and made her way into the room.

Me, being a man . . . well, I was much less astute and was, in fact, reluctant to go into the room. Jeff hesitated at the door, so I asked, "Where are you headed?" "Aww, I was going to tell Mama and Daddy a few things and then maybe go get some air," he muttered. His voice was low and depressed. "I'll join you," I suggested, and we turned and walked back down the hall. Two nurses passed us on our way, the first one asking, "Mr. Sellers, do you need anything?" and the other making brief eye contact and smiling slightly. We met Jeff's parents in the waiting room outside the ward. He told them Jennifer was doing "okay" and assured them he was, too. I could tell he wanted some refuge . . . some solitude. He turned and walked out the door.

Honestly, I still wasn't sure what was happening, nor was I entirely certain how I could be a friend to Jeff in the moment. I reluctantly followed him, fearful that I might be intruding on his desire to be alone but motivated by the fact that to not follow him might leave him feeling abandoned in a time of need. Men don't necessarily communicate well in hard times . . . at least it is something I have struggled with in the past . . . and there is a lot of guesswork with how we might best be a friend to someone in need. But as I followed Jeff down that hallway, all I could think of was

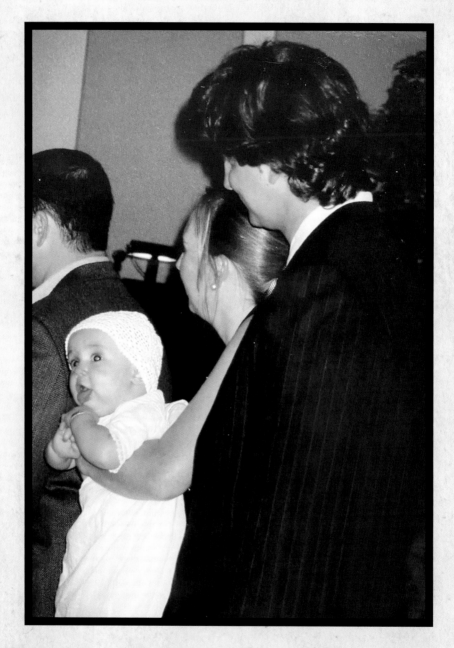

There's that tongue again . . . this time, at her dedication! All three of our girls were dedicated at Bethany Baptist Church. Baptized there, too. God has certainly been good to us . . . he gave us plenty of milk and honey.

Simon coming the aid of Jesus as he struggled up the hill called Calvary. No, I'm not suggesting Jeff is as Jesus was . . . but I know he was in need. And though the Romans compelled Simon to help, he did far more than merely offer assistance. Simon carried the cross, even but for a brief, few steps. So, I followed Jeff down the hall to his own personal Calvary . . . perhaps I could help him carry this cross.

A few minutes later, we found ourselves in the back parking lot sitting on the tailgate of a truck. "They can't find a heartbeat," he told me. His voice was shaky, and his eyes winced as he spoke. "A few days ago, he was fine. She came in for her last weekly checkup, and everything was fine. I just don't understand." I didn't understand either, and I felt ill-equipped to offer any logical or profound utterance that could soothe the heartbreak that one of my dearest friends was enduring.

I listened. I tried to encourage. I tried to comfort. But I knew nothing I could ever do would soothe his pain.

At some point during the night, Jeff and I prayed for Jennifer and for Hannah, their daughter . . . that was all I knew to do. Simon couldn't carry the cross all the way. Neither could I.

"In the morning, when I rise,
In the morning, when I rise,
In the morning, when I rise, give me Jesus.
Give me Jesus,
Give me Jesus,
You can have all this world,
But give me Jesus.
And when I am alone,
Oh, and when I am alone,
And when I am alone, give me Jesus.
Give me Jesus,
Give me Jesus,
You can have all this world,
But give me Jesus.
And when I come to die,
Oh, and when I come to die,
And when I come to die, give me Jesus.
Give me Jesus,
Give me Jesus,
You can have all this world,
You can have all this world,
You can have all this world,
But give me Jesus."

- S N A K E S   A N D   B A N K E R S -

Part One

Hannah and Bay celebrated Bay's graduation from high school *Thelma & Louis* style. They blasted out of the house around 3:30 a.m. on a Saturday morning . . . the night before, they had made every assurance that they would be quiet and not disturb anyone. I woke from Hannah's alarm before she did and lay motionless as she slipped out from under the sheets and got dressed. Soon enough, I heard something that reminded me of fond memories from years ago, and thus, this story.

We have always lived in old, wooden houses. Our first house in Covington County, Alabama, was owned by the former president of the First National Bank of Gantt. He left town not long after the bank closed . . . the Great Depression had collapsed the banks loans, and, in turn, its assets, too.

Uncle Pickens, Hannah's great-uncle, loathed that bank president. "I went down to the bank because we heard that banks were closing around the state. I just wanted to make sure our money was safe." Uncle Pickens said he drove his old Ford down to the river . . . "I never did care much for that bridge. It was one lane, and it didn't have any guardrails . . . wouldn't take much for a fella to drive right off the edge," he said. After waiting on an oxcart to cross, he made his way into Gantt.

Pickens found the president sitting at his desk. "That fella looked me dead in the eyes and told me everything was going to be fine . . . and there wasn't anything to be worried about," he said. "I felt pretty good about how everything would be okay." Pickens said they had a good visit, and after a few minutes, he stood up to leave. "The president put his hand on my shoulder as he walked me out the door. He patted me on the back and told me how good it was to get to visit. I agreed and offered similar hospitalities in return."

Pickens said that was the last time he ever talked to the president . . . a man whose name he would not even utter . . . "I walked out of the door and took two steps. He locked the door behind me and drew the curtains shut. That bank never opened again, and we lost everything we had in that bank," he said.

Anyway, our first house was built by that bank president, and I never could quite tell if Pickens was satisfied that our family now owned the last vestige of that fellow's remnant in Covington County, or if Pickens resented the fact that we brought the bank

Looking back now, I think Hannah and I were too young and dumb to appreciate just how big of a project we had taken on. Built around 1900—we think—this old house became our first family home. Bay was born here, and this is where Hannah and I matured from reckless newlyweds to parents. We sold this house some 20 years ago . . . and the memories from that home are still so powerful that I struggle to drive by it without getting flooded with emotion.

president back into the family, by way of his house.

No matter, I suppose. The house was built in the early 1900s, or at least, that was the best that we could document. It is average by today's standards, but, no doubt, it would have been the largest house in Gantt at the time. When we bought it, it was a lifeless shell . . . the only activity that occurred within its walls was from the wasps that called it home. "I don't think anyone has lived in it in 20 years," the owner told us when we bought it. The home's bones were good, though . . . the stamped tin metal shingles had done a good job of keeping the water out, but we were mere novices when it came to home remodeling. Hannah's parents, George and Brenda, though, had already bought, moved, and restored two old houses very similar to this. One house, some of you may be familiar with, is known as The Cottle House. Brenda operates a bed-and-breakfast out of it, still to this day.

George ambled around in the waist-high grass around the house. His eyes surveyed the roof and the exterior walls. He'd step up closer to each windowsill and door frame, occasionally picking at the wood to see if it was rotting. Rounding the second corner of the house, he pulled a piece of sedge brush from the tallest stem and put it in the corner of his mouth. The grass was a perfect complement to his straw hat and overalls. He looked the part . . . a large man, George stood over six feet tall, and his barreled chest had to be nearly as much in circumference. His eyes searched the wood . . . his fingers traced the intersections between boards . . . his feet tested the strength of the door thresholds . . . he questioned the integrity of every element of the exterior of the house.

Soon enough, he made his way onto a concrete slab that led to a busted-out sliding glass door. "Now, you know this wasn't original to the house," he chuckled. Above his head was an abandoned wasp nest the size of a basketball. He looked up at it, shuffled the straw from one corner of his mouth to the other, and said, "Those were hornets. That's the inside of the nest. The rest has fallen away. Let's just pray they are not in this house somewhere." I silently agreed and reminded him, "I am allergic to wasps."

"You are?" he pondered. "Well, technically, I'm allergic to anything that flies and stings," I answered, "and especially if they can do both at the same time." He belted out a one-syllable laugh, and then agreed. "I guess we all have that allergy, don't we?!"

George ducked under the busted frame of the sliding glass door and made his way into the house. I followed close behind, and Hannah followed close behind me. He examined the inside of the house with the same scrutiny that he subjected the exterior to. He tested floor joists with his bouncing weight, and he closely examined the intersection between the brick fireplaces and the wooden frame of the house. "If ever there was going to be rot in these ceilings and walls, it would be right there. Water hits those bricks, and, eventually, it will find its way into the house." I took the fact that we had yet to find any rot to be a good sign. He explored every nook and cranny of the house before venturing back outside. He had not said much during the inspection; he'd simply offered a few instructional tidbits, the likes of which I always appreciated. I was trying to learn . . . but I didn't want to learn underneath the house.

George laid on his back and shimmied underneath what he called "the rat seal." He picked at it with his pocketknife, testing it for rot. My mind was rotting with fear, for surely, he would not crawl deeper under the house. My mind raced. "It's summertime, and I bet there are a dozen rattlesnakes under that house," I thought. "Please, dear Lord, don't make me crawl under there . . ."

George shimmied a bit further. I could only see one foot and knee. I squatted down to get a better view. He turned his head back towards me and asked, "You got a flashlight?" "No, sir," I answered. "Good," he quipped. "Ain't no telling how many rattlesnakes are under this house, and I sure didn't want to crawl around down here with them." I found relief in his candor. His honesty let me know that I wasn't a coward or lesser man simply because I was fearful of the snakes that might be . . . instead, he affirmed to me that he shared the same apprehensions . . . and I took comfort in that kinship.

He slid back out into the sunlight.

Standing up, he dusted himself off and said, "There are two kinds of snakes—the kind you see and the kind you don't. Snakes are always around, just depends on which kind." I nodded my head attentively. He went on, "One of those kinds is much more dangerous than the other."

"The kind you can't see, right?" I asked. He shook his head in disagreement, "Nope. More people get hurt trying to get away from snakes they do see than actually get bit by snakes in the first place." (He was right. I researched the statistic later on. More people do actually go to the hospital for stitches and broken bones suffered from their reaction to a snake's presence than those who have actually been bitten by a snake.)

"You see, there are always snakes . . . no matter where you go," George said. "There are always snakes. The key is, no matter how dangerous they look, don't panic. Don't run. Just maintain your composure and stay focused. Pay attention and be smart. Most snakes—even the ones you can't see—can't hurt you unless you make the mistake." I nodded my head again. "You understand what I'm telling you, son? I am not actually talking about snakes. I am talking about people." I nodded my head again, and I was thankful I had not said anything stupid about snakes, for I surely had no idea we were talking about people. "Some folks will always be snakes," he added.

George walked back to the truck and pulled a Mason jar full of ice water from the front seat. Unscrewing the lid, he pulled a long draw off the jar. Smacking his lips in satisfaction, he said, "That's a fine house. If you can buy it cheap, then get it, and move it, and fix it up."

Soon enough, we struck a deal with the owners and hired our old friend, Jack Odom, to move the house for us. Upon hearing of our new project, Uncle Pickens insisted, "If you find any money in the walls, I want my money back, but I won't charge you anything for interest." Hannah and I laughed together that night . . . lying in the bed,

We never could have completed a project like this without George. He had the know-how, and we had the "want to." It was a great combination. When we first bought the house, I went to cut the grass and weeds around the outskirts, just so we could begin the tear-out and prep work. Hot and tired, I sat my Weed eater down near that blue-painted wall, just in front of my old Dodge truck. After drinking a glass of water, Hannah and I decided to call it a day, and we climbed into the truck, cranked it up, and promptly ran slam over the Weed eater. I have a love-hate relationship with Weed eaters. I'm pretty sure they are the spawn of the devil, and I love to hate them!

we fancied what we might do if we did find all of the bank's money stashed away in the walls of that old house. Tomfoolery, we both agreed, but isn't that what dreams are made of? Some notion of tomfoolery? And we sure made plenty of dreams come true in that old home. Bay was born while we lived there—and so was the Legend of Thunderfoot. That is, after all, the recollection that Thelma and Louis provoked as they readied themselves in the pre-dawn hours that Saturday morning.

Part Two

Jack Odom was a wrinkle-faced, white-haired, stoic man. I suppose you have to be stoic, though, to cut a house right down the middle with a chain saw, lift the two huge halves with steel beams, and tow them down the street with a couple of semitrucks . . . that's not something just anyone can do. But, Jack could, and he did.

"I'm putting that younger boy on the roof of the first half," Jack said. "He will make sure we don't rip down any telephone or cable lines." Jack didn't worry about the electric lines. "They always put them at the same height on the pole. We are way under the height." But Jack didn't think much of the cable company . . . "It's those dadgum cable guys that get ya. They don't care where they hang those wires on that pole." I just nodded my head . . . I had no idea whether everything he said was perfectly logical, or if it was lunacy to sit a man on top of half of a house while it's being pulled down the road. "You're the Captain. I just take orders," I told him as he loaded up in the lead truck. "Good," Jack offered. "At least I know one person out here will listen to me." I heard him laughing at his own joke as he fired the big diesel engine . . .

They used two semitrucks—hooked up back-to-back—to pull the pieces of the house from its 100-year-old resting place and out into the road. Sheriff's deputies blocked traffic for the behemoth loads, and a pilot car followed at a safe distance . . . and, sure enough, "that younger boy," who was, in fact, a grown man at least 35 years old, was riding on top of the first piece of the house. Hannah and I were out in front of the convoy . . . that seemed to us to be the best vantage point to watch the massive spectacle.

We spent a week taking all the tin off the roof and taking all of the gables and peaks down. The house was now flat on top, and, thus, considerably shorter. "You have two options," the man from the power company told us. "You can lay the roof down flat or pay us to move every power line out of the way. There are 26 on your route. It's $600 per line." "Oh, that's easy," Hannah said . . . "Somebody hand me a chain saw." The power company man did not understand her suggestion was to cut the roof off of the house. "Ma'am, you can't cut down the poles."

We busted a gut (that's a Southern expression meant to suggest that one laughs so hard that their belly hurts), and we laughed until tears fell from our eyes!

The convoy was a parade of sorts . . . deputies to the front and rear, blue and red flashing lights warning approaching traffic. Two men who worked for Jack drove just behind the lead deputy, asking folks to pull their car completely off the road to make way for the battleships floating down the highway. Folks were happy to oblige . . . kids hung out the back window of their parent's cars, watching intently as the house eased by at a brisk five miles per hour. A reporter from the newspaper jockeyed around the convoy trying to get a few good pictures . . . I searched for the write-up that the *Andalusia Star News* published covering the "Parade of Home," but it was to no avail.

It took about 40 minutes to travel 3.8 miles from downtown Gantt to the Valley of Shiloh on Gantt Lake. The trip was relatively uneventful, save one mailbox that was a little too close to the road. "It's got to go," Jack exclaimed. "I have 80,000 pounds of house sitting in the road. The only thing keeping us from moving forward is that 15-pound mailbox." Soon enough, Jack had the owner's permission to remove the mailbox. One of his men shimmied the post to and fro until it finally freed. After the convoy passed, the same man, armed with a bag of Quikrete, began resetting the post and mailbox. "That isn't the first time we've had to do that," Jack noted. The man who owned the mailbox was Marcell Gantt . . . he and I became fast friends in later years. He spoke with a thick, country accent . . . one that makes Hannah sound like a Yankee, and his gait of speech was slow and deliberate. Marcell could never be accused of talking too fast . . . sometimes frustrated by his deliberateness, I would answer the question before he finished asking.

Marcell liked a cold beer or two . . . and he was one of the strongest, most hardworking men I'd ever known. Standing 6 feet 2 inches and weighing 180 pounds or so, Marcell wasn't the physical specimen that struck you as a pillar of strength . . . but he was "country strong" . . . that is, he gained strength not from barbells and visits to the gym. Instead, he was raised strong because he had a lifetime of building fences and lifting hay bales.

And I'm sure Marcell and Hannah are cousins . . . seems too close in proximity . . . both families grew up within a stone's throw of each other. We will never be able to trace the lineage, though. How the Gantt name jumped from one family to another, thus merging the two families together, is forever lost in history.

A hundred yards farther down the road, I saw Jack stop and get out of his truck. He gestured to the truck driver (once the house was on the smooth asphalt and out of the yard where it was built, the movers used one semi per piece of the house) to ease the first piece of the house up to a line hanging low over the road. "There is no way it is going under that line," Hannah said in observation. I agreed.

Jack stamped around in the road for a few seconds and then perched, with one hand on his hip, the other pointing and directing the man on the roof of the house. Hannah and I were about 50 yards in front of them. I put the truck in reverse, and we started backing up . . . before we got to them, Jack threw a pair of wire cutters up to the

Jack Odom was as fine of a man as I have ever known.
Hardworking, dependable, trustworthy, and honest,
he taught me many a lesson in life . . . and we remained
friends for many years until his death. Even still today
though, his son Marty and I remain good friends.

rooftop sentinel. "I told them to move the wire, so cut it," I heard Jack yell as I got out of the truck. A sense of urgency and panic set in as I envisioned all sorts of calamity unfolding hereinafter . . . I hurried my pace. Before I got to Jack, he was on the phone with the cable company. "I told y'all . . . so now, I'm cutting it," he said. "Better send a truck out here to fix it."

And with a nod of his head, Jack gave the order . . . snip . . . the cable fell limp across the cab of the truck. Jack drug the cable off the truck and coiled it up on the roadside. "It will be alright . . . they've known for three weeks they needed to move the cable, and we can't just sit here in the road for half a day waiting on them to come do it now," he muttered, as he loaded back up in the truck. Then, like General Patton, Jack gestured with his left arm out the window for the troops to resume the slow march forward.

Fifteen minutes later, the trucks all grumbled to a stop in the midst of the clearing where we wanted to turn this house into our home. The two pieces of the house lay, perfectly aligned, a mere quarter of an inch from each other. "That's about as close as I can get them," Jack offered. Hannah and I were more than impressed, as Jack himself had navigated the two trucks within a snail's hair from each other, such that a casual observance would not allow one to conclude the house had been cut in two.

A few days more, all the trucks were gone, and our future home sat on its new and fertile ground . . . awaiting restoration and life.

Hannah and I worked tirelessly for nearly a year on that house. Certainly, we hired men like Tony Nall and his crew to work on it . . . they built the roof back and handled the structural mending that needed to take place from the house being cut in two . . . but Hannah and I worked for hours on end restoring that home.

And I can't wait to tell you about some of those special moments . . . and maybe I'll get far enough down the road to tell you about Thunderfoot. In the meantime, never forget the lessons learned from good men like Jack Odom. To this day, I've never let someone else's failure to do their job keep me from doing mine . . . I learned that from Jack Odom. He was a fine man and a good friend. God rest his soul.

Part Three

Hannah and I were poor to say the least. We'd just spent three years clawing and digging our way through law school. I say "we" because Hannah was as much a student as I was, helping me study, working full-time to pay the bills, and making sure our little home in Centreville, Alabama, was as good as it could be under those hard times. We moved back to Andalusia after I graduated, and this banker's house and the land it sat on would be the house that we made into our home . . . the house where we began our family.

We spent nearly a year living with George and Brenda while we worked on transforming the old skin and bones of the house into something more hospitable . . . from rotten wood to aged floors, the whole house had to be redone. Tony Nall and his crew took on the biggest work, but because we were poor, we did much . . . perhaps, most . . . of the work ourselves. I worked as a lawyer in town until 5 p.m. every day. Hannah was a social worker with the United Methodist Children's Home. We'd both get off work around 5 p.m., visit with George and Brenda at dinner, and then usher off to the lake to work on the house. Most nights, Hannah would call it quits around 9 p.m. Sometimes, I'd work until midnight. I fell in love with Hannah in a completely different way during those long summer nights. You see, I already knew her as the Southern lady that she was. Certain to wear a dress rather than slacks to church, never to serve guests from paper or plastic, firm in her beliefs and convictions and unashamed of who she was, and as good-looking as a tall glass of ice water on a hot summer day—she was who I fell in love with.

But this woman who slung a hammer like a cowgirl with a six-shooter? Or the seductress who carried lumber like it was a plate of dinner rolls? Or the woman who caulked and painted until she, herself . . . was covered? Who is she?

I'd never seen this side of Hannah. Sure, I knew she was hardworking, but this was next level hard work. And she tackled this sweat-laden dirty work without fear. It didn't matter if we didn't know how to do something, she forged ahead, and we learned as we went. We made mistakes along the way, too, but never too prideful to admit our shortcomings, we'd back up and regroup and go at it again.

And Hannah never faltered . . . and that was sexy to me.

I still remember vividly how she'd leave the top button of her denim shirt undone. It was hot (so was she), and she simply thought that the less restrictive clothing was more comfortable. I found the occasional glance at her cleavage alluring . . . a pleasant distraction from the late-night marathons, for sure. Every now and then, she would see "that look" in my eye . . . and she'd roll her own. Shaking her head and laughing, covered in dirt and dust, sweat and blood . . . "How could you think 'this' looks good?" she'd ask. I'd just grin sheepishly . . . embarrassed that she "caught" me.

But to me, she looked beautiful . . . still does.

There were certainly hard times. And I don't think we could have gotten through those hard times without each other . . . and there were certainly times that I wouldn't have made it without her. One Sunday afternoon comes to mind . . . we were hanging molding in what would be our bedroom. The walls in the bedroom were reclaimed tongue-and-groove heart pine 1x4s that we salvaged from another old home. We tore it down so that we could reclaim the salvaged lumber to use in this house . . . we wanted to preserve the authenticity of the era of the home during the remodel. We built a small nook area—meant to be a place for Hannah to have a vanity and dressing area—off our bedroom. Like a kitchen with a sunroom off to one side, our bedroom and the vanity nook were not separated by walls . . . rather, they shared the same exterior walls . . . and the "nook" is what distinguished the vanity from the bedroom.

The first corner leading into the nook was a 90-degree turn of the molding on a corner that stuck out . . . the corner turned away from the bedroom and into the nook. I positioned my ladder on the right side of the turn and finished up nailing the molding . . . "chachunk, chachunk," the nail gun hammered away. The compressed air forced the metal slide out of its resting place, and the slide came out with such force that it slammed the nail through the molding and into the wall. Satisfied that the end of the molding was well secured by those two nails, I lowered the gun to the ground, letting the air hose slide between my hands until it came to rest on the heart pine floor. From the same perch, I leaned around the corner and measured the next piece of molding. It was a short piece . . . about five feet in length . . . and the cut was easy to make.

Oftentimes, because the molding could be flimsy, I'd have to ask Hannah to help me cut it . . . with her holding one end as I measured and cut the other end on the chop saw. With short pieces, though, I could manage myself, allowing her to continue in her work, undisturbed. I finished my measurements and made the cuts . . . and eased back over to the ladder. In hindsight, I should have moved the ladder, but trying to hurry to finish the last few pieces of molding in the room compelled me to make poor decisions . . . such is often the case in life.

Shortcuts rarely lead to any fruit.

I climbed the ladder and leaned around the corner—molding in one hand, nail gun in the other, and leaning like Italy's Tower of Pisa. Even Otis, the town drunk on *The Andy Griffith Show*, could have seen that trouble was brewing. Ah, but I was aware of the danger of falling from the ladder . . . such a precarious position was easily identifiable . . . so I took measures to prevent such calamity. Aren't I smart? (You should be able to detect the sarcasm). Leaning and straining, I decided I simply needed to nail the nearest top corner of the molding, and then I could move my ladder to a better position to finish the rest of the board. I carefully positioned the board—my fingers wrapping underneath it for better leverage—and cocked the corner into the best position . . . I pulled nail gun over my head with my right arm and put it in the prime position . . . "chachunk..." and that nail found its mark. The board was nailed perfectly in place . . . and my finger was, too.

"Aaaaahhhhhh!" I yelled and probably said a cuss word or two also. Hannah came running into the room. "What's wrong?" she asked. Leaning around the corner, still on the ladder, with my left arm crucified in an almost upright position . . . blood trickled down my hand. I didn't fault Hannah for not realizing my predicament . . . no normal person would ever comprehend that this was even a possibility. Only I could accomplish such a feat! "I've nailed myself to the wall!" I felt stupid just saying it. And I could see from the look in her eyes that Hannah wanted to laugh . . . but thought better of it . . . until she could find a way to free me. I suppose there was some part of

My only regret about this "note" was that we did not give glory
to the One who deserved it all. I wish I could be a fly on the wall
one day when some carpenter tears that old mantel off the
wall during a remodel job and finds this. God bless America.

It was only a day or two before this picture was taken that I
somehow managed to nail myself to the wall . . . in nearly this
very same spot. I've been nailed to the wall, metaphorically, a
few other times, too. I've never been able to get down by myself.
That day in the Valley of Shiloh, Hannah had to pull me away
from the nail. Every other time, I needed help, too. I've never
been strong enough to pull myself off the wall.

me that wanted to laugh, too . . . but dadgum, it hurt. "Help me first . . . we can laugh later," I offered. I saw a smirk hit the corners of her mouth as she walked around behind me to inspect my carpentry skills. After a brief assessment, she retreated to the hallway, yelling, "I'll be right back . . . stick around!"

Comedian.

Hannah reappeared a minute or two later, and by then, my finger and hand were throbbing. She put a second ladder on the other side of the corner and climbed up for a closer look. Hammer in hand, she slid the claws up under the molding and leveraged the hammer against the wall. "This is probably going to sting a little," she said. I closed my eyes and braced myself. With one swift and fluid motion, she lurched down on the handle of the hammer. The back side of the hammer rolled on the wall, and the claws pulled the board straight out, away from the wall. The molding . . . soft pine . . . pulled straight out away from the wall just as intended and tumbled to the floor with a loud clamor. Trouble was that the nail simply pulled through the soft pine molding, and my finger was still nailed to the wall.

"This is really going to hurt," Hannah said. I swear I saw a smirk come to the corners of her mouth again.

Vixen.

She pushed hard on my finger with one hand and then slid the claws of the hammer in between the head of the nail and the flesh of my finger. It hurt like hell, but I was free . . . and free bleeding . . . "Don't you get blood on those floors!" she barked.

She ushered me to the soon-to-be kitchen and wrapped my finger with paper towels. Perhaps, I needed stitches . . . but, not to be encumbered by my own idiocy, I pressed on into the night. My finger swelled to about twice its normal size, and I'm pretty sure it got infected, but after about a week, everything returned to normal.

I'll never forget that day, though . . . not because of the blood or the pain, or even because of my own stupidity. Instead, I'll never forget that day because I don't think in all the history of humanity has a man who nailed himself to the wall had the pleasure of staring at cleavage while his rescuer used a claw hammer to free him.

If that ain't sexy, I don't know what is. Why, I even considered nailing myself to the wall again, but thought better of it, for surely, there had to be an easier way! I love you, Hannah Merrell . . . you dirty, sexy, hammer-swinging Southern lady!

Part Four

Work steadily progressed on our turn-of-the-century remodel. Windows, both new and old, were installed. George had salvaged some beautiful paned windows from the parsonage at the First United Methodist Church . . . they had had a sliding lock that allowed them to swing open to the right or to the left depending on how you hinged them, and with the locking mechanism, you could keep the windows open no matter the wind conditions. Not unlike the newer still slide on a screened door, the open windows invited the cool breeze of a spring afternoon into the house. They looked beautiful in our master bathroom, a claw-foot tub perched on a stoop just below them . . . Hannah would come to love this view in later years . . . she took many a bath gazing out these windows. Looking back, it still amazes me how such a simple thing can bring such joy.

William Merrill was a local craftsman and artisan. Regrettably, he died a few years ago, but before his death, he spent a considerable amount of time building a chandelier for our kitchen. Hannah had found two beautiful globes in an antiques store or at a yard sale . . . with mouths larger than basketballs and bases twice as wide, they were huge. Ribbed all the way around, the sharp points of each ridge line projected prisms around the room when lit from within. Of course, the tragedy was that there was no standard light fixture that they would attach to, so Hannah enlisted the help of Mr. Merrill. He built a beautiful, one-of-a-kind chandelier for the kitchen. It is one way he left his mark on this world.

He was a jolly sort, and with his long white beard, had he weighed another 30 or 40 pounds, he could've easily passed for Saint Nick. He liked to smile, and he liked to laugh, and he liked the challenges that Hannah always presented him with when she expressed her vision to him. You see, Mr. Merrill may have been a welder by trade, but he was an artist at heart. He oftentimes talked to me about how appreciative he was that he had the regular business of welding . . . usually consisting of building custom-made stair rails and repairing things that farmers or mechanics had broken . . . those things paid the bills. He appreciated those things because they provided for him and his needs. However, he cautioned us not to become too complacent with the mechanism of life. "Welding can be routine—sort of like breathing," Mr. Merrill said. "It just becomes the natural course of things. Life can be that way, too . . . and if life ever becomes routine . . . well, it seems to me that we have lost the true value of each breath that we take. That's why I look forward to seeing you pull up in the driveway: I know that whatever vision Hannah has, it won't be routine, and it will make me breathe deep." Of course, in typical welder fashion, whenever we settled our bill with Mr. Merrill for a particular project, he would also always add, "Now, this is the last one of these I'm ever going to do for y'all." Yet, every time we came back, he always welcomed us with open arms.

I breathe a little deeper because of William Merrill. Thank you, old friend. There is a piece of you in every house we've ever built and in our hearts, too.

Tony and his crew continued all along. They had done a fine job scabbing all the floor joists under the house and the ceiling joists in the attic so that, structurally, the house's wound of being cut into had been repaired. There does still exist a $1/8$-inch crack straight down the middle hall of the house where the chain saw ripped its way through the wood. I always appreciated the fact that Jack Odom went to great pains to cut a precisely straight line when he cut the house in half. I don't imagine it was easy to exercise such precision with a chain saw . . . he, too, was indeed a master of his trade.

Hannah and I continued in our endeavors as well. We finished replacing the rotten walls in the back hall. Tony and his men had repaired or replaced all the rotten structure . . . Hannah and I came behind them and put new, old stock, 1x4-inch tongue-and-groove heart pine on the walls to match the rest of the house. After a fresh coat of paint, no one would ever know that this wood came from an entirely different house.

From there, we moved to the laundry room. Space was an issue in this house. Despite appearances, it was only two bedrooms, and we had to engage in some intricate planning to create the space necessary for closets, bathrooms, and a laundry room. Remember that at the beginning of the 20th century, most houses did not have indoor plumbing, and they certainly did not have a laundry room or closest. Why, even in the 1930s, the setting in *To Kill a Mockingbird*, Mayella Ewell lured Tom Robinson into her yard with the promise of a payment of one whole nickel for busting up the chifforobe. The chifforobe, you see, was the equivalent of a closet for many homes . . . thus, like so many others, our banker's house had no bathrooms, closets, or other modern-day allowances within its walls.

We carved up what would have been a third bedroom, situated in the interior of the house, to create space for Hannah's vanity nook, the master closet, the laundry room, and a bathroom for overnight visitors.

Speaking of overnight visitors . . . the house was built with a traveler's room off the front porch. Though it was attached to the main house, the room was only accessible from a door that opened from the front porch. All these years later, the traveler's room was still only accessible from the front porch. We cut a hole through the wall, made the traveler's room our second bedroom, and put a window in where the door once stood . . . with a view to the porch.

The banker apparently rented the room to travelers passing through. The room was probably built with the intention of renting it to wealthy landowners coming into town to do business with the bank. Apparently, that banker found himself in a bit of a predicament when a sultry young lady came into the bank inquiring about renting a room. According to a few old-timers who heard the story from other old-timers, she was "quite a looker, red-headed, and big-chested, and she knew that money wasn't the only capital that could be traded." No doubt enticed by her feminine wiles, the banker rented the traveler's room to her for one night. After the second night, the banker's wife apparently protested to the pastor of the local church. He, in turn, visited with the banker and left with the assurance that the sultry redhead would be on her way the next day.

The next day came and went, and there were still one too many guests at the banker's house. Apparently, the wife wasn't putting up with it any longer . . . that third night, a group of men on horseback came in the form of a posse and met with the young lady. She assured them she would be on her way at first light . . . and she was. One old-timer said as she started up the road in her buggy, she looked back at the banker and his wife and thanked them for their kindness, but quipped, "Sometimes, you have to let your corset out and breathe a little."

Anyway . . .

The four rooms had been partitioned off and walled up. Next came managing the space in the most efficient manner. The laundry room was barely big enough to sit a washer and dryer side by side, so I used some of the framing timbers we tore out of the roof to build a massive shelf about head high above that space. As with any house of this age, the ceiling was extremely high . . . allowing the heat of summer to rise to the top of the room . . . 12 feet 6 inches to be exact. So, six feet off the ground, my massive shelf sat . . . waiting for its bride . . . the water heater.

I calculated that an 80-gallon water heater, when filled, would weigh around 500 pounds. "Hey, Tony, can you send your guys in here to help me for a second?" I asked. Two guys rounded the corner. "Climb up here and give me a hand, fellas." They obliged, but silently, I surmised that we collectively didn't weigh enough. "Hey, Tony, I think we need one more set of hands," I hollered. I heard the footsteps getting closer, and the biggest man of the crew turned the corner. "What are we trying to do?" asked one of the guys standing next to me. Ignoring his question, I gestured for "big boy" to climb up, and, in short order, he did. The four of us stood chest to chest on the shelf, and I was almost satisfied that my construction would survive the weight of the water heater. "Alright men, that's all I needed," I said.

"But what are we doing?" the same fellow asked. Tony hollered from the next room, "Y'all all standing up on that shelf?" The fellow to my left answer out, "Yeah," and Tony started laughing. "Y'all are human guinea pigs. He needed to see if his shelf would hold the weight," and he let out a belly laugh for good measure. "Don't breathe too deep, or you just might fall!"

Before Tony had finished talking, all the men had climbed down . . . each inspecting my work and assuring me it would hold . . . "Shoot, first thing I did was make sure it looked good," I said. "Ain't no way I was climbing up there unless I thought it would hold us." Each of them commended me for turning a corner in the world of carpentry . . . I was just glad they approved.

I breathed a sigh of relief, too, that the shelf was done.

William Merrill breathed his last breath a year or so after he finished work for us on a later house we renovated. Jack Odom breathed his last breath a couple of years back, too. And the old-timers told me that the buxom redhead breathed her last, too . . . a few towns over after she left the banker's house . . . shot by a jealous wife.

"I like to breathe the fresh air," Hannah said, as she scooped the water up and pulled it up over her shoulders. The smell of gardenias floated in through the open bathroom windows. She had filled the claw-foot tub with something lavender, and the two smells blended nicely. The neighbor next door was cutting his grass . . . and the smell of that

More 35-millimeter film and the pictures we took with it . . . it was always so authentic. You see that Hannah's eyes are closed in this picture, but that's part of what makes it so special to me. It's not perfect, and we weren't either, and neither was life, then or now. Today, folks take a hundred pictures to get the perfect one, and that winning picture suggests life is perfect, too. But the truth is, life is always hard, and there is always struggle. Here we stood in a house with no windows or doors, broke, and living with Hannah's parents while working on our dream home. Tired and hungry, we stopped for this picture . . . and it makes me smile every time I see it. Not because it was perfect, but because we had nothing but each other. . . and that was all I ever needed.

The bank of windows on the back of the house sat above a clawfoot tub where Hannah loved to take baths. Those windows opened out into the yard, and Hannah loved to soak in a warm bath listening to the song of the birds and the whistle of the wind.

fresh cut lawn occasionally drifted in as well. Hannah drew in a deep breath through her nose . . . "Isn't it beautiful?" she asked.

She could have been talking about our newly renovated house. Or, she could have been talking about the ornate antique fixtures on the tub that we salvaged from another old antebellum home. Or, she could have even been talking about the freshly laid sod in the yard or the birds singing in the evening shade . . . but she wasn't.

"Yes, it is," I said . . . and we both sat and stared out the open windows into the woods of the backyard.

Just breathe. The breath of life is abundant.

Chapter TWO

THE LINCOLN CHRONICLES 2

THE SENTINEL

O ur dog Lincoln was only about four years old . . . still young by most people's standards. He had broad shoulders and floppy ears, and a long, slender, muscle-toned body followed behind those strong shoulders. His slick black-and-brown coat gave him a rather sophisticated look despite his tenderly brutish physique . . . he had a kind of debonaire look about him. Sometimes, he presented himself like Rambo—ready to take on anyone at any time. Other times, he came across more like Thurston Howell, III —yeah, the rich millionaire on the SS *Minnow* with the Skipper and Gilligan and the rest of the stranded crew. Savvy, smart, and sophisticated, he might outwit you instead of brawl with you. And still other times, he made me think he was some combination of the two.

No matter what mood he might be in, though, he was always a protector . . . and he still is.

He has bitten three good friends. All of three of them were men, and they all unintentionally made the mistake of getting between Lincoln and one or more of my daughters. Sophisticated in his brawn, Lincoln identifies what he believes to be a threat, but instead of attacking head on, he sneaks up from the rear. His protective instinct has become well known around the neighborhood . . . so well known, in fact, that the UPS man carries a long pole in his truck that he calls the Lincoln Log. It's not meant for hitting Lincoln, but for keeping him at bay. The FedEx man just leaves the packages for us at the road. Most of my friends call and tell me they are in the truck in the driveway.

Lincoln is not ferocious, though. Don't let my words conjure images of *White Fang* . . . lips curled, slobber slinging, teeth showing, nose snarling. No, that's not Lincoln at all. In fact, he is rather unassuming for the most part. He just wants to do his job . . . be a protector and occasionally find a deer. Truth is, he is a good dog, a loyal companion, and a great friend . . . far from the menace that some dogs personify.

His status as protector has never been more exemplified than it was one warm spring day when he was four years old. Our girls, Bay, Cape, and Banks, wanted to go fishing that afternoon . . . or maybe I did. I have been known to drag them along against their will! Lincoln was staged at his outpost—the back door.

You see, whenever we are inside, he keeps guard very near the back door. That, he figures, is the best way to put himself in between us and a threat. If ever we venture out the door, he is always at my side, and he is ever vigilant to surveil the surroundings to protect the girls as well.

"The Sentinel" is a true story, as you can see from the picture. In fact, all my stories are well grounded in truth . . . though I admit I sometimes add a little flair here or there. Lincoln was shot not too long after this picture was taken. Being shot changed him forever, physically and emotionally. He was never again able to climb on top of my truck. In fact, he couldn't even get into the bed of my truck after that unless I helped him. But he grew smarter and much more discerning. Lincoln is the best dog I have ever had. Shoot, he is one of the best friends I have ever had. After he was shot by a man, he always kept the family safe from any unfamiliar man. He became a sentinel of an entirely different sort.

This day was no different. He met me as I came out the door, and he paced with me . . . matching me nearly step for step as I retrieved our fishing gear from the shed and loaded it in the truck. As I placed the tackle box down, I looked toward him just in time to catch him leaping up into the bed of the truck. I laughed and said, "Oh, so you thought you were invited?" He whined back at me and wagged his tail in excitement as I smiled and then laughed.

He loves the water, and he loves to go fishing at the pond.

That pond is maybe three acres . . . not huge, but big enough that the family can spread out and each fish his or her own spot. I parked the truck under the power lines, the girls and I up front and Lincoln in the bed. We grabbed our gear and headed to the water's edge. Lincoln followed closely behind Cape, as she was the last to leave the truck and move towards the pond.

Spring was in full bloom . . . dogwoods flanked the head of the pond where the water flows from up creek. The short trees blanketed the shore with patches of their white, cross-like blooms. Wild honeysuckles of orange and yellow also dotted the landscape, hopscotching down the shore nearest our truck. Black-eyed Susan, a yellow-blooming flower with a brownish-black "eye" in the middle of the circle of petals, littered almost every step of the shoreline. We keep our pond shores in a natural state . . . not manicured like a golf course but, instead, natural and just accessible enough that you can fish from the shores.

Bay stood on the boardwalk that George built. It follows the edge of the pond some 75 feet or so down one side before crossing the pond nearer the head. This boardwalk/pier combination is a great place to fish. Bream huddled in masses underneath its shade, and Bay was catching hand-size bream as fast as she could get her hook back in the water. We had not been there 10 minutes, and she had already caught several fish.

"I caught the first fish!" she teased.

Banks and I made our way to the pond's dam. From its peak, I intended to cast for bass in the deepest waters of the pond. Though I may not catch but two or three, these deep, dark waters held the largest fish in the pond. Bay may have caught the first, but surely, it wouldn't be the largest. Banks stood close by me casting her Barbie Princess fishing pole. She wouldn't fish long . . . too young to stay too interested. Soon enough, she'd be picking flowers or laying in the grass, and that was okay.

Cape stood on the opposite shore where she'd already caught her first bass. And she would catch several more—she is quite the angler. She worked her way in and out of the dogwoods, easing towards the top end of the pond, weaving around the honeysuckle as she went. Periodically, she would disappear into the woods as she weaved further up the pond. Her apparent absence made Lincoln uneasy.

Thus, he continuously made his rounds. He went to each of the girls and nervously said "Hello" in his own way. Then, he was off to the next girl . . . surveying the landscape as he went. In a few minutes, he'd be back, and the process would repeat.

I could tell he wasn't comfortable. "Relax, boy." I tried to encourage him, but my words offered him little consolation, and off he went, back on the circuit.

A few minutes went by, and Lincoln had not returned, and I realized, after scanning the pond, that he was not with any of the girls. Curious it was . . . but I kept on fishing. "He's off in the woods," I thought to myself. But a few minutes later, Banks started laughing and hollered, "Daddy! Look at Lincoln!"

I turned to find him sitting on top of the cab of the truck. Perched like a watchman in a guard tower, the sentinel had found his post. And from then on . . . as long as he was able, he would climb up through the bed and atop the cab of the truck whenever we went fishing . . . because that way, he could see all the girls at one time.

Did I mention he is a great protector? Because he is.

Aren't you glad you have a sentinel in your life, too? The Father watches over us all . . . and He does so with a great eagerness to provide protection and comfort. Take comfort in that today, friends. Just like we take comfort in knowing that Lincoln will always intercept any coyote or stray dog that makes its way towards one of the girls, the Father is watching over all of us and desires to provide for us as well.

He watches over you, too . . . right now.

DOGS GET ALONG PRETTY WELL

My black-and-tan coonhound, Lincoln, had a friend . . . she was some sort of bulldog. She was white in color and about half his size. Her name was Biscuit. Lincoln is a big dog. When last I weighed him, he came in at just shy of 110 pounds. He eats a diet of almost exclusively table scraps . . . and he is a bit snobby about that, too. Often passing up smaller pieces of meat sitting too close to a vegetable—he prefers only meat—and maybe a potato occasionally. At the end of every meal, Hannah or I scrape all the "good" dog scraps onto a plate. He is almost always lying at the back door waiting . . . he's no dummy. He smells the good home cooking. Hannah always scoops the scraps into his dog bowl. I always sit the plate down and let him eat off the plate. Hannah hates when I do that. I don't do it to make her mad, but I want my dog to know that I value him.

So . . . he eats well—very well. He has fat rolls instead of abs. He was once a lean and muscular sniffing missile. Now, he is a stout and barrel-chested keg of sniff on tap. He spends much of the day sleeping, likely dreaming of biting the UPS man. But his intentions are good. He is not vicious. He only acts aggressive toward outsiders to protect our family, as he sees any visitor as a threat. That is one of his character flaws . . . assuming that every man is evil.

The bulldog, on the other hand, had a more discerning bite. Biscuit generally sized people up before she decided to pounce, and she was usually fairly accurate in her discernment. The UPS man was safe in her eyes . . . that's because she had figured out that he is a really good guy and a good friend. The mail lady was much the same, but there were a few folks who came to "talk to Mr. Walt about my son being in jail" that she didn't care for too much. We didn't talk long, either.

The two dogs were buddies, but that is all. Lincoln is too old for a "pretty young thing," and frankly, he can no longer sire offspring. Oftentimes, they went on adventures together . . . leaving the house early in the morning and not re-emerging from the woods till near noon. You could always count on Lincoln to come home when someone was cooking . . . that hound could smell a pan of cornbread from six creeks away.

They ate together, too. Unlike many dogs I know, they never fought over food.

Lincoln has a generally pleasant and subdued disposition, especially as he has gotten older. He prefers to lie around and watch the world go by, occasionally getting up to survey the yard or inspect the perimeter, only to lie back down again under the shade of the big hickory tree. In that respect, he gets along pretty well, but pull into our driveway in an unfamiliar vehicle, and he transforms from sleepy-eyed hound to vigilant protector. He would never let anything happen to my girls, and perhaps me, either, and that is why he and I get along pretty well, too.

They'd share, and they seemed content enough to know that the other of them was well taken care of. Usually after they ate, they'd recline together, too. Imagine the dog equivalent to unbuttoning the top button of your pants and laying back on the couch after lunch. Well, that was them on most days. They'd lie around on the porch together and exhale long, exaggerated, "Oh, I ate too much" sighs. Sometimes, I could almost hear them trying to convince one another, "Oh no . . . I ate way more than you did!"

Point of it all is that whether they be at play, at rest, or at work, there was no doubt that they found value in each other's companionship, despite their differences.

But the bulldog was a special dog with a special temperament. You see, Lincoln was a true jerk to her for a while . . . growling when she came near, barking from afar, and even an occasional scuffle where she got roughed up. The fact was, Lincoln did not like her when they first met. But being the true Southern lady that she was, she persisted, and her kindness prevailed.

Sometimes, I am a jerk. I've bit a few people in my lifetime, and I always regret it. More than anyone, it's my kids and my wife . . . we always seem to bite the ones we love most. I think it's because we are overly confident that they will forgive us. But my wife has a patience and a kindness that is unparalleled, and she always finds a subtle way to remind me that it's not nice to bite the UPS man.

There are a lot of jerks in the world. Pilate, Barabbas, Judas . . . just a few that quickly come to mind. Lincoln and I act more like them than we should, but there is one named Jesus, and He always wins with kindness and compassion. He always finds a way to bring me back.

We could learn a lot from these two dogs, but more from Jesus about how to act and how not to act . . . dogs aren't nearly as dumb as we think. I see evil in the world, but it always starts in the hearts of men. We can control that, though, because we have an example to follow.

Be kind. No matter what. It's just that simple. Then, there won't be murders; there won't be looters; there won't be hate. Be kind.

Size doesn't matter. Color doesn't matter. It is only the heart that matters.

By the way, Biscuit died about a month before I wrote this. Lincoln hasn't been quite the same since. He mopes, meanders, and seems to be lost. She was a valuable companion . . . like so many of the people in our lives. Let's not take them for granted either . . . for they are a temporal gift.

GET OUT OF THE TRUCK

"Load up, boy." My dog Lincoln just wagged his tail and looked at me. Given the fact that his tender years were well behind him, I suspect he was thinking something along the lines of, "I weigh 145 pounds, and I have bullet fragments in my foot. You really think I can still jump that high?"

He was probably right. "Hannah, will you get me that chair off the porch?" I asked. She obliged and handed me the small, khaki-colored wooden chair straight from the *Leave It to Beaver* kitchen. Studying the situation—fat dog, tall truck—I placed the straight back of the chair next to the tailgate of the truck and gestured to Lincoln. He was eager and excited, wagging his tail furiously. He loves to ride, but he didn't seem to understand the significance of the chair turned stepping stool. I encouraged and patted and even climbed into the truck at one point . . . but all he did was look at me and wag his tail.

Sometimes, it takes a woman's touch . . . so, Hannah did us both the favor of picking up his torso and sitting his front feet up in the chair. "Thank you," I offered, somewhat embarrassed. Though I knew she just saved my blue pinstriped suit and color-coordinated tie from the utter filth of a 10-year-old mud, guts, and barbeque sauce hound dog who is allergic to taking a bath, my pride still didn't like the fact that my wife just did the heavy lifting while I stayed pretty in my fancy clothes.

But her solution was wise. Lincoln certainly appreciated it, for almost as if he wanted to say "Thank you," he looked at her and ducked his head and whimpered slightly as he shook his tail even harder. Then, slowly, he climbed into the truck and excitedly searched every corner of the empty bed.

Grateful to have a wife who knows how to find the solution and isn't afraid to get her hands dirty, I kissed Hannah goodbye, shut the tailgate of the truck, and loaded up . . . finding it more difficult than it once was to get in the truck myself. With that, though, us two old dogs—Lincoln and I—were off. Where, though, he did not know. He was just excited to be going and seeing and smelling. In a way, I was, too.

If you know anything about me, you know that I juggle many hats in my effort to maintain this ministry we call *Shepherding Outdoors*. By profession, I am a full-time, elected district attorney. I usually work 50 or more hours a week. More importantly,

At first, we didn't realize Lincoln had been shot. We could see the wound on his foot . . . a laceration that was maybe a centimeter long. It appeared to be more of a cut than a puncture, but our best guess was that he had been bitten by a snake. We kept him asleep with Benadryl for the first few days, but we could tell he was in intense pain as time went on. He only got up to drink water or to use the bathroom, and that might have been twice a day, at best. He would hardly eat. Soon enough, we sought out the help of our veterinarian, and a few X-rays later, we could easily see the fragmented bullet lodged in the bone in between his foot and leg. Surgery likely meant amputation, but even in the best-case scenarios, we couldn't afford it as an option anyway. We treated him for pain management and infection at first, and then shifted to arthritis later. He never ran through the woods with the same freedom after that. He was a changed dog, and it broke my heart. Simple things like getting in the truck were no longer independent options . . . but even in a suit and tie, I never minded scooping him into my arms just so he could ride with me.

though, I am a father of three daughters, two of which are still at home. Our middle daughter plays almost every sport you can imagine, and most nights, we are at a game somewhere. Our youngest daughter is just coming into her athletic career. She recently made the junior high volleyball team, but I suspect her first love is still ballet. Recitals are commonplace for our household.

Our oldest daughter is at Ole Miss. She has a bright future ahead . . . and though we don't see her nearly as often as we prefer, our relationship is strong and fruitful. Above all else is my commitment to and relationship with my wife. And though we are each other's first priority, life sometimes forces us to serve each other the leftovers of our time . . . still, though, we manage.

All those ladies are my best friends. The Lord knew what he was doing when he gave me Hannah. But I know that Lincoln has a place and a purpose in our family, too. Make no mistake, though, Lincoln is not more valuable to me than my wife or my children. But he's a great companion. He greets me every morning when I leave the house to go to work. Though his bed is at the far end of the porch, he is always sitting at the back door, tail wagging . . . waiting to say "Good morning" as Banks and I leave for our ride to school and work.

On those days when I don't have on a suit, I try to love on him. On those days when I do have on a suit, I'll try to scratch his ears and talk to him. I don't think he at all appreciates the difference between a suit and a pair of blue jeans . . . and I know for certain that the dirt and oil on his skin does not care one bit which it gets rubbed on.

And, at the end of the day when I drive up that driveway, no matter where he is or what he's doing, he comes home and greets me. He hears my truck just as well as he smells cornbread when it's in the oven . . . and nothing will stop him from coming.

Whether I've been gone for 30 minutes or three days, he is always just as excited to see me, and he always acts as if we haven't seen each other in years. Seeing him wag his tail and simultaneously lift his paw and lower his head always warms my heart. It's a curious thing, his greeting. I don't know what emotions dogs experience . . . I like to think that he is happy to see me, though I have no idea if he truly understands what happiness is. Perhaps, he simply wants me to scratch his ears. Either way, I'm good with it. He brings me joy.

Thinking he has joy from seeing me brings me joy also, and that is enough.

Lincoln had been sick for several months. Back during the summer, the veterinarian told me that if he lived seven days, it would be a huge victory. She is a fine Christian woman, and to hear her say, "I'll be praying for you both," let me know this was serious. After seven days of her studious and diligent efforts, she then cautioned me that 30 days might be the next objective. He obviously lived 30 days. And, while he is enjoying much better health, he is still sick. That being the case, we loaded up in the truck that morning because his breathing was labored, and his movement was slow and cautious. I can tell . . . he is failing.

Pulling up to the vet's office, I parked right at the front door. I could see there were no other patrons in the lobby. "So, it is safe," I considered. Because he is so big, other dog owners usually get very nervous when we come through the door. Truth is, I get nervous, too . . . he could eat a lap dog in a single bite. So, sometimes we take the back door.

On this day, though, the lobby looked clear. Getting out of the truck, I met him at the side of the bed. He stuck his cold, wet nose to my cheek. His tail wagged like a machine gun. I couldn't help but laugh. I asked, "What? Are you excited to see all your girlfriends?"

You see, Dr. Walker and her staff treat him like a king . . . sometimes, I think he'd rather live there with all those ladies. They keep him inside. Give him a soft mattress to lay on. Feed him everything he wants. Pet him on demand. Shoot . . . if I thought he'd eat a grape, I bet they would peel them for him. Fact is, I know he doesn't go more than a few minutes without some form of attention while he is here. So, who could blame him? I'd be excited, too.

Funny how little things can change a mood, though.

His tail-wagging quickly stopped when he caught a glimpse of the leash I held behind my back. Lincoln does not like a leash at all. That hatred for the leash goes back to tracking deer. The confines of the leash keep him from the object of his nasal affections, and he resents how slow and lumbered I am as I snake my way through the narrow pathways he weaves in the woods. Seeing the leash, he retreated as far away from me as he could and sat down in the far corner of the bed of the truck.

I was in a suit. I'm pretty sure he recognized that it was unlikely that I would climb back up in the bed of the truck and wrestle with him. So, we were in a standoff.

I can only imagine what passersby thought, seeing me standing at the end of the bed of the truck begging him to come out. "Come on, you jerk," I jokingly offered in frustration. He looked at me from the corner of his eye and wagged his tail sheepishly. His expression said to me, "I know you want me to come . . . I am not. I hope you're not mad."

Perhaps I should've beckoned for one of his lady friends inside . . . he probably would've quickly come to them. "Ungrateful dog," I laughed to myself, imagining him lying in a dog bed smoking a cigar and surrounded by all those women.

"Look, I have got to get to work!" He moved to the other corner. I had no choice . . . I had to resort to bribing him—giving him the last few bites of my breakfast biscuit that Brenda gave me coming out of the driveway. When he took the sausage and bread from my hand, in Spiderman-esque fashion, I wrapped the leash around his fat-rolled neck.

He is old, fat, sick, and achy . . . yet, show him a leash, and suddenly, he becomes a bowl full of energy and agility. "You crazy dog."

Lincoln is my companion. He walks with me through the woods. He sits with me on the porch in the morning and enjoys the sunrise as the coffee brews. He rides with me in the Jeep on the weekends, and he tracks deer for me every winter. We have a special bond . . . unlike any I have ever shared with a dog before. To say we are buddies is an understatement . . . but we are.

Everybody needs a buddy.

One day, and likely one day soon, Lincoln will pass on from this earth. I'm not certain he will not join me in Heaven. There is no biblical reference to dogs being in Heaven . . . but I know Jesus will be there . . . for He walks with me in the woods also. Why, He even goes hunting with me. And I am a firm believer that Jesus is also a Jeep man. He, too, is my buddy.

Like Lincoln, so quick to jump in the truck and ready to ride, lots of folks are quick to want to embrace all the wilds of this world. But when the world wraps its tentacles around them and they begin to wither, they are reluctant to withdraw . . . to get help. Lincoln wanted the wilds of those fun-time women at the vet's office . . . but he didn't want to be obedient to the restriction of the leash. I see lots of people do the same things. They want relief from the pain of addiction or strife, yet they don't want to embrace the submission and obedience necessary to free themselves from the bonds of their life.

And, like Lincoln, sometimes, I see people run to the far end of the bed of the truck of life. They crouch in the corner trying to get away from what they know is good for them . . . all because they might have to surrender.

Get out of the truck.

TRUST THE DOG

Our dog Lincoln's nose is remarkable. He certainly knows how to track blood and the smell of a deer. But it's much more than just a meat seeker. Where I might only smell an onion after Hannah has sliced it and the tear-provoking odor has permeated the house, Lincoln smelled the same onion when she got out of the car and it was still wrapped in the plastic grocery bag. It's not just that he can smell blood or animals . . . he can smell everything.

What you and I simply smell, he absorbs, like a computer storing data. His ability to store and recollect smells has always been remarkable, and his data storage capacity within the read-only memory (ROM) of his nose has saved me on more than one occasion . . .

Banks was turning 11 years old. The house was full of fifth graders, all there to celebrate that almost-teen milestone with her. My ambition at every birthday party we've ever had is two-fold. First, don't lose any kids. Second, make sure everyone has a good time and doesn't end up crying. This night, the hayride was to be the main entertainment. A good hayride followed by good food and tasty, sweet treats . . . how could it go wrong?

I already had the tractor and the wagon ready to go. It was parked just up the hill from the house . . . hay bales lined each outside edge of the wagon, making for perfectly suited bench seats for the dozen or so girls to rest their tails. Hannah hollered, "Who's ready for a hayride?" and a chorus of little screaming girls celebrated with squeals of glee. Herding them out to the old beat-up wagon might have been more of a chore had there been much light in the yard, but fear of the dark outskirts kept the little wigglers close to home . . . and conveniently close to the illuminated wagon.

The old red Massey Ferguson tractor came to life as all six of its cylinders roared in the darkness. A billow of jet-black smoke blew up and shrouded the tractor as it first fired up, adding to the mystique of the moment . . . through the growl of the tractor, I heard the girls make spooky noises as the black veil fell over them. Then, hearing a few coughs in the thickness of the diesel exhaust, I considered better of the situation and hollered, "Allllll aboooooard!" Turning to get approval, I saw Hannah and Banks both giving me a thumbs up, but Lincoln stood at the back of the trailer wagging his tail.

"He wants to go, too," I thought to myself. "Ever the faithful guard dog." Some years back, Lincoln had been shot in the foot by a hateful landowner who didn't appreciate

Lincoln chasing rabbits across his property. His injuries weren't life-threatening, but the bullet remained lodged in his foot, so jumping up or down was something he was reluctant to do. I noticed from time to time that, with just the right angle and pressure, he would recoil off that foot because of an unexpected jolt of pain through a nerve or the joint. Standing behind the trailer, he wagged his tail feverishly and stared straight at me. "Are you going to help me up or not?" was essentially what he was saying. So, I climbed down off the tractor and picked up all 110 pounds of that old black-and-tan coonhound. Realizing that Lincoln was joining them, the girls clapped and clamored for his attention. True to who he was, though, Lincoln moseyed right over to Banks' feet and laid down. "He knows what his job is," I thought to myself with pride. Climbing back up onto the tractor, I put it into gear, and I slowly let off the clutch . . . and into the darkness, like flour falling through a sifter, we disappeared.

Of course, there were lots of squeals and giggles along the way . . . Hannah told the story of The Headless Woman of Sweetgum Bottom—reporting to the wide-eyed girls of the times the villainess had been spotted in these very woods—and the ride itself was a perfect success. It, too, is perhaps, a story for another time. For now, though, the tractor lumbered up the last hill and slowed just a bit, coming to a stop at the crest near where we originally departed. After several alleged spottings of The Headless Woman of Sweetgum Bottom, the girls were eager to not only stay in the light but get in the house! I had barely called for all the girls to disembark before they scurried down the drive over the short distance towards the light of the house. Chuckling at their flight of fright, I cranked the tractor back up and revved the throttle as hard as it would go. Black smoke plumed, and the big diesel roared louder than ever before. The girls instinctively all started running—in mob-like fashion—and screamed all at once! I couldn't help but laugh as I took the tractor to its "spot" and then walked back toward the house.

I don't know why tractors have a "spot," but they do. Mine has parked in the same place for years . . . as do most tractors I am familiar with. The tractor would have been just as well left at the crest of the hill. I'm just a creature of habit, I suppose. But I do believe there is comfort in always knowing where something is and knowing that it is where it is supposed to be. There is also comfort in the light . . . for all Hannah's talk of boogeyman tales and The Headless Woman had even me suspicious of the cracks and rustles I heard in the nearby woods. Perhaps I even sped my gait ever so slightly as I sought out the comfort of the light.

The darkness of the driveway gave way to the light of the back porch and the windows in the house. The living room was full of rug rats. I could see them through the elongated windows on the back porch—some danced, others huddled in serious girl talk, and a few ate cupcakes and drank lemonade. The house was a bustle of activity . . . much like a beehive, the girls scurried about, to and fro, talking and singing, dancing and running, giggling and laughing . . . about what? Only the Lord would know.

Once I learned to trust Lincoln's instincts, I relied on him often. Bumps in the night were often investigated by a whistle, summoning him to the door, and then like Lassie, sending him off to survey the yard. A minute or two later he'd return wagging his tail, and I knew all was well. Likewise, and on the trail, more than once Lincoln alerted me to a rattlesnake as we meandered through the woods. And he was better than any character test man ever administered . . . if he liked you, I knew you were alright, and if he didn't take kindly to you . . . I kept a sharp eye on you, too. Trust your dog.

I stepped up on the porch and wiped my feet as I had been well-trained to do. Turning the doorknob and pushing the door open, 13 little girls rushed past me as if they were making the last lap at Talladega Superspeedway. Coming through the door like the famed last-place racer, Dick Trickle, Hannah scolded me and demanded, "Did you brush your feet off?" I nodded my head in affirmation and eased into the house thinking to myself, "I know she didn't make them brush their feet off when they ran inside trying to get away from The Headless Woman." But discretion was the better part of valor that night . . . I kept my mouth shut and smiled.

A minute or two later, they all came bursting back through the door like someone had set their britches on fire. "The Headless Woman, The Headless Woman!" they yelled almost in unison. Watching them breeze past the doormat with no regard, I then made eye contact with Hannah—she shook her head and rolled her eyes. I'm not sure if the headshake and eye roll were directed at me or were a consequence of the girls. Nonetheless, the girls scampered around like pinballs bouncing off bumpers from one side of the room to the other, as the excitement of the festivities was welling up inside of them. Hannah, ever the mother hen, did a quick head count and realized that we were two girls short. With the gaze of a sow grizzly bear studying an approaching threat to its cubs, Hannah's eyes pierced right through me as she asked, "Did you lose some of the girls?"

"What?" I asked, with a quite convincing and almost indignant assurance, even though I had not done a head count to make sure. "Of course, I didn't!" I answered. "They must be in the bathroom or hiding," or so I hoped. Hannah stood up and began a sweep of the house. She quickly emerged from one bathroom and then the other, with no girls in her brood. Her pace quickened ever so slightly, and the notion of disapproval grew on her face as she made her way to the back door.

"Who's missing?" she asked. Honestly, I had no idea. I wasn't even sure I could name all of their names to begin with. Banks piped up, "Maddie and Jane Ruth." Then, one of the other girls chimed in. "They are missing?" And you could hear the estrogen begin to pump through the air, coursing through their little veins like tiny anxiety molecules, destined to find fault and lay it squarely at my feet. All eyes turned to me. "Mr. Walt, where are they?" "Daddy, where did you lose them?" "Where did they . . ." "How could you . . ." The chorus grew to a deafening decibel. If ever I wanted one of those "Calgon, take me away" baths, it was then.

I retreated to the porch and left them to their chaos.

We had been back just a few minutes. I knew those girls were there somewhere. I never stopped on the hayride . . . the only way they could have gotten off would have been to jump. Had they, Lincoln or Hannah would have surely taken note. Simultaneous to my backtracking thoughts, I heard Hannah ask the rest of the girls, "Did anyone see them on the hayride?" A song of squeaky voices all affirmed they were on the hayride and several recounted sitting next to them in the wagon. I breathed a slight sigh of relief.

Again, Hannah commanded the room as I eavesdropped through the back door. "Did anyone see them jump off the hayride?" she asked. "No, they were on there until the end," Banks assured Hannah.

"That's my girl!" I thought to myself . . . saving Daddy's butt!

"Are you sure?" Hannah said, doubling down.

"I am sure, Mama," Banks responded. She was followed by several others, all attesting to the same facts. The room grew silent for a moment . . . I paced on the back porch. "Hey, let's go look for them! Let's form a search party!" Banks insisted with a particular intensity in her voice. And, with that, the pitter-patter-rumble-tumble of little feet scurried about the hardwood floors of the house as they all gathered their necessary supplies. I heard talk of flashlights and walking sticks "in case we see The Headless Woman." Others filled water bottles and grabbed snacks as if the trek would lead them across the Sahara.

I stayed on the porch until they all came bumbling through the door like bumper cars bouncing off each other. Some had backpacks. Others had raincoats. One had a walking cane, and several had umbrellas . . . held not upright to guard against the seemingly invisible inclement weather, but as spears to guard against . . . "Did she just say Sasquatch?" I thought to myself. They managed to find more flashlights than I even knew we had . . . amazingly, each had batteries that worked, protecting all those little commandos against the invisible Sasquatch, or even worse. But, let the power go out tomorrow night, and every battery in the house will be as dead as the Crimson Tide's chances of winning the National Championship without Nick Saban.

The troop looked like little Vikings going to pillage some nearby unsuspecting village, but they also looked like a horde of zombies, one seemingly unwilling to follow another, and none of them wanted to lead into the darkness. One would muster the courage to lead the charge, but three steps into the darkness, she'd declare a reason to return. The next little Napoleon would lead the way, only to return in similar fashion. It seemed the darkness presented the girls with a barrier I wasn't sure they could pierce. Banks stepped to the forefront—she is quite the commander when need be—she gets it from being bossed around by older sisters. After a minute or two more of chatter and chaos, she assembled some order and divided the girls into four search groups, each with their group leader and a designated side of the house to search. Banks was assertive in her command, and fearless. She compelled the other girls to move without fear, too. I envisioned her riding alongside Teddy Roosevelt as they charged San Juan Hill with the Rough Riders . . . she took charge and meant she would find her lost friends—even if it meant battling Sasquatch or The Headless Woman. Inspired by her motivation, the groups separated and disbursed.

I was quite confident at this point that the other girls were hiding. I had recollected through the events of the hayride, and there was no way they got off while we traveled. Several key witnesses attested to my innocence in the Living Room Court that was conducted by Judge Dredd (don't tell her I said that) and assured the court that the missing girls were present when everyone off-loaded from the wagon. Surely, I should be acquitted of any wrongdoing. With that critical testimony, the only conclusion left to be had was that when the girls all barreled out the door—and then scared themselves back inside—these two remained outside in hiding.

I eased open the door to gauge Hannah's temperament . . . I wasn't sure I had been acquitted in her mind. She was nowhere to be seen. The living room and kitchen looked like a clutter bomb exploded . . . drawers left open; hiking boots strowed out; glasses half empty and sweating on the table; camping paraphernalia scattered in front of the closet door; and a big, rich, birthday cake sitting in the middle of the breakfast table. It was obviously homemade, one of Hannah's recipes. The bag of White Lily flour, a couple of remnant eggshells, and the now-sweating jug of buttermilk all sat at the end of the kitchen counter. And the cake was slathered in Hannah's famous homemade buttercream icing.

"Well, heeellllloooo . . ." I seductively said out loud to the cake as I made my way toward it.

"Who are you talking to?" came a bark from the next room. Hannah's voice scratched the record playing in my mind of the enchanted moment I was about to share with the unguarded cake.

"You, sweetheart! You . . . that's who," I answered.

I dragged my left index finger through the cake's buttercream icing as I passed by it on my way to the other room. It was an easy crime—there were far too many little munchkins in the house for me to ever become a suspect. I sunk my finger deep and dragged it through the icing like a Massey Ferguson bottom plow turning the first field of spring. Once the icing climbed to my middle joint, I pulled away and immediately started sucking my finger like a newborn goat latched on to its mama's ninnie. "Heaven," I thought to myself. "No one makes icing like Hannah does." I stopped momentarily to savor the last sweet taste and then wiped my finger forward and backward on the back of my jeans . . . best to destroy the remnants of the evidence.

As I turned the corner, Hannah had her head in her hands. She looked up, and I could see the desperation on her face. "You know they are just hiding," I offered, and I leaned down and kissed her forehead. I held the kiss for a moment, trying to comfort her, and to gauge whether I was still under indictment. "I know. It's not that." She stood and wrapped her arms around my waist. I could tell she was troubled. "Nothing is going like I wanted it to," she said.

I was beginning to understand. I leaned in to kiss her, and we held close for several seconds. I wanted her to know that she was not only safe in my arms, but that everything would be okay. I was sure this would be long remembered as a hallmark moment in our marriage, so I touched my nose to hers and kissed her again, holding the kiss for several seconds. I waited for some kind of passionate reaction from her, and I felt her lips wiggle, ever so slightly. Then, her head recoiled like a diamondback rattlesnake preparing to strike. "Did you eat some of that icing?" she asked. I pulled away in shock. "How could such a good plan go so desperately wrong?" I thought.

"What? Of course, not. I've been outside!" I declared with righteous indignation as I headed toward the door. She was on my heels with a quicker step, inspecting my hands and chin as I marched. "Let me go see if I can find these two knuckleheads and see if we can restore order," I said, and away I went.

Pulling the door shut behind me, I knew Hannah would soon inspect the cake. "I danced too close to the flame, and I'm about to get burned," I thought. There was only one thing left to do—finding the girls would surely restore order and absolve me of my finger-dragging sin. I knew better than to dance so close . . . I should have quit while I was ahead . . . but Adam would have never resisted that icing, for the apple held nothing to it. I may have already received absolution and acquittal for any part of losing the kids that I might have been responsible for, but that cake was like the Sirens beckoning for Odysseus and his men. As Robert Palmer once sang, "She's simply irresistible." No man should ever be held responsible for finger-dragging through homemade icing.

The yard was pure chaos. Though it seemed longer, I had only been inside a couple of minutes, but Banks' four search parties seemed to be restricted to the perimeter of what some might say is our yard. That is, we don't really have a yard. We have thin woods and thick woods around our house. Most associate the thin woods nearer the house as our yard. That's as far as Lincoln will go to pee on trees . . . so that makes it official. That's our yard . . . the girls refused to venture beyond, no doubt frightened by the conjured notions of The Headless Woman or Sasquatch that they had surely been contemplating since they last passed me by.

"I don't blame them. He is a big, hairy joker," I said under my breath as I started out into the yard.

The girls saw me coming and swarmed me like summertime bees to a jar of sugar water. Buzzing all around and never standing still, they peppered me with questions and utterances, the likes of which I couldn't understand. Rotating in and around one another, they made a circle around me . . . I was trapped. I tried to quiet them with hand gestures and a calm, soothing tone . . . realizing that wasn't going to work, I thought it appropriate to escalate my tone, ever so slightly. "HHHHEEEEEYYYYYY!" I yelled at the top of my lungs. Okay, maybe it was a tad more than an "ever so slight" escalation.

I could hear crickets chirping. How beautiful they sounded amidst the otherwise silent night. "Okay," I whispered. "Listen very closely." My Sunday School teacher taught me the value of whispers. Amidst the wind and rain and earthquakes, the Lord whispered to Elijah. Why? Because it forced Elijah to listen closely . . . so, I whispered to these girls. "Where have y'all searched?" All at once, nine voices erupted like the

It's easy to talk about Lincoln as a hunter or a guard dog, but more than anything else, he is a friend. Fact is, he is my most faithful companion outside of my family. We joke sometimes that Lincoln and I are best friends because we are otherwise surrounded by women. Somedays, it's not a joke! He loves our girls though. Banks is at that age where she stays home sometimes by herself. Old enough to take care of her own needs, we will leave her for short stints, but only with the comfort of knowing Lincoln is with her. He would give his life for her and her sisters . . . no doubt. And that gives me great peace and gratitude because that's what a good friend would do.

sound of NASCAR engines on pit road after the Grand Marshall declared, "Gentlemen, start your engines!" I held my hands out as if I was about to part the Red Sea myself, hovering my palm over the closest ones' heads . . . they began to mumble . . . then chirp . . . then silence. "Quieting this group of talkers was as much a miracle as the Red Sea," I thought to myself with a grin. Too bad my kids thought of me more as Elmer Fudd than a miracle worker on most days. For now, though, I had command of these other little girls, and, even if but for a moment . . . I would savor it.

Parental control is oftentimes an illusion for me in my house. At the time, I had an 18-year-old, a 15-year-old, and, as you already know, an 11-year-old . . . all females. I am also married to a female. My last hope of male companionship on the homestead was my boy dog, Lincoln. But . . . Judge Dredd had him neutered. Poor guy doesn't even have his crown jewels anymore. I suggest that my parental control is an illusion because, while the girls often do as I instruct, we rarely understand each other. At times, they bring me into the fold to talk about prom dresses and toenail polish, but I'd much prefer to talk about the deer rut and crappie fishing.

Truth is, there are four of them, and, with Lincoln, one and a half of us . . . well, wait a minute . . . I've been neutered, too, so together, Lincoln and I make one. Four to one. No mere mortal man can survive that ratio. Whatever parental influence and control I might have in this household is only because the grace of God makes it so, but isn't that truly the case with any teenager? We'd do well to remember that.

At that moment, though, I was a miracle worker. They all came to a pause under my outstretched arms. I jutted my chin a little just for effect. "Oh, Daddy, would you stop it?" Banks muttered. I giggled. She did, too. She knows my sense of humor well, and, while I am pretty sure she secretly thinks I am funny, she rarely admits it in public. I obliged her request, lowered my arms, and resumed my normal posture. Over the next few minutes, I extracted from them precisely how unproductive their four search parties had been in their efforts. Essentially, they all reported back that the missing duo was not anywhere within the light cast of the house, and that had they gone beyond that distance, they surely would have been beheaded.

The longer we discussed the matter, the more drawn to me the girls were . . . especially when we discussed The Headless Woman. "No doubt, she is out there," I affirmed. Banks, again, knowing my sense of humor, chimed in, "She is, y'all. Daddy was down in the holler hunting squirrels one time, and she chased him back to the house. Mama had to shoot at her to scare her off." It was one of those proud father moments . . . my baby girl had learned how to spin yarn with the best of them. I just stood back and nodded my head. The girls drew a tighter circle, and, by this time, every twitch in the woods caused the entire pod to shift like a bait ball of menhaden in the Gulf blue. As one little girl lurched when the woods would begin to speak, all the little girls lurched the same way. When the woods spoke from the opposing side, the entire bait ball of little girls would circle back around to the other side. Somehow, every time they shifted, I always found myself between the bait ball and the imposing and mystical spook in the woods.

About this time, Lincoln nosed up to the bait ball. Curious about all the excitement, he weaved through the girls and took his place by my side. His tail wagged furiously. He sensed the excitement of the group and was intent on being a part of the chase . . . whatever it may be. When Lincoln gets excited, he bows his head and shakes it from side to side, as if he is trying to get your attention. He's never been one to speak . . . unless he is barking at you as a warning . . . so when he shakes his head, he whines until you satisfy whatever demand it is he makes of you. His whining captured the girl's attention, and they suggested, "Let's take Lincoln with us."

Banks had moved past her Commander-in-Chief role and transitioned to concerned friend. "Dad?" . . . she only calls me "Dad" when it's serious . . . "I'm starting to think we should be worried. They've been gone forever." I could see the concern well up in salty expression in the corner of her left eye. She was genuinely worried, and I didn't want this search party to turn into something more estrogen-driven, so I held out my 'miracle worker' arms. "It worked again," I snarked to myself, almost in disbelief. Banks was serious now, too, shushing the other girls and telling them, "This is serious, y'all."

Lincoln sensed Banks' troubles and shifted his weight from one side to the other to lean on her. He sat on his haunches and lifted his head to meet hers. He looked up into her eyes with a curiosity all his own. He saw the hurt in her eyes and understood the stress she was under, just the same as I did. He leaned his head into her body and forced her to pay him some attention. He didn't do it, though, out of selfishness . . . I'll remain convinced that he demanded her attention to compel her to think of something other than her troubles. It worked, too. She began scratching his ears, and, quickly, her countenance changed.

"Tell you what, girls," my voice captured their attention. "I want y'all to go back to your areas and resume your searches. Lincoln and I are going to form our own search party." On my heels, Banks put her little Napoleon persona back on, and she quickly led her group to the other side of the house. Once they all dispersed and I had some semblance of quiet, I squatted down next to Lincoln.

"Here's how I see it, boy. Those two girls are hiding somewhere. They think it's funny. And they wouldn't hide too far out into the woods or the dark. They are too scared to. No, they are really close by. Can you find them? Huh? What about it, Lincoln? Find 'um," I urged.

With that, he put his nose to the ground. He knows "Find 'um." That's what I tell him when we start any track. Deer? Rabbits? Coyotes? Little girls? "Find 'um" is always the command, and he loves to hear it. Hound dogs like Lincoln live for the track. Tracking a deer for Lincoln is like cooking the perfect biscuit for Brenda or making the winning shot for Cape. It not only brings him fulfillment, but joy, too. He finds purpose in the track . . . and so he longs for me to say it.

"Sniff, sniff, sniiiiffff." Following abruptly was a long and exaggerated exhale. Dirt blew clear of his exhale as the air leaving his lungs pushed the smallest of the dirt away. Realizing he was simply sniffing right in the middle of where the bait ball had just dispersed, I thought we ought to find a new place to start. "Come on, boy. Let's walk up to the tractor." I started back up the hill, and he followed, his nose to the ground the entire time. I walked to the back of the trailer where I was certain that all the girls had off-loaded. "Find 'um, boy." His tail wagged furiously, and his nose went straight to the dirt . . . sucking and blowing so hard that one might confuse him for a fat man running a sprint . . . he tracked right down the path that the girls took as they made their way inside.

He made two circles at the door to the house, his nose hardly lifting off the porch floor, and then he tracked back out into the yard. He stopped just a few paces out into the yard . . . and it was not merely coincidence to me that he stopped near where the girls thought better of venturing past when they rushed out of the house earlier. He circled twice more . . . never lifting his nose. Then, he walked straight back to the porch and the door.

Frustrated, he whimpered slightly. His black coat shimmered in the light of the porch, almost as if he was wet . . . but he wasn't. His chest bulged as he took short, rapid-fire, bursting breaths and exhaled prolonged exasperations as a consequence. His eyes searched out in front of him as he scoured the area for the scent . . . the scent of what, I did not know. But he did. And I learned a long time ago to trust the dog . . . he knows. Whimpering again, he walked back off the porch and then to the same spot in the yard and circled again.

By now, Banks had returned with her search party. I sent them inside, save Banks. I thought the other girls might be a distraction and felt this might be a good opportunity to do a little shepherding. "Dad," . . . she was using her serious tone. "They've been gone like an hour. Maybe we need to call the police."

"Banks," I sat down on the edge of the porch next to where she stood and looked at my watch so that she, too, could see the face. "It's been about twelve minutes since we got off the tractor. It may seem like a longer time, but stress has a way of exaggerating time." Banks nodded her head. "And you know what all of this emotion will resolve?"

She knew the answer because we've had this conversation before. "Nothing," she responded. "That's right," I said. "We need to use logic—not emotion—to solve problems. Remember, we don't do drama in this family." Although, I must admit . . . any family with four women and two neutered men is going to have its fair share of drama. "They are out there right now, giggling and laughing . . . watching us worry and fret. That's why it's fun to hide from people. And they are not far away. They are too scared to go deep into the darkness. Don't you remember how much y'all all squealed in the dark of the hayride?" She nodded her head in agreement as she watched Lincoln peel off and come back up on the porch.

Lincoln walked up and nosed me in the ear. He sniffed hard into my ear three or four times before I pulled away, laughing as I did. "They ain't in my ear, buddy. Find 'um!" He stuck his cold nose to Banks' cheek and then back to the ground. He lapped around us one time and then sniffed his way down the porch to the tool closet. Around the edges of the closed wooden-planked door, I could see that the light was suspiciously on inside the closet. The light fell out of the closet through the cracks around the door like the sun peeking over the horizon on a brisk, fall morning. Lincoln stood at the door for a few seconds and then turned to look back over his shoulder. His expression was well understood . . . "Well . . . you comin'?" he beckoned. By now, he had begun to wag his tail slightly . . . as if he knew . . . "Found 'um."

I nodded to Banks, and she walked over to the door. Silently, she stood listening to anything that might giggle or shudder inside the tool closet. She then grinned from ear to ear and nodded her head to me . . . quickly waving me over, she silently acted out a monster pouncing on the occupants of the closet. I nodded my head in agreement, and as she reached for the doorknob, I reached for the light switch and turned off the closet light. On the silent count of three, she snatched the door open, and the monster in me roared to life . . . "AAARRGGGGGHH!" Again, my arms stretched out—this time over the tops of the two almost-teens hiding inside the closet. Their shrills pierced the night, and then we all melted into laughter. Banks was satisfied that the girls were safe and humored that they have been made to suffer a little for the torment they had caused . . . and all was well again in their world.

And, without any more fanfare, the girls evacuated the tool closet and ran to the edge of the porch. Banks yelled, "Found 'um!" as loud as she could to the remnants of the search parties in the yard, and the rest of the swarm of buzzing bees quickly appeared from around the corners of the house. Then, as quickly as they came, they all disappeared into the light washing over the living room where they danced and laughed the night away.

Lincoln, though . . .

He moseyed over to his cedar-chipped dog bed and laid down. He rested his head on top of his crisscrossed front legs and let out a long and exaggerated exhale . . . then he closed his eyes. I walked over and stooped down, scratched his ears, and quietly told him, "Good boy, Lincoln. Good boy." He thumped his tail about three times on the porch floor, and that was that.

To him, he was simply fulfilling his purpose. The contented expression on his face suggested he was not smug or arrogant in his accomplishment, rather, he was simply satisfied that he got to fulfill his purpose. "I could learn a thing or two from him right now," I said to myself as I sat back down in my porch rocker. He peeled one eye open to see if I was going to talk anymore. "Yes, I could…" and then I considered all the times I felt pride in accomplishment instead of satisfaction with the purpose. "I'm gonna work on that, Lincoln." And I have . . . and I will.

Hannah is a stay-at-home mom. Early on in our marriage, we agreed that her being at home and pouring into our girls before they were old enough to go to school was vital to their development and spiritual growth. As it happened, that plan turned into 12 straight years of staying at home with at least one of the girls. Along the way, Lincoln and Hannah became great friends, too. Now that everyone is off at school, the two of them find themselves spending lots of time together. And as he has done for years, Lincoln still follows Hannah around the yard and the garden all day long as she does her daily routine. Why, he even likes to lie down in the leaves as she rakes them into piles . . . we think he is under the impression she does that just for him to have a soft spot to rest!

"Trust the dog…" I thought to myself. "Trust the dog. Not only will he teach you a thing or two . . . he will always seek his purpose." Sitting on the lightless porch listening, the crickets' song was drowned only by Lincoln's snores from just a few feet away. Hannah was inside, finishing up with the last few dishes from the party. An occasional clank of the dishes caused a momentary cessation of the cricket's serenade. "Trust the dog," I reminded myself again. "For even if they are too old to learn new tricks, they are never too old to teach us one or two." In that moment, I wasn't sure if I was talking about my relationship with Lincoln . . . or Banks . . . but I knew that in both, the same was true. "Trust that ole dog."

From the dark of the porch behind me came a familiar sound . . . "Thump, thump, thump."

Chapter
THREE

CREEKS, STREAMS, AND RIVERS

A SWEET, SWEET SOUND

"A maa-yzeing gra-ece, how swee-yt the sound," Bay, my sometimes sinner, sometimes saint oldest daughter sings to her heart's content. She does every Sunday in church and most other days of the week, too. She sings loud enough in church that I can always pull her voice out from the others, and it is beautiful music to my ears. She sings just loud enough to be distinct and purposeful, but not so loud as to be commanding. She worships. She has no desire to draw attention to herself such that she is worshiped. She is a soprano for most songs . . . occasionally an alto, but the soprano suits her voice best. Sometimes, I get so focused on listening to her voice that I lose myself in her. I close my eyes and just listen. I hear her voice to the exclusion of all others, and it pulls at my heart strings.

Don't misunderstand me; Cape and Banks both sing majestically. They have voices that can rival most anyone in our church choir. Theirs are certainly beautiful melodies—perfectly in time, hitting every note, the highest of highs, and the lowest of lows. The two younger girls have been blessed with their abilities.

But Bay . . . when she sings, it is special to me.

Who does she sound like? Cher—maybe if you were under water? Perhaps, in the right setting, she would sound like Adele. But the best way to describe her voice? The sound a cat makes when its tail gets caught under the rocker. That's what best describes her singing style. Yes . . . you read that right . . . and it's okay to chuckle a little. I wrote it and meant it to be funny.

Bay can't sing at all. She is tone deaf if I understand that term correctly. She can't hit the notes, and she never sings in key. She gets it honest. I can't sing a lick either.

Bay often sits in between Cape and Banks in church and, oftentimes, a similar scene repeats itself. Mid-song, after Bay's voice cracks and she misses a note, Banks looks up at Bay with the glare of 11-year-old frustration. Banks might even nudge her in the hip with her elbow, further scolding her for not being able to sing. Cape, a bit more discerning in how she responds, as a 15-year-old, will usually just grin, glance at Bay, and resume singing. Others—teenagers around us—sometimes will turn and look in her direction, too, giggling in friendship and love on those occasions where her voice is particularly out of tune.

Our firstborn has always held a special place in our hearts. Not only does she have her own unique personality, different from her sisters, but she also marches to the beat of her own drum. I think that's why she worships so unashamedly . . . because she simply doesn't care what anyone thinks of her singing, or her worship style. And that makes it even more beautiful to me.

And I close my eyes and soak up every word she professes . . . as it is, often, the most beautiful voice I hear when I worship.

Beautiful, not because she is my daughter. No, the beauty of her voice has nothing to with fatherly pity or kinship's thick blood. Instead, the beauty of her voice stems from who she is. You see, Bay doesn't sing for you or for me. She sings for the Lord. And she sings to bring glory to Him with the voice that He gave her. And because she doesn't sing for our pleasure or for her own glory, she remains ever faithful to offer every out-of-tune word to Him. When others poke fun at her and suggest she should stop, she keeps on singing, for she doesn't seek the approval of men but of her Father. And that is beautiful—more beautiful than the most melodical voice, more beautiful than any soprano master, more beautiful than any voice—because it is the song of her heart.

In the Bible, we read that, "God created mankind in His own image, in the image of God and He created them; male and female He created them" Genesis 1:27, NIV. We also find in verse 31 that God reflected on His effort and found that it was "very good." And we know that we are "God's handiwork, created in Christ Jesus to do good works, which God prepared in advance for us to do" Ephesians 2:10, NIV.

You see, I know God made Bay just the way she is. She does, too. Singing isn't her strong point . . . that's nothing to be ashamed of. God made her in His own image, and she is His handiwork. She is not a bad singer, she is God's handiwork, created by Him for a purpose. She knows that, and that is what is so beautiful about her voice.

Bay can hear herself singing. She knows that she doesn't sound as good as her sisters . . . and she is certainly thankful she has my off-key complement to help distract others . . . but she also knows that her voice is a "sweet, sweet sound" to the One she sings for.

And there is no more beautiful song than that.

In Acts 4, Peter and John found themselves in jail, and then in the court of the Sanhedrin, for doing good works in the name of Jesus, the Christ. The Sanhedrin were not entirely sure how to handle the charges against the men, for they admitted that they were guilty of preaching and teaching the name of Jesus as the Savior. To the Jewish hierarchy, this was a serious crime, but the Sanhedrin were fearful of causing a revolt—because the two men had been quite persuasive to the masses. A crowd of believers who had seen the good works that John and Peter had accomplished stood in court. Thinking they could satisfy their own interests and deter the crowd of onlookers from further belief, the Sanhedrin told Peter and John to never preach or perform an act in the name of Jesus again.

Peter responded that it is better to be judged right in the eyes of God than in the eyes of men.

And he nor John ever stopped preaching the Gospel of Jesus Christ.

Bay will never stop singing . . . because she sings for the Lord. She doesn't sing for you—or for me. And that's what makes her voice the most beautiful voice I've ever heard. Hers is a song of the heart . . . not for the ear, but for the soul.

What say you, friend? This Sunday, will you sing a new song unto the Lord? When is the last time you sang from your heart? From your soul?

Or when is the last time your heart sang at all?

There is joy in the Father. Sing to Him this morning and every day. He hears the beauty in your voice, and He loves you and your song . . . even when others don't. Keep singing . . . sing, Alleluia!

Never let the scornful voice of man keep you from your voice, your faith, or your Father.

And thank you, Bay, for showing the rest of us what faith undeterred looks like. You are a mighty warrior and a beautiful singer. I love all that you are.

Hannah captured this moment . . . our first embrace after Bay's graduation ceremony was over. I didn't want to let go and still don't. There are so many elements and layers captured in this one image . . . the light filtering in from above as a representation that the Father is always watching over her; one of Bay's lifelong best friends stood behind us and to the left, as if to suggest, "I'll always be here, too;" the watch on my hand prominently taking center space in the frame as if to say "time marches on;" and the gentle smile on my face with my eyes closed . . . because I was happy for her—so I smiled—but I was sad about losing her, so I also cried. So much captured in one image . . . but most of all, the image captures a beautiful girl being transformed into a beautiful woman. God is good.

AFTER THE RAIN HAS FALLEN

I taught her to hammer a nail. I helped her build her first birdhouse. Through that, I taught her to overcome obstacles and adversity. A few years later, I taught her how to use a skill saw and how to rip a board. I taught her those things.

We were together when she killed her first deer. I was standing next to her when she pulled the trigger. I saw the tears roll . . . a mixture of joy and sadness at the taking of the animal and the implication of death. We drug that fine seven-point out of the woods together and ate of his bounty together, too.

I was with her when she summited the highest mountain east of the Mississippi. I was with her each step of the way . . . heavy breaths and long steps . . . all the way to the top, all just so we could gaze at the wide wonder of God's creation.

I was there when the first drop of rain fell. I watched as the storm brewed and the clouds built . . . I heard the thunder roll. I stood by her side, never giving an inch, as life threw everything it had at her . . . and I watched in awe as she learned that, like Esther, she was made for a time such as this.

I was there when the green thunderstorms of Arkansas rolled in . . . hail columns and tornadoes . . . windblown trees and debris flying all around. I held her tightly in my arms, vowing to never let go while hell reigned supreme all around us . . . clutching firmly to the gift God gave me.

And I was there each and every other time the rain fell. And now, after the rain has fallen, I'll still be here, too, waiting for her to come back.

Today, the rain rolls gently off my cheeks, stirred by the winds of emotion and the lightning of memories brought on by receiving this photograph from a friend. It captures that perfect moment in time where I am lost in my recollections of her. Yes, lost in those recollections . . . today it rains again.

I've been there for plenty of mountaintops and even more storms, and I'll still be here, waiting, after this rain has fallen, for I know there are more mountain highs to come, and perhaps, even a few more valleys to cross, too.

But that's what parents do, right? No matter how hard the rain falls, we make sure that the way back home will always be visible . . . after the rain has fallen.

—— HAVE I TOLD YOU —— LATELY

All of Bay's first days of school were fairly unremarkable, at least from her perspective, until she reached the second grade. She had mastered the school line in kindergarten, and by first grade, she was an old pro and a veteran, confidently sashaying up the sidewalk every morning. As a first grader, she was a "big girl," and that meant she'd sometimes carry a purse to school as an awkward, mismatched accompaniment to her backpack. She strutted in like a peacock as she walked from the truck to the doors of the school. Sometimes, she'd gather an entourage as she went, and, huddled like bees clamoring around the hive, they'd all pile through the doors together.

Our ride to school back in those days took about 20 minutes, and that was "our time." Her school was just a few miles from my office, so it was out of convenience that I started taking her every day, but it soon became a matter of the heart. It didn't take long for me to realize that those were special times . . . just she and I . . . together to talk and laugh and sing.

During those early days, I tried to teach Bay the value of classic rock. Growing up in a home with either no television at all, or at the very least, no cable, she had very little exposure to things outside of our world. So, instead of chasing the fanfare of the latest Disney pop star, Bay and I sang along to the songs of my youth. She knew every word to Bad Company's "Shooting Star," and she loved Van Morrison's "Brown Eyed Girl" because "she's my . . . brown-eyed girl." She also loved to belt out the up-tempo Jimmy Buffett classic:

"I like mine with lettuce and tomato
Heinz 57 and French-fried potatoes
Big kosher pickle and a cold draft beer
Well, good God almighty,
Which way do I steer for my
Cheeseburger in paradise?"

But the best song of all in those days of riding to school and work, holding hands and singing songs off that first-generation iPod—which I still have and use every day—was our song:

We hunted a lot more than we fished, but fishing was still a part of our lives. This day, we ventured down to Choctawhatchee Bay to fish for speckled trout . . . otherwise referred to as sea trout by folks who aren't from around here. We caught a good mess of fish that day, and I think all the kids had a good time, and that was what it was always about . . . them having a good time. My friend, Chris Jackson, and his boys joined us on this trip. I don't even remember if Chris or I wet a line that day. We probably spent all our time helping our kids . . . my girls and his boys. We threw the fish back, too . . . most of them juveniles that day. All were too small to keep but that was okay, because catching Bay's smile at this particular moment made it all worthwhile.

Ahhh, the Buffalo River and the very first "12-Year-Old Adventure." If you're unfamiliar, I realized as Bay approached teen-hood, that I would lose most of my influence in her life. I also realized that hormones would rage, and if my girls were anything like Hannah or me as teens, we were in for a rough ride. So . . . the Lord laid it on my heart to have a special time for just Bay and me before she entered the minefield booby trap of the teen years. The concept was simple: a low-cost, low-tech adventure in the wild that was within a day's drive of our house. For Bay, we drove 10 hours to the Ozark Mountains of Arkansas and spent nearly a week paddling one of the most majestic rivers I have ever seen! The canyons and cliffs settled in over the crystal-clear waters were unlike anything we had ever experienced . . . we fell in love with the river that week, and the depth of our love for each other grew deeper, too!

"Have I told you lately that I love you
Have I told you there's no one else above you
You fill my heart with gladness
Take away all my sadness
Ease my troubles, that's what you do."

Rod Stewart's classic had long been our favorite. I oftentimes sang it to Bay as she drifted off to sleep at night. She knew it was more than just off-key notes from my voice . . . she knew it was my heart singing to her. Almost every day, she would find it on the iPod, and we would listen—holding hands and singing—on the way to school.

Bay learned about Vanilla Ice and Bon Jovi, too. She still sings, "Livin' on a Prayer" at random times as she passes through the living room. She mastered Jimmy Buffett, as any Coastal Alabama kid ought, but we always came back to Rod Stewart. It was our song . . . and it still is today.

Of course, we would go over spelling words and talk about history from an overly masculine perspective . . . I never could understand her lack of interest in tanks and battleships. We'd talk about her sweet teachers—and the mean ones, too. We'd talk about physical education, music, and art classes . . . those were her favorite. Bay is a great artist—though she doesn't cultivate her craft nearly enough—and if you want to know about her musical talents, refer back to the story "A Sweet, Sweet Sound."

Our pediatrician once cautioned us that: "Deep thinking children will come to an awareness that there is evil in the world at sometime between second and fourth grades." He went on to suggest that this awareness creates within them a recognition that people die and that bad things happen. Our trips to school remain some of my most beautiful and precious memories with Bay . . . straining to sit high enough up in the seat so that the sun visor kept the sun out of her eyes . . . but one day, she became aware, and the trips became some of the most excruciating moments of my life.

I once dug rocks out of my knees after a bicycle wreck. I once had to have a fishhook cut out of my ear. I have endured countless lost hours in the Everglades searching for camp through all hours of the night. I've endured a lot of hardships, pain, and suffering in my life, but nothing prepared me for this.

I knew she was distant that morning. I wasn't sure why, but she seemed disengaged. She held my hand a little tighter than normal, and she didn't let go. She sang occasionally, but she didn't seem as interested this morning. Because we were in about our third week of second grade—with three "first days" under our belt—this was old hat by now, so I had no cause to believe anxiety was setting in for Bay. But I could sense something was off . . .

"Baby, everything okay this morning?" I asked her. She forced a grin and nodded her head yes, but being the classic rock girl that she was, even she knew she couldn't "hide her lyin' eyes." I fumbled through the iPod . . . Eagles . . . "Lyin' Eyes" . . . the song started to play in the background.

"Bay, what's wrong, baby?" I asked.

"Nothin', Daddy," she said. "It's fine."

It took me years to learn this, but "It's fine" is her distress signal. Even today, when she says those two words, I know something is wrong.

I tried to joke with her a little and sing along to the music . . . but she never really engaged that morning. She was clearly preoccupied. As I pulled into the school line, she would always let go of my hand and begin to situate all of her girl paraphernalia—purse, hair bow, backpack. She was a fashionista by this point in her life, so she was going to make sure everything was right before she got out of the truck. Not this morning, though . . . she just held my hand and kept her gaze fixed forward.

As was the custom, the line would stall its momentum so the cars at the front could unload . . . and, after 15 or 20 seconds, it would resume. It usually took three good surges for us to navigate through the maze and get to the unloading area. With each forward push, she tensed more and more. I tried to be lighthearted and cheerful, but my awkward efforts were feeble.

I took my foot off the brake, and the truck began to roll forward. "Daaaddddyyyy," she quietly cried out. Turning to her, I saw tears as big as figs rolling down her cheeks. Her eyelids squeezed tight against each other, and her mouth grimaced downward at the corners. She gritted her teeth trying to fight the emotion within her . . . but it was just too much. Like an idiot dad, I had no idea what was going on.

We pulled forward to the unloading area. "I don't want to go to school today," Bay said. "Let me just come to work with you." Her eyes were wide, and they begged me to agree. She took both her hands and cupped mine within them. "Please, Daddy, please?" I couldn't comprehend what was happening, and I didn't know or understand what to do. A teacher opened the truck door, and Bay clutched my hand tighter. "Just one day, Daddy? Please?" Tears bellowed from her eyes as her voice cracked. Everything within me said she had to go to school, but everything within me also said, "Don't make her go."

Mrs. Bryant took Bay by the hand and gently coaxed her from the truck. The decision had been made for us, no doubt, by someone who had dealt with this before. "It's okay, Dad. I'll take care of her." Mrs. Bryant was a great teacher and a sweet lady, and I trusted that she would. But I'll never forget the look on Bay's face as I drove off. Her hand reaching for me . . . her eyes trained upon mine . . . desperate for me to come back.

"I failed her." Driving away, that was all I could think. "I failed her." Pulling out of the parking lot, I wrenched with emotion over the desperateness of my daughter. I didn't understand . . . and I was supposed to be her lion. I called Hannah as I drove down the road and explained the horrific emotions of the morning. She tried to reassure me, but she, too, was concerned. "I'll call the school and see," she offered. She called me back a few minutes later and said Bay would be fine. "Mrs. Bryant said she is already calmed down and getting back to herself." It was little comfort, but it was all I had.

This picture is from our first real family vacation: Hawk's Cay on Duck Key in the Florida Keys. We went snorkeling, swimming, fishing, and boat riding . . . we spent the entire week in the great outdoors. But Hannah still talks about this restaurant every time we go fishing. "Remember that time we went fishing in the Keys, and we took the fish we caught to the restaurant? And they cooked that fish just an hour or two after we caught it?" I always smile and nod my head. "That was the best fish I have ever had in my life." I guess it was because she is still talking about it all these years later.

The next few weeks, that scenario replayed itself every morning. It was brutal. Soon enough, her pleas transformed into questions of my love and loyalties. "Why, Daddy? Why can't I just stay with you?" Her words were like daggers through my heart. "Why won't you let me stay?" Her eyes pierced me. "Why are you leaving me? Don't leave me, Daddy, please!" Her tears were like acid on my soul. "Why are you leaving me?"

Those words still ring so firmly in my ears today. They were too much . . . secretly, I'd cry as I pulled away from her every day . . . fighting with all I had to not show a tear before we parted. Pulling away as she strained her arms toward me while Mrs. Bryant or Mrs. Watson held her tight was, perhaps, the hardest thing I have ever done in my life.

But I knew I had to . . .

"I just don't think I can do this anymore, Hannah," I said. "You just don't understand how hard it is to leave her when she is begging me to rescue her." Hannah hugged me tight and assured me I was doing the right thing. I always trusted her parental instincts over my own, but I cautioned her. "I can't keep this up very much longer." Thank the Good Lord, Bay worked through the anxiety within a few weeks.

I had to leave her . . . so she could grow. The fact was the best fatherly thing I could do for her was to let her work through it on her own. She needed to learn . . . and soon did . . . that we aren't in control, and we simply must trust the One who is.

And grow she did into a beautiful young lady, confident in who she is, in who her Lord is, and with little fear of taking on the world and all that comes with it. She is her own lion now . . . and a fierce one at that. I doubt she will need me to rescue her, but I trust that she knows that I will if ever the need arises.

Ironic though, all these years later, second grade comes full circle. For as I type this, all I can do is hum the tune to "Have I Told You Lately" as tears roll off the end of my nose and onto the keyboard as I think to myself, "Don't leave me, Bay. Don't leave me."

But I know she must.

I used to think driving away from her crying eyes at the school was the hardest thing I had ever done . . . now, I know I was wrong.

God give me strength to let go and to trust that she is ready and that You will shelter her in the storm. Amen.

"Fill my heart with gladness
Take away all my sadness
Ease my troubles, that's what you do"

BEST PART OF WAKING UP

If you are old enough, you remember that *"The best part of waking up is Folgers in your cup."* You also remember the Folgers commercial where the college-aged son comes home from college early one morning and makes coffee for his parents. The mom was ecstatic, the dad was grateful, and the son grinned from ear to ear.

I also remember the "Messy Marvin" Hershey's Syrup commercials with the grandiose tree houses. And I remember all the commercials that aired around Christmas always seemed to be the best . . . electric trains zoomed around the Christmas tree as the whole family ate Nestlé Toll House cookies in front of the fire.

Wouldn't it be great to have one of those made-for-TV moments? Except they don't really exist . . .

Try as I might through the years, I've never managed to recreate that perfect moment. My tree house never looked nearly as impressive; my coffee is pretty good, but I have never found a morning where everyone in my family was in a good mood at the same time; and, if someone makes Toll House cookies at our house, they are eaten by a pack of ravenous wolves long before any fireside chat has time to transpire.

Point is . . . life is real. We can't compare ourselves to television or to the internet . . . we will likely never measure up. Instead, let's find joy in the imperfection of what we have—each other. This morning, I wrapped Cape's shoulder in ice packs and Ace bandages because she is hurting. She wasn't mean, but the pain prompted her to be ill-mannered. I feel her pain, too, almost literally—my back is cramping—I slept on the couch last night. Hannah and I had a fuss, and, though we rarely go to bed mad, the truth of the matter is, sometimes we do. I spoke with Bay yesterday on the phone. She seems to be adjusting to college life well, but my heart hurts. I still miss her desperately. Banks is upset, too, because we are going to be late for school, and she thinks she'll get in trouble.

All the while . . . I drink my Folgers.

It's a bit cooler outside this morning, which is nice. Banks just used most of the hot water, though, by taking a 30-minute shower. The girls are starting to stir and arguing over who gets to wear what . . . and I'm still drinking my Folgers.

Soon enough, we will all depart for work and school. I'm certain Banks and I will have at least one fuss before I feel how cold the water is . . . for, in my selfish imperfection, I intend to tell her of my displeasure.

Someone will be running late. Someone might even cry—maybe me. We will eat breakfast too fast. We will forget a belt or a purse or a lunchbox, or Heaven forbid it be garbage pickup day!

And when I walk out the door, I will still be drinking my Folgers.

Yes . . . I probably drink Folgers because that commercial resonated with me. I always wanted those perfect family moments. It took me 45 years to realize that I have always had them . . . every morning . . . no matter the circumstances.

I like Folgers, but it is not the best part of waking up. The best part is my family.

Thank you, Lord, for the coffee, but most especially for the beans of life that are my family. I love them in their perfect imperfection, and I am especially grateful that they still love me despite my imperfections.

I even love them when they make me wear ridiculous pajamas on Christmas morning . . . and when the older girls refuse to wear theirs for the picture.

Remember, friends, life is not a fairy tale, it is simply life. The best part of waking up is knowing Jesus lives. Beyond that, there will never be perfection. Don't read these stories and think we are the perfect family . . . unless you understand that the only perfections we have are in our imperfections.

God is great. Coffee is pretty good, and hot showers are, too.

Remember friends, life is not a fairy tale; it is simply life. The best part of waking up is knowing Jesus lives. Beyond that, there will never be perfection. Don't read these stories and think we are the perfect family . . . unless you understand that the only perfections we have are in our imperfections. God is great. Coffee is pretty good, and hot showers are, too.

THE LAST DAY
OF SCHOOL

Bay was five years old on that first day of school 12 years ago. The peaks of Andalusia Elementary School seemed large and looming, towering over the tiny "dots" that lined the sidewalks. The procession of the carpool line advanced ever so slowly . . . with some kindergarten parents opting to drop their kids off instead of parking and walking them inside. I imagined the conversation the parents in front of us were having with their "first day-ers." I imagined lots of tears and big, tight-squeezed hugs and clichéd utterances from parents—much like Hannah and I—who wanted to offer assurance and convey confidence during what was surely to be an intimidating time for a child.

I hoped to find the right words when our time came near . . .

And while I remember with some vividness the occasion, there are parts that are admittedly blurry. I wonder if it's the emotion of it all that suppresses the memories. Perhaps, it's simply the passage of time and old age. Much has changed in the Merrell family in the last 12 years. What will remain unforgettable, though, is what a vibrant child Bay was. She always smiled . . . and her smile was so inviting and warm that if ever it disappeared, it took a little piece of me with it. Some children are, by nature, shy. Others, outgoing. Some pleasant and some ornery. Bay was not only pleasant, but she was one of the most loving and compassionate children I've ever known.

Axl Rose penned perhaps the greatest tribute to the vibrancy of a girl's smile when he wrote:

"She's got a smile that it seems to me
Reminds me of childhood memories
Where everything was as fresh as the bright blue sky
Now and then when I see her face
She takes me away to that special place
And if I stare too long, I'd probably break down and cry."

Music is such an important part of my life. I listen to music when I write, when I worship, when I study, when I work, and often, when I spend time with my girls. And because of my love for music, I give "it" to my girls. From Guns N' Roses and James Taylor to Jimmy Buffett to Adam Crabb . . . my girls know music.

"Whenever I see your smiling face
I have to smile myself
because I love you, yes I do..."
—JAMES TAYLOR, "YOUR SMILING FACE"

I love you, Bay Merrell.

Just minutes before we took this picture, Bay and I hunkered down under a picnic table to escape a deluge of hail, rain, thunder, and lightning. Trapped on the Buffalo River in Arkansas, we had nowhere to run to when the thunderstorm engulfed us. Tornado warnings rang out, but we never heard them . . . for we were so remote that no warning system was near. All we had, and all we needed, was a small clearing in a state park and a picnic table. That was enough . . . the Lord provided.

Rose was reminiscing of a beautiful woman he once loved when he wrote "Sweet Child O' Mine," but the song speaks to me and conjures images of my girls and their childish antics. Bay is the bright blue sky, and she always takes me away to that special place. Even on the most grueling of days, I often seek comfort in the memories of her sweet smile and cheerful disposition. Her smile can part the clouds during the fiercest of life's storms.

We pulled around the semicircle drive to the school that morning. Her face told me all I needed to know . . . the corners of her mouth were drawn tight, there was no smile in sight, and her eyes spoke of nervousness and anxiety. I could see redness forming around her eyes—she was struggling to hold back tears. I gently patted her knee, and she took my hand in hers and squeezed my fingers.

A few more cars advanced in the line. We opted to drop her off instead of walking inside. We knew it would be difficult no matter the method of separation, but we ultimately decided that the closure of the car door would be most effective. The finality would make it easier, we thought. Waiting for the line to advance, I recalled watching *The Chronicles of Narnia* with Bay. A great movie adaptation of C. S. Lewis' series of books, most notably *The Lion, the Witch, and the Wardrobe*, the plot follows the adventures of three children in a fantastical journey in the land of Narnia. Lewis, a famed Christian author, never hid his faith in the book, and it remains a great demonstration of who Christ is in an alternate storyline . . . watching the movie creates a great opportunity for anyone to talk about the Messiah to their children.

As the movie came to an end, Aslan the lion, the King of All Kings in Narnia, laid down his life to save the children. Bay cried crocodile tears as the hero of the movie gave himself to save others . . . and her tears provoked my own. With the thought of comforting her—and probably myself, too—I squeezed her tight against my torso and whispered in her ear, "I will always be your lion."

I don't think she understood . . .

A few more cars advanced in the line. She squeezed my hand even tighter, and I saw a tear roll down her cheek. I looked up to catch Bay's eyes, and they were wide with anticipation. She gazed out the window and gawked up the line of cars, straining to see if there was anyone close by that she might know. "There's Hannah!" she exclaimed. Hannah was a longtime childhood friend of hers. Her presence on the breezeway headed into the school seemed to calm everyone. "Hurry, Daddy, maybe we can catch her!" Bay urged. I considered ramming the cars in front of me out of the way for, surely, that is what any good lion would do, but common sense got the better of me, as I knew I could not be anyone's lion from prison.

"A good lion builds a child into capability," I reasoned to myself. "We've prepared her for this moment. She will be fine." I looked at Hannah, who was in the back seat, and nodded in assurance. She smiled and nodded back.

And, in an instant . . . it was time. The Safety Patrol student opened the door to the truck. A teacher stood nearby and closely monitored. Hannah offered a few words to Bay as she unbuckled her seatbelt. I saw the redness in her eyes . . . the fear of the separation that was to be was very real and very present. I felt it myself as my throat burned with emotion. I leaned over and looked Bay in the eye, told her how much I loved her, and reminded her, "I will always be your lion." Hannah gave Bay a big hug and a kiss, told her how much she loved her, and gave her every ounce of confidence that she could muster.

And with that, Bay was gone. I still remember her walking down the sidewalk . . . perhaps just a "dot" to some, but she was my everything. She looked back over her shoulder and smiled from ear to ear . . . it was the most comforting smile I had ever received from her. With it, she conveyed so much: "I'm okay. I love you, too. I am ready. I know you'll rescue me if I need you." She made eye contact with me for an instant, and then she set her gaze upon Hannah. Still walking away, her smile and her eyes conveyed so much in that moment.

The door shut, and Bay turned to face her very bright future. With that, Hannah squeezed my hand tighter than she had before, and the redness of her eyes turned to tears. For, you see . . . it was not Bay who was riddled with anxiety . . . it was us. And we cried tears of joy and of sadness as we pulled out of the parking lot.

It was not the first time the joy that is my firstborn daughter brought tears to my eyes. Pulling out of the school parking lot, I recalled making our way down the sterile white hallways of what was then called Andalusia Regional Hospital. Hannah, nine-and-a-half months pregnant, asked, "Do you think you'll cry when you see her for the first time?" Confused by the absurdity of such a question, I quickly disavowed any inclination to cry at the sight of a mere mortal baby. Early the next morning, Olivia Bay Merrell was born. Seeing her and holding her for the first time, I couldn't help but realize that childbirth is a miracle in and of itself, and children truly are a gift from God. Holding Bay for the first time, I was overcome with joyful emotion and could do nothing but weep.

Letting go of her for the first time at Andalusia Elementary School, though, I was also overcome with emotion. I wept, and Hannah did, too.

And as I write this story, I draw nearer to letting go of her, again. Yesterday was her last day of classes as a senior at Andalusia High School. She graduates in less than a week. Tears cover my cheeks as I type this. As a means of comfort, I try to remind myself that, "A good lion builds a child into her capabilities." I know in my heart that she is ready, just as she was on the first day of school at Andalusia Elementary School. She is an all-A student and a leader among her peers, and she maintains virtue and is a compassionate friend. But above all else, I know that she carries the true King of Kings with her wherever she goes.

And though I know she is ready to walk the Grove at Ole Miss, where she will no doubt make a mark that will stand the test of time, I know I wasn't ready to let her go when she was a 5-year-old, and I fear I am not ready now.

As much as she knows that I love her, I can never take the place of her mama. Theirs is such a special bond.

Maybe Hannah will hold my hand and let me squeeze her fingers from time to time in the coming days. Even the mightiest of lions will whimper on occasion.

And though I might weep today, I know she now understands that I will always be her lion. I love you, Butter Bean.

WHERE'S BANKS?

If you've never been to the Grand Hotel just south of Fairhope in Battles Wharf, Alabama, you really should just go for a stroll through the summertime azaleas and camellias. Cobblestone paths lie beneath sprawling live oak branches that reach towards the horizon such that the weight of the appendages pulls to them back down to the ground. Draped in windblown Spanish moss, these 500-year-old trees blanket the grounds of the historic hotel. In the small and quaint marina, boats rock gently from side to side as waves from Mobile Bay dance along the jetty walls and find their way into the safe harbor. The southern wind blows most days, fresh in off the Gulf of Mexico, touching your face with warmth and tickling your nose with the inviting smells of the salty sea. Seagulls seem to hover, nose to the wind, in disorganized flocks above the marina . . . hoping a fisherman or tourist might offer them a snack. Pelicans, the majestic kings of the nautical air, glide in an almost attack-like formation, one behind the other, so low to the water that their wing tips nearly touch and at such a brisk pace that even the fastest Stauter-Built boat would struggle to keep up.

Redfish, speckled trout, flounder, mullet, and even an occasional blacktip shark pass through the marina's waters. Many a fine fish has been caught off those same jetties. Trust me . . . I know. I grew up on these waters . . . when Jimmy Buffett wrote of "mother, mother ocean," he was here, and I heard her call, too.

The acreage at the Grand Hotel is a truly a microcosmic representation of the finest of the natural beauty Alabama has to offer. Alabama, by the way, has more natural diversity than all but four other states in the country and ranks first amongst states east of the Mississippi River. Mobile Bay, flanking the hotel grounds on three sides, drains fourteen percent of the nation's freshwater from four different states. It is the second largest freshwater delta system in the country and one of the largest in the world.

Our family visits the Grand Hotel occasionally . . . sometimes just for Sunday brunch with my mom . . . other times, for the weekend. And while the Grand Hotel is spectacular in its splendor, it is not the amenities that set it apart from all the rest—it is the surrounding natural beauty, and especially, the people.

We finished our fireside outdoor meal at Bucky's, one of the hotel's restaurants, and began our leisurely walk back to our room under the moonlit night's sky. The waves lapped against the seawall; the wind tussled in the trees; the lights of the city of Mobile danced and shimmered on the water; and our girls ran back and forth like fireflies on a hot summer night. Bay was about 13 years old at the time. Cape was 10, and Banks was six or so. They were still young enough that they would "play" without fear of scorn from the others, and this was one of those moments where they were all playing together . . . all seemed right in the world.

Hannah and I held hands as we made our way off the bay and onto one of the cobblestone paths leading to the building where our room was. The girls followed not too far behind. We talked of how miserable we were from eating far too much and how good we would sleep tonight . . . Bay and Cape—who, by now, had passed us and were 30 feet ahead—conversed on their own, and Banks bounced between us and the girls, not entirely sure which group she wanted to walk with.

Bay turned and yelled, "We are going ahead to the room. We want to change and go swimming."

"Okay," Hannah yelled, and the two older girls accelerated their pace.

Banks, only a few feet in front of us, turned and asked, "Can I go with them?"

"Sure, baby, but hurry and catch up," I told her. "Wait on your sister!" I yelled up ahead.

Soon enough, they all disappeared around the curve ahead. Hannah and I walked a little slower . . . enjoying the alone time together, even if only for a few minutes.

The elevator doors opened, and we stepped onto the third floor of our building and turned down the hall toward our room. Advancing toward us came Bay and Cape, towels draped around their shoulders. They were shivering because they both put on bathing suits still wet from an earlier swim and stepped out into the hall where the air conditioner had to be running full blast. They pranced down the hall to make better time, desperately wanting to find the warm outdoor air.

"Where's Banks?" I asked.

"What do you mean?" Bay asked. "She was with you."

A shiver ran down my spine at that moment, but not from the cool air. There wasn't any time to talk . . . recounting the story would do little to help find her.

"You haven't seen her at all since we were walking back?" Hannah asked.

"No," the girls said in unison. I could detect worry in their voices. They were old enough to know.

Now, with a heightened sense of urgency, I told Hannah to retrace our footsteps, and I would circle around to the bayside on the front of the buildings. We would rendezvous at almost the very location where we last saw her. Before I could even finish, she bolted off.

"Girls, you check in the parking garage downstairs and around the pool and meet us there," I instructed.

Once we got outside, the chorus erupted. "Banks? Ban . . . BAAA . . . BANKS . . . Ba . . . Banks?"

We sounded like crickets that couldn't get in time with each other. If she was within ear shot, she would surely hear one of us. I scanned furiously in the bushes, the

Surrounded on three sides by Mobile Bay, the Grand Hotel has long been a favorite for our family. In the off-seasons, the rates are more affordable, and so we often find ourselves there in winter or fall, when the north wind might be a little bitter, but the warmth of a family hug makes all of the cold disappear!

hammocks, the horseshoe sets—anywhere a child might wander—as I called out for her. Nothing. Rounding the corner of the next building and turning back to the street where we last saw her, I found Hannah with desperation in her eyes. The two older girls came right behind me. Nothing.

Hannah said, "I am going to find someone who works here and tell them."

"Maybe she went to the wrong building?" I panted, still trying to catch my breath from jogging.

Bay added, "Check the third floor. She knew we were on the third floor because she always pushed the button on the elevator." Hannah took the girls to sweep the nearest building. I went to the next nearest to do the same.

Soon enough, I encountered a hotel employee—an older gentleman with salt-and-pepper hair and comforting eyes. I could hear the walkie-talkie blare . . . it was security, and they were executing the "missing child protocol." Hannah had obviously found someone to report to and ask for help. This gentleman must surely have seen the panic on my face. He put his hand up as a means of reassurance and asked, "Are you the father?" I nodded, and he put his hand on my shoulder. "It's going to be okay. We will find her." We were on the third floor. "Come on, let's walk to the other end and see if she is up here," he said, letting me know he was already one step ahead of me. He walked briskly, but not such that he would incite fear. The radio chatter continued, and as we turned down the far stairwell, he reported our location, and that this hall was clear. We stopped on the second-floor hall, and he called down the hall for her. I prayed as I waited to hear a response but heard nothing.

That may be the most deafening silence I've ever experienced. There is no greater silence than calling for your child and hearing nothing in response. Already, nightmares from work were setting in. I've seen too many children go missing in my lifetime. "Don't worry," he assured me. "We've already shut down the entrance gate. No one will get in or out until she is found." The radio chatter picked up. More people reporting locations "cleared," and I felt comfort from knowing the hotel was responding with a clear and concise plan.

"I have her," an angelic voice squawked over the radio.

I stopped. So did my new friend. He held the radio up closer to his head and held his hand out. "I have her," the voice repeated. "We are on the third floor of the Bayside North Building."

Tears pricked my eyes. In fact, the memory is so haunting to me that they came to my eyes as I typed this. My mind raced. "Is she okay?" I asked. "This way," my friend ushered, and we rushed to the next building.

We went through the lobby doors, and Banks and a beautiful elderly woman sat cradled in a chair. Banks was crying, and the woman held her close, reassuring her everything would be okay. Hannah came through from the other side of the lobby at almost the same time as I did. Banks jumped forward, and we all reunited. I could see the relief in her eyes as she sprang toward us . . . and I saw the curl of her cry turn into the glimmer of a smile.

I could only imagine . . . that was as close to what it would feel like to be face to face with Jesus as I will ever experience on this earth. The joy, the relief, the rescue.

"I can only imagine.
Surrounded by Your glory
What will my heart feel?
Will I dance for you Jesus?
Or in awe of You be still?
Will I stand in your presence?
Or to my knees will I fall?
Will I sing Hallelujah?
Will I be able to speak at al?l
I can only imagine."

In joy, we all fell to our knees.

There is so much here, in this "God moment" as my friend Steve Yelverton later dubbed it. In an instant, we thought she was gone, and it happened under our watchful eye . . . such a simple mistake . . . innocent yet nearly catastrophic. Life can be that way. We think we are in control, that we have the power or authority, and even under our watchful eye, catastrophe can strike. All we need to do is run toward a Father who is waiting to receive us with open arms. No matter the catastrophe, He is our rescuer.

The amenities at the Grand Hotel are nice . . . but it is the people who are the heart and soul of the place. They rescued our daughter, just like He will rescue us. And even though she knew enough to go to the third floor, such as in life, sometimes, we find our way to the wrong building. And thank the Good Lord above Banks remembered two things we taught her: stay put and look for help. She did just that.

Parents, be vigilant. Let us talk to our children about things that might happen. And remember . . . a shepherd never rests until every sheep is safe and accounted for.

Chapter
FOUR

A FATHER'S OUTDOOR JOURNAL

——— A L L I G A T O R   S E E D S ———

I went alligator hunting a few nights ago . . . it's become a tradition for our family and a small circle of friends. One of those friends—Travis Martin—well, he is a special sort and one of my most treasured friends. I want to tell you a short story about him, because I think it will change your perspective on those small and curious opportunities that life sometimes presents.

At the time, I had been the district attorney for four years. Hannah and I were building a pier at our lake house, and we were considering adding a fireplace for the ambience and the warmth. I love to sit on the pier on cold winter days. It is . . . absolutely quiet. Searching through Facebook Marketplace, I found the perfect solution. You might recall those bright orange cone-shaped fireplaces from the 1970s? Well, someone had one for sale, and they lived just up the road from our house. That someone was Travis Martin.

Through trial and error, Hannah and I realized that, while the construction of the fireplace on a pier was certainly possible, it was probably not the best conceived plan. I figured that the structural requirements to support the weight of the hearth were likely more than I was capable of . . . so we decided to scratch that plan. And aside from talking about that cone-shaped fireplace, Travis and I had never talked before nor after.

And that was the end of that. Or so I thought.

Six months later, I received a Facebook message from Travis.

"Call me when you can," he wrote.

Maybe "that" was not the end of "that." Curious, I dialed Travis' number. As it rang, I speculated that he was eager to sell the cone-shaped fireplace and perhaps wanted to talk about a better deal. Travis answered with his casual, Southern drawl. "Hey, man," he offered. "Someone told me that you know a little bit about alligator hunting?"

The DA in me was cautious. The man in me wanted to be boastful. "I've been a few times," I responded. Travis dug a little deeper. "Think you might be interested in going again?" he asked. I wasn't sure where the conversation was headed. I was not much of a mind to go hunting with perfect strangers . . . that seemed a good way to end up on a boat with some angry son whose dad I had put in prison. Hell-bent on revenge, he'd be sure to make gator bait of me.

"I don't really like to go hunting with other folks, much," I answered.

"Much." I couldn't believe I had added that one word to the end of my decline. I had

The Alabama Grand Champion Cypress Tree is a true treasure.
Hidden deep in the murky swamps of the Mobile River Delta, it
is massive . . . spanning 27 feet in diameter and some estimates
put it at over 1,000 years old. It dwarfs all the other full-grown
trees around it, and it commands the forest. We paddled about
five miles that morning, from whence I shall not say. I was
raised to hold the tree's location close . . . for the reason it has
stood for so long is because most don't know where it stands
at all. As the story was told, "loggers passed it by a hundred
years ago because the tree's top was gone." You can only get into
where it is by boat—either a canoe or kayak—or perhaps a
sturdy welded boat. The dry land swamp is thick with vegetation,
and navigating from dry island to dry island is best done by
looking up to the trees. I always find my way, not by looking
down . . . because every palmetto looks the same, but by looking
up to the treetops, for the unique trees that show me the way.
Such is life, is it not? We spend too much time looking down,
and not enough time looking up. I've found that whenever I am
lost in life, struggling to find my way . . . if I'll just lift my eyes
up to Him, He will show me the way.

no intentions of going gator hunting with this guy who I'd only met face-to-face one time, much less with his rabble-rousing friends.

"Why did you say 'much,' dummy?" I scolded myself silently.

"Well, it would just be me and a couple of guys from the power plant," Travis explained. "We just need an extra hand, and we know you're familiar with the Delta, so we thought you might like to join us if you didn't already have a trip planned for yourself. Truth is, we heard you had killed some big gators, and we thought we might could pick up a few pointers along the way."

Now, I felt as though declining the invitation would be rude. I didn't exactly know what to do. I was excited about the opportunity . . . Alabama only issues about 100 or so alligator tags per year. Without that tag, you cannot hunt legally. I did not draw a tag that year to hunt alligators, and so, this was a second chance of sorts . . . on the other hand, I have been pretty diligent through the years to never go hunting with people I did not know. Aside from the fact that there are plenty of people who hold vendettas against me—and the fact that I don't want to get shot—I'm also pretty particular about hunting safety. No drinking and guns. No drugs and guns. No morons and guns.

Looking back, I have no idea why Travis called me. There are plenty of good alligator hunters who would've been a great asset to his team. Instead, he reached out to me. I'm also not sure why I used the word "much." You see, by doing so, I allowed for the possibility that I would go. I had no intentions of doing so. Travis went on to explain that I might know some of the guys who were going . . . I knew of a few. Nothing bad . . . just all-around regular guys.

I was reluctant, but ultimately, I felt obliged to go.

And so, I did. A few weeks later, I boarded a boat with three men I did not know. After several nights of hunting, we had no quarry for our toil to speak of. A close call with a nice 11-footer. A short jaunt with a six-footer out of sheer boredom. But nothing tagged yet. And so, it was . . . the first three nights of our friendship seemed fruitless.

But, just as with any seed, growing fruit takes time. Since that first odd conversation from the long-haired, skinny guy whose last name I struggled to remember, I have traveled the country with Travis and our kids: crossing the Everglades with Tyler, Cape, Anna, and Gracyn; conquering the Mobile River Delta with Bay, Cape, and Anna; navigating the full length of the Apalachicola River with Tyler; and camping in more places than I can recall with some combination of Bay, Cape, Banks, Tyler, Anna, and Kaitlyn.

There are too many times and moments to capture them all . . . hiking through the Delta to the Alabama Grand Champion Cypress Tree is certainly one of the more memorable adventures. Estimated to be over 500 years old and more than 29 feet in diameter, the tree is the largest of its kind in Alabama. And to think . . . it started as a seed no larger than the tip of a man's finger. Now, it is wider than any man can reach around, and it is the tallest tree for miles around . . . all because it was given a chance.

Likewise, ours is the grandest of friendships, expanding beyond anything I ever imagined when I first offered that reluctant "yes" to a hunting invite. Travis has taught me to be a better father, a better husband, and a better man. And it all started with the smallest of seeds . . . we went hunting again those few nights ago. We didn't kill anything on that trip either . . . but with every passing day, the friendship grows stronger.

Curious, isn't it? How the Lord opened doors to an awesome friendship, all because of a fireplace and one wrong word. Sometimes, the bounty is not in the thrill of the hunt or the kill itself . . . but rather, sometimes the bounty is in the oddest of journeys.

God is good, and "all things work together for good," Romans 8:28, KJV.

CAHABA RIVER EXPEDITION

Part One

The Cahaba River is one of the last untamed rivers in Alabama. It is a beautiful vixen, originating somewhere outside of Birmingham and making its way down to Selma, and there are no true dams that stop or restrict its flow. In the river's upper reaches, rocky shoals and small rapids are commonplace, and the closer to Selma you paddle, the slower the run of the river becomes. We put in towards the upper end, between Montevallo and West Blocton at the canoe launch at Living River retreat center.

Bay, Cape, and I, along with my dear friend Chris Jackson and his two youngest boys, Jake and Grey, all struck out. Bay and Jake were both in the eighth grade at the time . . . Grey and Cape both younger by a few years. Chris and I became the best of friends years earlier, and, if anything, life taught us both that spending time with our children should be paramount.

Rain drizzled on us at a sprinkle's pace as we unloaded the gear from the truck and loaded the kayaks and canoes down. From the looks of our boats, we were set for what would surely be more than a "three-hour tour." My kayak was loaded down with about 200 pounds of gear, plus Cape and I . . . probably pushing 500 pounds total. Contrary to what most men buy, I opted to forego the sleek, fast, missile-like kayaks, instead opting for something that was sturdy and steady. I bought the kayak for this purpose in mind . . . carry enough gear that the girls won't be miserable, and still get to experience the majesty of God's great outdoors. It has done well.

This would also be Bay's first long-distance paddle under solo power . . . she had a different kayak. In years and trips past, she was always in the kayak with me. Now that Cape was older and growing bigger with every spoonful of chocolate pudding, two kayaks were necessary. And plans called for this trip to be some 40-plus miles . . . this would be a coming-of-age paddle for Bay. I was already proud, and though her paddling this trip by herself would make my heart swell, I am proud for who she is, not simply what she accomplishes.

It was after lunch before we ever put the first paddle in the water. The upper Cahaba cuts through the granite and limestone outside of Birmingham, Alabama, near the foothills of the Appalachians as they birth from the floor of north central Alabama. Most of the river here runs through canyon-like crevasses cut through the valley floor where two high rising foothills meet . . . "Where their toes touch," as Bay once explained. The hills loomed large and steep . . . pines and hardwoods clung by their fingernails to the sides of the steep inclines. Granite outcroppings lorded over the river below like guards at the entrance of the palace hallway, their breastplates of armor bulging forward and hanging overhead of all who approach.

We stopped at one such outcropping because its appearance suggested we might find a cave within its bowels. Instead, we found a coal vein. The vein was thick and rich—dark black—probably six or eight or maybe as many as 10 inches thick. Chunks of coal lay on the stone floor below the rock face. The vein tracked along the rock face, zigzagging its way out of reach and sight. The cave was not to be, but the roof of the outcropping provided a nice shelter and relief from the drizzle . . . it hung overhead and protruded just far enough out to act as an umbrella of sorts. Previous passersby had built campfires here . . . no doubt because the coal was plentiful and, obviously, a great source of fuel for a fire. Imagine their dismay when they woke the next morning to find their skin, tents, clothes . . . everything soot covered . . . and this time of the year, the river runs cold . . . no doubt they must have debated taking a bath or suffering through the misery of being covered in soot from their fire.

The water was crystal clear and cold . . . made colder by the overcast skies and drizzle. This was to be the worst of the weather for us, we hoped. We expected it would clear up that night, and the sun would shine for a brief time in the morning . . . after that, we weren't entirely sure. Rocks dotted the water's edge. Some fell from above, others revealed from below . . . some were massive bus-size boulders, and others were pebbles. Occasionally to the inside of a river bend, we'd find a small Buddha belly of rocks big enough to stop and walk about for a bit . . . stretching our legs and grabbing a snack.

On one such rocky sandbar, we flushed two spring turkeys . . . our first wildlife sighting of the trip. The turkeys, standing at the water's edge, had no doubt come down from the hilltops for a drink. Seeing us, they walked away, but when they felt we were pursuing them . . . simply because we were floating downriver towards them . . . they flushed. Seeing a 20-pound bird take flight is not unlike watching a helicopter lift off. It would seem impossible, yet with the combination of lift and wingspan, those awkwardly large birds always find a way. They lifted high and fast . . . we could hear the "flap, flap, flap" of their wings slapping through the air as they tried to gain momentum. With seven or eight strokes, they rose around the bend and behind the next granite outcropping. "No turkey for supper tonight. It is spring turkey season," Cape said, disappointed.

Every river trip must include a few good jumps from high places. Sometimes, it's a rock face or a cliff . . . most times, it is a good tree. We call them good "kerplunking" trees. Named so, because when you jump out of it and hit the water, the sound you make is "kerplunk." Cape found a good kerplunking tree just a few miles into our trip. This tree was stout and tall, and erosion at its base had drawn it down to about a 45-degree lean out over the river. "It's a perfect kerplunking tree," Cape said as she shimmied up its trunk to its upper reaches. Standing some 20 feet above the water, I watched her contemplation. She was brave and showed the courage of a warrior . . . she was, after all, only 11 years old. Twisting around each side of the tree's trunk and craning her neck to look below, she checked for rocks or logs or anything else that might hurt her if she landed on it.

While she looked on the left side, she talked of how cold the water was . . . she looked on the right side . . . and talked of how cold the water was. She shimmied back down just a bit, to a "better spot," and she talked of how cold the water was. And she was right . . . it was cold. No way would I jump in! Of course, cold water has a way of dampening even the most adventurous spirit... and she ultimately declined the kerplunk, instead satisfied that she had conquered the climb. "Good for you, Middle Princess," I thought to myself, "for doing what you wanted to do and not falling to pressure to do otherwise. I'm proud of you just for making the climb."

We made camp about five miles downriver from where we launched . . . not a bad day's journey for an afternoon trip and a few stops along the way. An open clearing built as part of the Alabama Scenic River Trail, the camp was open to the public and came with fire rings and a picnic table.

I challenged the girls to set up the tent on their own, and they managed . . . I say "managed" because I thought they were going to kill each other in the process. I forced them to smile for the picture. As soon as they heard the camera "click," they were back at each other . . .

Nothing soothes ill tempers like good food. Isn't that what my mother-in-law, Brenda, always says? And whenever I take the girls camping, good food is a must. I can hardly expect them to tolerate my camping notions if I don't treat them to some finer niceties while we are "in country." Steaks are always on the menu . . . in fact, they are the traditional first-night meal. This night was no different, complete with macaroni and cheese and some green beans . . . and Chris cooked a fantastic camp dessert . . . the name of which, I can't remember. It seems it involved a Dutch oven, blueberries, lots of fresh dough, a couple of pounds of sugar, and at least a tub of butter. I don't remember the specifics, but it was divine.

We ate our steaks with a Case Hobo knife. Years ago, I bought each of the girls one . . . and every camping trip, we have carried those same knives and eaten with them. They are as much a part of the tradition as anything else . . . and I hope one day they bury me with mine in my pocket. I hope that years after I am gone, they hand their Case knife to their kids and say, "Your Granddaddy gave me this . . . and it carries with it a lifetime of memories . . . and now, I give them all to you."

The Hobo, for the unfamiliar, is a knife/fork/spoon combination, and it is about as American as American can be . . . every kid should have one. Holding it invokes thoughts of Daniel Boone and the frontier, Lewis and Clark and their expedition, or even John Wayne sleeping on the open range. Sure . . . none of those guys had a Case Hobo knife, but that doesn't stop us from pretending, now does it? Even if they lose it one day . . . my daughters will never forget it. My girls are now full-fledged collectors of Case knives, but that has as much to do with George Gantt as anyone. He signed them up for the Case Collectors Club before they were even born. I just add to the collection along the way. The Hobo knife is one of the best additions, and my hope is that one day, they will hold the knife in their hand and rub the bone-handle sides as they tell their kids stories of our adventures.

We sat around the campfire that night telling booger tales and campfire stories. Campfires are a great uniter. Marriages have been reconciled, wars settled, and disputes resolved . . . all over a campfire. Best of all, though, many an awkward father found a way to bond with his children while roasting marshmallows . . . myself included. Even princesses are drawn to campfires and enchanted by the dance and flicker of the flames. Many a good bond has been forged over a campfire, and our first night on the Cahaba was no different. We talked about the day's adventures . . . the turkeys, the ducks, and the geese . . . the fish clearly visible on the bottom even at depth through the crystal-clear belly of the river. And, we talked about the rain. We knew it was coming . . . storms and rain . . . but we were OK with that, for the next day would be a day of great celebration.

It was to be Easter Sunday, the day our Savior would rise from the tomb for us . . . for me, for my daughters, and for you, too.

Part Two

The first night in the tent was a little rough. It always is . . . I've been on dozens, if not more, of these trips, and the first night is always low on sleep. Nevertheless, a nearby creek made for soothing white noise, but even that turned into a torrent of noise like Niagara Falls at some point during the night.

We set up two twin air mattresses in the tent. To make it all work, we slept on them sideways, such that the seam of the two mattresses was at about my waist . . . to begin with. It only took a few minutes for the girls to fall fast asleep. And, if you've ever slept with a child, you know they root. And root, they did . . . so effectively that it only took them a half an hour or so to root the lower mattress away such that my waist was now bridging the Grand Canyon between the two mattresses. Cape was curled in a ball at my head. Bay was half on and half off the mattress, and it did not seem to faze either of them in the least.

To make matters worse, the "below the waist" mattress was slowly leaking. "Great," I bemoaned.

As if that wasn't enough, Bay, who was on one side of the mattresses and I on the other (with Cape in the middle), was not familiar with what I call "the trampoline effect." That is, the effect of bouncing on your side of the mattress to then catapult whoever is one the other side of the mattress straight off into the oblivion of the night. So, every time she decided to roll over or adjust, she would raise up and then collapse all her weight abruptly back on to the air mattress. The resulting compression of air on her side of the trampoline forced all the air to the other side of the mattress. The result? Each time, I was sent flailing into the side wall of the tent!

Imagine, if you will, walking through the peaceful meadow of your dreams and, suddenly, a lightning bolt the size of a battleship strikes directly on top of you. Or you wake from the sleep of your dreams on the operating table and the doctor yells, "CLEAR!" and then he sends 100,000 volts through your body with cardiac paddles. Or even worse yet, you're walking down the quaint country dirt road of your dreams, and without warning, a whisper-quiet Mack dump truck plows into you from behind.

Each time I fell asleep, my dreams would transcend from peaceful and serene to hellish chaos . . . and I would wake up in an instant, with my face smooshed to the side wall of the tent. It was only on the fourth of such occasions that I realized what was happening . . . she catapulted me again before I fell completely back asleep. I slid off the air mattress and onto the flat earth. At least this time, I might sleep uninterrupted. Yet, the white noise of the creek had now grown to the roar of Niagara Falls in my impatience for lack of sleep. I lay, eyes wide open, rock in my back, watching Cape and Bay sleep like newborn puppies nestled to their mama's bosom.

"Jerks."

Then, to add insult to injury, a "water faucet" turned on about five feet away from the tent. I think it was Chris. "How much can one man pee?" I pondered. A full minute later, "Apparently, a lot." That only made me have to go, too. Double great.

Sunrise brought relief.

At sunrise or shortly afterwards, Chris and I got up to begin the day . . . Easter Sunday.

"Thank you, Lord, for Your sacrifice," I said a quiet prayer to myself as I watched the clouds roll overhead.

We stoked the fire back to life and then made breakfast. Hannah "made" breakfast for us before we left. Breakfast burritos—sausage, eggs, cheese, and bacon wrapped in flour tortillas—once the fire had a nice bed of coals, we heated them to piping hot. By now, I had had a couple of cups of camp coffee—some of the best coffee you'll ever have—and the kids were all starting to emerge from their tents. One by one, they stumbled to the fire, stretching their arms, squinty-eyed and yawning. It was cooler this morning . . . and overcast.

The hot fire and the warm food were soothing . . . breakfast was quiet.

But this was a day of celebration, and we would not let it pass without worship. I read Mark and Matthew's accounts of Christ's resurrection . . . that is, the Son of God

Chris Jackson knew a lot more about expeditions than I did. He knew a lot more about camping, canoeing, fire starting, everything. If there was such a thing as an expert, it was him. When our kids were still waist high to a grown man, I knew how to get lost in the woods; how to tie a knot that had to be cut to get undone; and how to roast marshmallows on a fire. We were a great combination because he knew everything, and I knew nothing! Chris was a longtime scout and scoutmaster. I was a cub scout for one year. Together, we were certainly a dynamic duo! But that's really the point, isn't it? Too many men are intimidated by the outdoors because they don't know what to do. The consequence is that the child is never given the benefit of camping or fishing. Find a mentor. Find a resource. Find a way. Don't be intimidated . . . your kids have no idea how long it takes to set up a tent—they have no idea you are not an expert!

Bay cut a sweetgum ball in half and suggested it represented the Crown of Thorns that Jesus wore. She talked of His death on the cross and how He suffered and died for us.

who came to earth, lived a blemish-free life, was crucified unjustly, and died as an atoning sacrifice for my sins and yours. Well, three days after His body was secured in a tomb and put under guard by Roman soldiers, the tomb was found to be empty. Christ rose to life. . . and He did so on what we Christians know as Easter Sunday.

After I read the Scriptures, Chris delivered a powerful devotion that left all of us thankful and grateful for what God has done in our lives. Then, Chris pulled out a bottle of grape juice and some unleavened crackers . . . he broke the bread and gave it to us. He then poured portions of grape juice into cups and gave us each a share. Reading from Scripture, Chris recalled the Lord's Supper, and we took the bread and the "wine" and partook of it, in remembrance of what Jesus did for us.

It was a special moment . . . for in those few minutes, a break in the clouds developed overhead. Blue sky broadened. Rays of the sun parsed through the clouds on the quartered sky. Birds chirped and chattered back and forth . . . all coinciding with Chris' Easter morning devotion and the Lord's Supper. I'm not suggesting God revealed Himself in those moments . . . He could have . . . I'm just telling you it was special.

And, of course, we had to have an Easter egg hunt! But this was no ordinary Easter egg hunt. After we took the Lord's Supper, Chris reached into his backpack and retrieved a menagerie of colored plastic eggs . . . pink, green, yellow, blue . . . the full spectrum of pastels was represented. He handed each of us an egg and then asked us to open them. "It's empty!" one of the kids exclaimed. "That's right," Chris said. "This is no ordinary Easter egg hunt. Your job is to go out into the woods and find something in nature that in some way symbolizes Jesus and Easter and the sacrifice He made for us. Then, put it in the egg and bring it back. When we all get back to the fire, we will show what is in our egg and tell the story of why "it" is significant."

Everyone was excited at the prospect and departed quickly to find the treasure of Easter. I wish I could remember everything the kids brought back . . . it was such a special morning . . . to hear their creativity and faith spelled out by the warmth of our fire. While I can't remember every detail, I wrote in my journal these words:

"Bay cut a sweetgum ball in half and suggested it represented the Crown of Thorns that Jesus wore. She talked of His death on the cross and how He suffered and died for us. Cape dug through the 'pantry' until she found a pack of salt. She emptied the salt into the egg and reminded us of all that Jesus calls us to be Salt and Light . . . and she is."

Chris did a tremendous job shepherding that day.

Not long after we adjourned from the morning services, the clouds rolled back across the sky, and the rain soon followed. Our latest weather update confirmed the bad news . . . rain and storms for most of the day. We decided to stay put and enjoy the day, rain and all, with some measure of shelter.

But sitting in camp all day could be the death toll in a child's mind . . . sitting idle, boredom will quickly set in, and complaints will soon follow. So, fishing became the first order of business. The girls and I fished for an hour or more without so much as a bite. It was fun fishing in the rain . . . none of us had ever done it before. Chris, on the other hand, caught a monster! Although, looking back, I don't recall anyone seeing the monster in the water... "Hhhmmm." After Chris clearly schooled everyone with his expert fishing skills, we passed the next couple of hours with checkers and cards around the table. I told a couple of stories from my youth . . . about when I was "Wanted . . . Dead or Alive." Can you believe the girls still, to this day, don't believe that I used to be part of famous rock band, Bon Jovi? I even sang the song to prove my claims.

Nothing.

The kids also did not believe Chris and I captured Chewbacca one time and shaved him down . . . turns out he is really a French poodle with an extraordinary amount of hair! After all that, who could resist a little chicken salad for lunch? Hannah's secret family recipe. And you'll note from the pictures that, for whatever reason, Cape refused to use the Case Hobo to eat her pudding!

After lunch, we set out on foot during a break in the rain to do a little exploring. We soon found a crystal clear, stream-fed pond, and everybody decided to go for a swim. Cold was not the word for it. Maybe a little too cold for me . . . And we also did a little puddle jumping in the stream. Cape and Grey opted to do a little kerplunking, and then we settled back into some dry clothes, a warm campfire, and a little relaxation. Somewhere in there, I took a fantastic nap, too. "Thank you, Lord, for the little things and for letting me have the air mattress to myself for a couple of hours."

Chris made "Tacos in a Bag" for supper that night . . . yes, you read that right: "Tacos in a Bag," and then it was off to bed again. And oh, the joy of sleeping on the ground once more.

Part Three

Night number two was much better than night number one... but, only because I was on the verge of sheer exhaustion. My body had no choice but to find rest. The girls said I snored loud enough to keep even the angriest bear at bay, and I must confess, their complaints the next morning gave me a little satisfaction . . . payback for the trampoline the night before. I also got a little revenge with Chris. This time, it was I who "turned on the water faucet" at about 3 a.m. Clearly, I drank too much water the evening before . . . I woke up about to burst. Shortly afterwards, I heard the familiar but faint sound of a distant tent zipper. Chris or one of his boys fell victim to the old familiar truth—the sound of running water will always make you have to go, too.

Campfire cooking is, perhaps, the best. The next morning, the aroma of the link sausage wafted to my nose as the smoke from its sizzle curled up in loops over the top of the skillet. Pork always has the most appetizing smell when fried . . . this

I don't remember where we were when this became a camping
tradition . . . maybe the girls will one day remind me, but for
years we ate pudding snacks when in country or on the river,
and we always did two things: First, we licked the lid because
there was too much good pudding to be ignored stuck to the lid,
and two, if we didn't have a spoon, we just used our tongues!
One of the best things about being on the river is that mom's
table manners rule book often gets tossed to the side.

We've had many photo shoots for the sisters in our lifetime. Seems whenever I want to take a picture, they hate it. But if either of them wants to take pictures, they will take a hundred, and then a hundred more!

sausage had the warm hint of hickory smoke and the subtle suggestion of sweet brown sugar. This was Southern sausage made with pork, fat, sugar, and a few other secret ingredients . . . there is nothing like it. The smoke danced above the pan. I leaned in over the top and soaked it all in like a sausage-smoke-sauna. The warmth of the fire rose around my neck and cheeks and tickled my ears. The warmth of the fire . . .

As an additional comfort, the sun was piercing through the trees behind me. Two days in the wilderness without feeling the sun seemed like an eternity. It was cool that morning, but the sun warmed the back of my neck and my shoulders as the fire warmed my cheeks. I closed my eyes and just bathed in it.

The river swirled. I could hear the current wrap itself around a tree that stood at the water's edge. I could hear the pop and gurgle of the swirls and burls of the water as it rounded the bend. I could hear the snap and the pop of the eddies as they reversed course and went against the grain.

I could hear the wind. It sifted its way through the trees overhead. Few leaves had formed yet, so the wind went through the treetops with a familiar sound . . . it reminded me of the noise my mama's switches made as she swung them towards the backside of my childhood legs. That sound was not one I cared to recall. But the wind was as peaceful as the water. Gentle. Caressing . . . if not just a little bitter cold with its breath.

As the sun rose higher and brighter, I felt surely this was going to be a good fishing day. Some men fish for records. I fish for fish of character. I want to catch fish of great character. So, I typically forego such trivial things as size and weight, especially when I don't catch a big fish. And this day, I caught several fish of great character!

To that point, though, too many men shy away from taking their kids fishing or hunting for one of two reasons: first, fear of not knowing "how." Second, fear of not meeting the child's expectations.

Men, those two things . . . fear because of inexperience and embarrassment for not being a trophy slayer . . . are killing the sports of hunting and fishing, and they are keeping us from teaching our kids the value of God's great outdoors. I have never gone hunting or fishing with my girls when I was fully competent in what I was doing. Which lure to use, or which tree stand to sit in are, oftentimes, just luck. And I've never gone hunting or fishing with my girls when we didn't catch or kill a trophy—because, to us, the trophies are the memories.

Take them . . . shepherding outdoors.

On into the afternoon, we stopped and scouted the beginning of the "mile-long shoal." The name was somewhat intimidating, and from the top of our vantage point, it looked somewhat daunting. It wasn't Grand Canyon daunting, but for Alabama—and Bay's first serious solo shoal—this was enough to cause a little anxiety. We hiked down the riverbank to scout. As luck would have it, we found a great old logging road and ATV trail just downriver. We followed the trail for almost the entirety of the shoals. Along the way, wild azaleas of pink and orange flanked us on both sides . . . a perfect complement to an Easter trip. Confident we had identified the best route through the "mile-long shoal," we launched back into the sun-shone water. Bay did great . . . tracking a perfect line and avoiding the boulders and the sleepers . . . that is, a rock hidden just below the water's surface. This shoal gave her confidence . . . and she would need it.

The morning's stretch of the river was one set of shoals after another, with more than one waterfall and plenty of fault lines. Drops of six feet over the course of a few hundred yards were not uncommon. The water was a bit high, and the flow was fast. The rain of the past two days gave the river plenty of volume, and it also gave the last set of shoals of the day a menacing growl. We stopped at the top of the shoals to survey the river's run. These were, no doubt, the most treacherous shoals of the day we had faced. There was a substantial drop which would force all of us to paddle diagonally across the river while also traversing the midsection of the rapids. Failing to make this crossing would mean disaster, as one would then have no choice but to ride over the falls. They were not tremendously high—about four or five feet—but going over the edge would not only be dangerous, but it would also certainly spill gear everywhere. Once we made it through the belly of the midsection of river . . . all should be fine.

White waters bounced over rocks scattered about throughout the river. Like pimples on a teen's face, the rocks were plentiful, but not unavoidable. The water boiled behind some of the larger rocks . . . with vacuum-like eddies rolling in behind the boulders, the areas were surely dangerous . . . for, to flip inside that boil could mean prolonged bouts under the water. I sat silently at the top of the shoal and prayed a prayer of safety for all of us . . . the water raged in my ears as the winds whipped overhead.

We huddled the kids altogether, and with a certain measure of concern in our voices, Chris and I gave the final instructions . . . then we launched. Bay and Jake went first. Chris and I were not too far behind with Cape and Grey. I preferred for them to let us go first through the shoals, but their confidence was beginning to outshine their judgment . . . they pressed into the mouth of the churning water.

At the top of the shoal, the water flowed straight for a few hundred yards . . . Bay dodged a boulder here and a sleeper there and was grinning from ear to ear. I watched nervously but found comfort in her smile. "This is why I come," I thought to myself. Seeing your child smile broadly or hearing them give a belly laugh . . . well, that's the stuff that dreams are made of. But my joy was but for a moment . . . she craned her neck to look for the passageway through the middle of the shoals. She dug hard with the paddle to the left side of the boat . . . she understood and was handling the navigation well. "Dig, dig, dig," I chanted with each stroke she took. Now into the top of the shoals myself, I had to turn my attention away from Bay.

A few seconds later, Chris said, "Bay is in trouble." I looked up to find her hung sideways on a rock. The water was pushing her broadside, and before I could even yell, I saw the fear in her face. Few things strike at your heart more than experiencing the fear and anguish of your child. I could see her eyes . . . wide and searching, turning to me as the kayak rolled, as if to say, "Daddy, help!"

"Oh, and I want to, and will always rescue you . . . with every ounce of my being."

I dug hard with my paddle, but she could only hold on for a second or two before she rolled. She emerged from the water, now separated from the kayak. Fortunately, the water wasn't too deep, and she stood up in the waist-deep water. She managed to grab the bow line of the kayak before it darted downstream, but the churning river pulled hard like a madman tugging on the arm of a child. The kayak flailed about as Bay held tight to the rope. No doubt, the friction burned as the rope slid, an inch or two at a time, ripping the skin from her palms. Despite the pain, she held fast and was tough, as she knew that kayak was her lifeline. I preached and preached, "You can never lose your kayak in the wilderness," and she remembered. Bay wrestled the kayak like it was a wild bronco, kicking and snatching at the rope . . . doing all it could to get away . . . but she held on until I could get to her. It seemed like hours, but it couldn't have been more than 15 or 20 seconds.

She was exhausted. I got out of my boat and grabbed both her line and that of my own. Cape helped Bay get into my kayak. Her knees were banged up and her hands were rashed, but she was okay. I told her she had to paddle on down the river. "I don't know if I can, Daddy."

She was scared and beat up and understandably reluctant to go without me. I made sure she was physically okay and reassured her. "You can't quit, Bay," I said. "It's not an option. I know you are hurting and a little scared, but you can't quit." Even though she was rattled, I was confident that she and Cape could navigate the rest of the way through the shoals. This was an important lesson in life for her to learn . . . sometimes, immediately after the fall comes the hardest test of all. I knew she could do it . . . she is not a quitter. Never has been. It's not in her to quit. So, I let go of her rope; she had to do this on her own, for there will come a day when I won't be there to rescue her from the struggle after the fall.

Bronco defeated, she had prevailed the champion . . . and she had the battle scars to prove it! And Cape, calm, cool, and collected, ever the hero herself, took control of the kayak and paddled them through the shoals and to the safety of a downriver sand bar. Bay's kayak was full of water. I saw little hope of flipping and draining it, so I simply lay down on top of it—the water was freezing, and the warmth of the adrenaline rush was fading—and floated on my belly on top of the nearly submerged kayak down the rest of the shoal.

A mile or so downriver, we made camp for the night, batteries dead—both in ourselves and the camera. Tired, wet, and sore . . . but oh, the stories we could tell! We made a big fire, ate hot dogs, and slept hard on the sand bar.

Part Four

Our third and final night on the river was bitter cold. We made camp at the tail end of the shoal that "Bay almost died" in. That's what we renamed it . . . the "Bay Almost Died" shoal. Of course, she was nowhere near death, but the drama of the new name made for a good story. A spreading sand bar, layered with driftwood—perfect for a warming fire—lay at the bottom of the shoal. When we went to bed, I hung most of our clothes on a line near the fire, with the hope that they would dry by the heat of the fire. They did . . . sort of. Because they were "on a line," the clothes were folded over the top of the line. The fire side of the clothes on the line were dry. But, at some point during the night the fire went dim, and the other side of the line froze solid.

Did I mention it was cold?

During the early morning darkness, our once "slow leak" air mattress had breathed its last breath . . . flat as a fritter, but we adjusted. Bay and Cape shared the one good mattress while I slept on the ground. I laid the flat mattress out for a little insulation from the weeping effects of the cold earth below, but still I shivered through the night . . . the girls had a sleeping bag each, but I made the poor decision to only bring a blanket. It was one of those, "Lord, if you'll get me warm, I promise…" kind of nights.

I was roused by an alarming sound not too far from the tent. A few screaming babies perhaps . . . a couple of old fire engine sirens maybe . . . at least those thoughts might adequately describe the sound. It's springtime, though. I knew the sounds well . . . I've heard them before. Two bobcats had fallen in love and were courting or commencing, I'm not sure which. Yet, even knowing what it was, the screeching noise was still chilling. In the still dark of the deep woods, your mind begins to wander when startled . . . "Was that really two bobcats?" "What if they are aggressively defending their territory, and we have encroached?" "What was that? Footsteps outside the tent?" By now, I was shivering enough to mimic a wounded jackrabbit . . . "Great," I worried. "Now, I am the prey."

To make matters worse, the cold was bone chilling. I pulled another shirt and an extra pair of pants from my bag and layered up to the size and shape of the Stay Puft Marshmallow Man. I could see my breath in the moonglow of the tent, and my toes ached in the painfully thin pair of cotton socks . . . the only socks I had for the trip. At times, I shivered uncontrollably. My teeth chattered like woodpeckers in a dueling pecking contest. And my ears . . . they burned. I could feel how red my earlobes were as the frostbite must surely be creeping up from the dangly depths. "I don't know if I ever remember being this cold," I thought to myself. And looking back on it still today . . . I don't think there was another cold that abused me more than that night.

Eventually—and thankfully—the sun rose. While I built the fire and found comfort in its flame, Bay decided to take a few early morning "sleepies"—a selfie with someone who's asleep—of her sister . . . Cape was not impressed. The fire, though, I could feel

Oh, the unfettered joy of taking an embarrassing picture of your sibling!

the blood warm in my toes as I lay my brittle feet upon a log at the edge of the pit. The flames licked at my toes, and my hands hovered above, and my knees touched the edge of the fire as I was all but immersed in it. I had made a dreadful camping mistake—I underestimated the weather in an effort to save space in the kayak. Warmer sleeping bags take up more space. I let my bravado replace common sense. I swore to myself— as I thawed my rock-hard, iced-over clothes that hung on the line—that I would never make this mistake again. Unfortunately, though, a few years later, near the peak of Mount Mitchell, North Carolina, on a blustery, cold March night . . . I made nearly the same mistake. But that's a story for a different day.

Chris and I saved the best breakfast of the trip for the last day. Pancakes and sausage . . . pancakes always have a way of soothing even the coldest soul. There's just something about flapjacks and some good, old-fashioned, sweet, sugary cane syrup . . . add in some link sausage—dang, that's good! Somehow, the flavor from the sausage drives into the syrup and adds just a little kick to the pancakes. And I always take the sausage and drag it through the remnants of the syrup as the last tasty morsels go down. Warm and sweet . . . syrup and sausage always soothe the soul of a Southern boy.

While we ate, a pair of bald eagles flew overhead. Their outstretched wings spanned six or more feet, and their bright yellow beaks pierced the chilled air . . . unmistakably, they are the king of all that flies. Low enough that I thought we made eye contact, that yellowed squint was intimidating . . . he read my soul as he looked deep into me. As our eyes parted, I felt the chill grow a little thicker in the air, and somehow felt inadequate in the majesty of this bird. It is not hard to understand why our forefathers thought it appropriate to name this raptor as the national symbol of freedom and independence. Gliding down the river's trail, scouring just beneath the surface for the unsuspecting bass . . . it was an amazing sight.

We broke camp and tiptoed into the blurry cold water. The air was still frigid . . . as the sun had not long crested over the opposing canyon wall. We had a few more rapids to traverse—and then several miles of still water through the Bibb County canyonland—to our final port of call in Centreville, Alabama.

It should have been an uneventful and relatively easy paddle that morning . . . just as the night before should have been a comfortable night's sleep in a warm sleeping bag on a comfortable mattress. But neither were to be . . . a few miles downriver, Cape and I were dashing across trying to make it to what appeared to be the safest passage through a small shoal, and we hung up on a sleeper. The current was vicious, and it happened before I could even react. We flipped at the edge of the three-foot fall line. When I emerged, I first thought of her, knowing she did not have on her life jacket . . . I had grown complacent in the security of what I thought I knew. Stupid, I know . . . she should have had one on. Let my ignorance be your lesson, please. Thank the good Lord, a PFD was floating right in front of my face, so I grabbed it, and, like a professional baseball pitcher, threw a perfect, God-enabled strike! It landed right in her outstretched arms! She grabbed the life jacket, and I turned my attention to our gear. Fortunately, all was still secure . . . except my cell phone. I knew time was of the essence . . . I snapped a few quick pictures of the falls from a nearby sand bar . . . and then the phone died.

And, as predicted, the rest of the paddle was relatively uneventful . . . until Centreville.

Sitting around the campfire the night before, we all agreed that every time any of us told a tale about this trip, the story had to end with, "and Bay almost died." It was meant to be our humorous way to pay homage to her first solo kayak wreck . . . but what happened at the end of our trip forever changed all of us . . . and how we would always finish this story.

Centreville is a quaint town sitting on high bluffs above the Cahaba River. The takeout at Highway 82 is on a high bluff, too. You can drive under the bridge and stage for loading, but the incline from the river's edge to the staging area is horrendous . . . steep and long. More upright than any set of stairs, one must look for toeholds to find footing sufficient enough to climb up the incline, and it was about 60 or so feet from the water's edge. Getting gear and kayaks up this slope was proving to be gruesome.

Ten minutes into our gear tote, a kindly sheriff's deputy approached. "Sir, would you mind stepping over here away from the little ones?" I obliged, though I was puzzled. "Were we not supposed to be under the bridge?" I considered before he started talking.

"Are you familiar with the Bibb County Correctional Facility?" he asked. I told him I was and advised that I used to live here. "Well, sir, a very dangerous man has escaped from the facility this morning. He is 6 feet 6 inches tall and weighs approximately 250 pounds. He should be wearing an orange jumpsuit. Right now, a team of tracking dogs is pushing him up this bank of the river, and unless he gives up, it's only a matter of time before he gets here."

A shiver ran down my spine. I looked around to make sure I could see all the kids, and as I did, for the first time, I noticed deputies and state police standing on top of the bridge and spreading a dragnet along the tree line on the upriver side of the bridge. "You folks can keep loading your gear. I think you have enough time before he gets here—and I understand that you can't just leave it—but if he comes through the tree line, I need y'all to immediately take cover in your truck and lock the doors," the officer advised.

"Yes, sir," I replied. "Don't you worry. We are going to get loaded up and out of here as quick as we can. Thank you."

I spent a minute telling Chris what the deputy had advised, and we decided to tell the kids, as they had to know the danger that might come. We didn't want to scare them, but we felt we had no other choice but to make them aware. "So, if you see a man wearing an orange jumpsuit, or any man who is taller than both me and Mr. Chris and looks strong, and he is running, you jump into the truck immediately," I said. "If he comes to the truck, lock the doors. Does everyone understand?" My voice was

Our last full day on the river and we stopped for lunch just below this shoal. A long, one-laned dirt road led us out to this vantage point, and our smiles were weary, but the sun was bright and warm. A trip with memories for a lifetime. No ride at a theme park will ever compare to what God gives us in the great outdoors.

stern. They knew this was not a joke. This was serious. They all nodded their head in understanding.

The officer stood close by, ever vigilant. I appreciated his presence. After another trip down the bank . . . and then a labored strain back up and to the truck . . . I could hear hounds. They were faint but increasing in volume. "I had hoped he would turn," I lamented to myself. I headed back down for the next load, telling the kids as I passed them to be very alert, pointing out that we could hear the hounds. "Those are the tracking dogs," I mentioned to one of the girls.

I was nervous and near exhaustion. My heart raced as I sensed the danger of having an escaped convict come running from the woods and him identifying our truck as a means of further escape. My heart also raced because my pace had quickened significantly . . . normally, I make sure the girls load their fair share and shoulder their portion of the work. This was not such a time. I raced up and down the Mount Everest-type slope from the river to the truck carrying far more than I would normally be capable of. No doubt, adrenaline coursed through my veins.

On the second trip back up, after hearing the commotion from downriver draw nearer, I put my pistol in the side pocket of my shorts. "Chris, there is a rifle behind the back seat of the truck." He nodded. The hounds still seemed distant . . . but I understood that they were behind the escaped inmate. So, he was between us and the hounds. I scanned the tree line . . . we only had one more trip, and all the gear would be secure. I looked over the gear left to be toted up the hill and saw, among other things, a machete and several paddles. "There are plenty of things there that he might use as a weapon . . . let's get it, girls, and then get in the truck."

Jake, Grey, and Chris grabbed up their last load. Bay and I headed towards our last load . . . Cape stopped and stared into the woods. The dogs were close . . . as if they would pierce the veil of the woods at any moment. "How did they cover so much ground so quickly?" I wondered. I saw Cape standing there, idle . . . and frustration poured through me at her refusal to make haste. "Cape!" I demanded. She didn't look at me . . . standing motionless and staring away . . . just as I was about to get onto her for not getting the last of the gear, the dogs' barking became unmistakably present, and I realized she sensed something the rest of us did not.

"Daaaaaad! There he is!" Cape yelled, her eyes, wide and focused, her finger pointing to the convict bursting through the tree line. He was a huge man—bulging from underneath the white tank top. His orange jumpsuit was tied around his waist, and I could hear his pants and gasps as he burst through the trees. The dogs were so loud they seemed as though they howled at my feet. How I heard his gasps, I'll never understand. My hearing, though, was heightened in the intensity of the moment, and all silence evacuated. Chaos ruled the sound waves. Chris started yelling at the kids to "Get in the truuuuuck!" and police officers from everywhere were screaming and giving commands. Cape turned and started running. Looking back over my shoulder to find Bay, I ushered her in front of me and then fell in behind Cape.

Everyone started running toward the truck. The escapee was not more than 50 feet away and was running nearly full speed. He would be upon us in a few seconds. All four of the kids piled into the truck, and Chris and I took up a defensive posture— that man would only get to the kids over our dead bodies—and we meant it. I pulled the pistol from my pocket . . . he was dead-eye focused straight on the truck. For the briefest of moments, I knew I would likely have to kill this man to protect my children. To this day, I get nauseous thinking about what might have been . . . I'm so thankful for the Lord's protection.

He took three full strides into the clearing under the bridge, and, before the he could get within reach of us, the Bibb County Sheriff's deputies and the Centreville Police Department's officers (and others I'm sure) descended on him from on top of the bridge like Navy Seals. Guns drawn, rifles, pistols, shotguns. I breathed a sigh of relief, but instantaneously, my next worst fear flashed through my head. "Please don't kill him in front of my children." I turned and yelled through the glass, "Put your heads down!" They all immediately did as I instructed.

"Get down! Get down! Get down!" The commands from the officers were unmistakable. The dogs barked liked raging noisemakers, and there was no peace in the moment . . . like the raging river, the tranquility of the flatwater had been shattered. And thankfully, the chaos of the moment was enough to overpower that man's resolve. Looking straight at Chris and I, he threw his hands up, fell to his knees, turned his head to face the nearest officer and said, "I ain't did nothing!" Officers descended upon him like ants marching, and they took him into custody without anyone being hurt. "Thank you, men, for a job well done."

"Breathe," I had to remind myself. I slid my pistol back into my pocket, adrenaline coursed through my veins once again. For the first time in a long time, I felt that I had stood nearly at the edge of not being in control, and it was unsettling. Like staring into the eagle's eyes, that man's gaze of desperation and determination was very intimidating . . . unsettling. Thankfully, Chris suggested a prayer of thanks. We had experienced so much, and there was truly much to be thankful for. During the prayer, I found peace and comfort.

And now, every time we speak of this trip, the story will end with, "Bay did almost die . . . but there was that escaped convict . . . and God is good."

—— D E L T A T I L L D A W N ——

Part One

Nighttime on the Delta feels like swirling around the dark circles of a black hole . . . its inner sanctum is dark and somewhat intimidating—a darkness that even an owl's eyes cannot pierce—ever lightening from its center, with bands of light at its outer reaches. The boat glided over the glass of the water briskly. My eyes strained against the darkness searching for apparitions in the waters ahead.

"You want the spotlight?" my friend, Travis Martin, asked. I shook my head no . . . the light of the beam draws to a pinpoint focus of the eye, and you lose sight of everything outside of its reach. "Better to drive by the moonlight," I suggested.

The apparitions I strained to see were not alligators . . . though I suppose one might have crossed our path. Instead, I strained to see logs floating in the river. Trees and stumps dislodged and uprooted from points far upriver, the silent sleepers slowly make their way downriver. Some sink to the river bottom. Others make their way to shallow water and settle in. And still others sleek their way down the river channel . . . sometimes only revealing a knob here or there . . . waiting to attack the bottom of a boat.

Cape, the Middle Princess, Travis' daughter, Anna, and his son, Tyler, all rode up front in the bow of the boat. The girls' hair followed behind them like wedding streamers on the back of an old sedan. They chatted back and forth about Lord only knows what. Tyler's gaze was fixed on the passing banks of the river. Occasionally, he would light up a set of eyes near the bank with the spotlight, and all our eyes would divert, trying to determine whether the gator he shined was large enough to stop and pursue further.

Gators sit low in the water when they feel encroached upon. At times, all you can see of them is the tip of their nose and the crown of their head. When they sink low, there are only two ways to determine the gator's size. Either you estimate the distance between the tip of his nose to his eyes, or you simply estimate the width between his eyes. The former calculation would suggest that for every inch between his nose and eyes, a foot of length is what he carries with him underwater. Thus, if you speculate that there are 10 inches between his nose and eyes, then he is surely a 10-foot alligator.

There is no such litmus test for the secondary calculation . . . we simply know and understand that the further the gator's eyes are set apart from each other, the bigger he is. Such crucial estimations are difficult, at best, when running 25 miles per hour down the river and glancing at a spot 50 yards away. The determination has to be immediate, for the gator doesn't appreciate your advance towards his position. He won't wait long before he submerges, disappearing into the murky waters below.

Tyler's Q-Beam spotlight pierced the night air like Luke Skywalker's light saber. He shined the left bank, and the reeds on the bank illuminated like the front line of a forest fire. I turned to look for myself, but he turned off the light before I could get a good look . . . Cape yelled out, "He's small." We continue up the river to our destination . . . we came for monsters . . . not babies.

I grew up in these waters, especially the south end of the Delta. As a teenager, I spent many a summer afternoon running the rivers here chasing largemouth bass. The south end of the Delta is a stunning expanse of saw grass, sprinkled with acres of river cane and other marshy aquatic vegetation.

"I always try to be aware of the nearest group of trees," I reminded Travis. "Growing up, we knew of plenty of times when sunken logs—we called them sleepers—were struck by boats running full speed down the river. It would pull the motor and the transom clean off the boat. Of course, the boat sunk in no time. Whether the boat's unfortunate occupants had figured out ahead of time where the dry land was often meant the difference between life and death."

I could see Travis' head pivot as he scanned the horizon for the hammocks. "Hammocks" is a South Florida swamp term for an island of dry land amidst the vastness of the swamp . . . a place to string up a hammock and rest, for you dare not sleep on the ground.

The rivers and creeks of the Delta snake their way through the marshy grasses where the freshwaters of the north collide with the salt waters of Mobile Bay. That collision slows the water's flow southward . . . sediments drop out of the water column and settle . . . and over thousands of years, these marshes developed. The Mobile River Delta is the second largest freshwater delta in all the United States. Its watershed reaches well into Georgia, Tennessee, almost all of Alabama, and, yes, it even steals a little thunder-flow from Old Man River to the west.

When crossing the Delta at night, there is no doubt that we are but men . . . not the gods that men so desperately seek to be. This is the place where men are consumed without a second thought. Alligators large enough to engulf grown men, buzzard colonies that would make Hitchcock's birds flee, bull sharks patrolling the waters interspersed with the gators . . . the Delta is the place where men disappear . . . and no one ever notices.

We men sometimes fancy ourselves the apex of the animal kingdom. And, perhaps, because we have souls—and some even have some intelligence—we are the apex in that regard. But if left in the Delta to challenge Darwin's theory, I fear we are not the fittest creatures in these swamps, nor are we likely to survive.

Travis and I have raised our kids together . . . mostly through their teenage years. He and I are two different men . . . he can fix anything with his hands, and I can fix many things with my words. His strengths compensate for my shortcomings, and vice versa. Like our family, he and Heidi would much prefer their kids be outside under the blue sky than under the spell of a computer screen. And ironically, like us, they use digital media to promote a message that promotes all things outdoors. Be sure to follow them on Facebook at Martin Homestead; on TikTok @martinhomestead; and YouTube at Martin Homestead.

Beyond that, the expanse of the Delta is awe-inspiring. Hardly an imprint of man . . . just towering cypress trees, scrub oaks, swaying saw grass, gentle southern breezes, and so many stars—the likes of which you will never see anywhere else.

At night, the sky here is as vibrant as any Fourth of July spectacular. Orion's Belt always anchors the Alabama night's sky. In the Delta, his belt always shines a little brighter.

This night, the moon was just cresting the horizon . . . its orange glow like the eye of a tiger, peering through the thin veil of cloud smoke on the horizon. "It's a spooky moon," I said to Travis. He nodded as he watched it climb. Its orange glow was enough to illuminate the path before us.

We slowed and turned into an old familiar creek. "It has been a few years…" I remembered aloud. Cape asked if this was a creek I had been to before. I nodded my head and grinned, "Let me tell you a story, girls." They both turned—Tyler, too—and listened intently as we eased up through the two-lane highway of a creek, dodging blown down trees and log jams as we went.

Years ago, my buddy Danny . . . well, he and I were up here fishing. About a half mile ahead, this creek opens into Little Bateau Bay. We were fishing our way to the creek. We had caught a few fish and seen a few alligators . . . but nothing spectacular had happened.

It was a beautiful blue-sky day. It had to have been springtime, as I recall, because it wasn't hot, but it wasn't cold either. I remember that we both had on T-shirts and shorts, and I remember how bright the sun was and how clear blue the sky was. The sun's warmth felt good on my skin. I also remember that a few bright, white, puffy clouds dotting the sky, but otherwise, it was blue as far as the eye could see. The wind was blowing out of the east, gentle and refreshing. Not too stiff, but just enough to keep the skeeters at bay.

We were fishing just up here around this next bend . . . Danny had just caught a bass that weighed a pound or so . . . nothing fit to eat but still fun to catch. He threw the bass back, and it flipped its tail hard when it hit the water. I guess the noise of the tail flip centered my focus because I heard something . . . rustling . . . in the saw grass? I strained my ears to draw out distinctly what the sound was. It sounded loud but distant. I couldn't quite make it out. It wasn't mechanical or man-made . . . definitely natural. The saw grass was tall and thick, browning at its ends where it seems to naturally die as it gets too tall and too long. When the wind blew, the saw grass blades clattered and chattered together, and it made a distinctive rustling sound . . . and this noise . . . it sounded almost like that.

"Do you hear that?" I asked Danny. He stopped reeling and let his soft plastic worm sink to the bottom. We both strained our necks to get just the right angle to zone in on the loudening noise. "Is that something coming through the saw grass?" I asked. "I can't quite tell . . . what is that?" Danny pondered.

The sound was coming . . . I could tell that for sure. "It's coming towards us," I

offered. He nodded, and neither of us wanted to speak . . . I suppose for fear that "it"
might hear our voices. My mind searched to explain the curious noise my ears heard . . .
"Pigs . . . a whole bunch of pigs? Maybe it's an alligator dragging something . . . a deer
maybe, through the reeds? Could it be something coming for us? A bear?" "Naw . . .
we are too far south." "Coyotes?" "Doubtful . . . its mighty soupy out there."

By now, the rustling was undeniable, and the source of the noise was only 50 yards
through the reeds, definitely advancing on us. I'd be lying if I didn't tell you that, by
that point, I was a little scared. And Danny . . . he has this "he-hey" laugh that he
made when he was nervous . . . and he gaped his mouth just a little as he looked at
you. Well, when he made that laugh and gaped his mouth a little . . . I got really
nervous.

I reeled my line in and considered the options. Whatever it was wasn't far from
being in that boat with us. Danny wound his line in, too. "Should we crank up?"
We both started trying to put stuff away . . . with thoughts of leaving the fish . . . and
whatever monster roamed the landscape. The rustling was nearly upon us . . . the hairs
on the back of my neck stood up, and I braced myself for whatever was about to part
the reeds. I raised my hands halfway up and spread my fingers . . . preparing to catch
or wrestle or push or hit whatever it was that was about to overtake us.

To my distraction . . . Plip. Plop. Plip-plip. Drop. Drip. Plop-plip-drip-drop. The
water in the creek slowly began to dance as the sound surrounded us. "Rain? Is that
rain?" We both looked skywards . . . both of us puzzled because there had been no sign
of rain at all. The bottom fell out, and a bombardment commenced, the likes of which
we had never experienced. The waters around us danced steadily now as each bomb
struck its target. The reeds sang as the mini-explosions rocked them back and forth . . . they
"cha-a-a-a-tt-tt-tt-er-er-er-ed-ed-ed." I got hit right in the eye. Danny took a direct hit
to the forehead and us, the boat, and all of our gear was being decimated by the deluge.

The noise was almost deafening.

"Start the boat!" I yelled. Danny jumped behind the wheel, and I held fast as he
fired that Johnson 35 up . . . we gave her hell for a quarter of a mile or so up that creek.
Like Mario Andretti burning through turn four at Indianapolis, Danny navigated the
twists and turns of the creek at top speed with the skill of even old man Stauter himself.

After a minute or two, the deluge subsided . . . and we slowed the boat to a stop. We
stared at each other in disbelief . . . and then all we could do was laugh!

"How did y'all let the rainstorm slip up on you, Daddy?" Cape asked.

"Oh, it wasn't rain, baby girl."

"Well, what was it then?" Everyone in the boat turned to hear the answer. They all
had a curious look that told me they were so sure they understood the story . . . and now
were lost in it.

That night, the wind was still, and the air was moist. I could see a thunderhead far off to the south. "Probably in the Gulf and won't even make it to us," I thought to myself. Lightning flickered occasionally from within its marshmallow body. The lights of the city of Mobile lay almost directly ahead of us, and we could see the tops of the tallest skyscrapers over the reeds and saw grass off the bow of the boat. Though the skyscrapers were miles away, they still loomed large on the horizon. Curious, isn't it? That God calls us to be the light. And even more curious that it only takes the smallest spec of light to pierce the broadest expanse of darkness. Be the light.

Well, you see . . . when we looked up to see the rain coming down . . . what hit me in the eye was pure white. Same for Danny's forehead . . . and all of the boat. Because above us were several hundred well-fed buzzards in a column of dark circles, like a black hole of death-eating scavengers . . . and they let bombs fly on the swamp that day! I have never before, or after, seen that many buzzards in one place in all my life.

I'm not sure what the apex predator of the Delta is, but I know on that day, we were nowhere near the top of the ladder!

And let me tell you, buzzards don't poop like mockingbirds! It was the most disgusting thing I've ever experienced. It was gobs, not drops!

The girls reeled in disgust. Tyler laughed and looked upwards, I think to make sure no buzzards circled in the night sky, and Travis just eyeballed me.

"True story," I said to him. I still don't know if he believed me, but it is.

Part Two

That night, the wind was still, and the air was moist. I could see a thunderhead far off to the south. "Probably in the Gulf and won't even make it to us," I thought to myself. Lightning flickered occasionally from within its marshmallow body. The lights of the city of Mobile lay almost directly ahead of us, and we could see the tops of the tallest skyscrapers over the reeds and saw grass off the bow of the boat. Though the skyscrapers were miles away, they still loomed large on the horizon.

The horizon was busy tonight . . . towering structures of cloud and steel dotted the distant landscape. I often used these man-made structures as navigation aids for nighttime travel in the Delta. Not that they could keep you from running into a log or even keep you in the main river channel, but generally advancing towards the lights of Mobile simply reassured me tonight . . . that I was in the right creek and headed to the right place.

Everything looks the same in the dark in the Delta.

Such is life, isn't it? I've lost friends to duplicity of the darkness. Not here in the Delta, but in life. Be it suicide or the even slower death of lasting depression, the darkness is a powerful foe. And, when everything has the same haze of despair and loneliness, the dark can be overwhelming. To make matters worse, when lost in the throes of depression, the horizon seems so far away . . . glimmers of hope seem so far off in the distance that one can barely focus.

We've all heard the expression that we should all be kind because we never know who might need a smile. Well, it's true. A friend once confided to me that he was depressed. I did my best to be a leaning post, but I could tell he was slowly getting lost in the darkness of the marsh. One day, he called me and told me through his tears that he, "wanted to get better but didn't know how." I asked him what happened, hoping to comfort him. He explained that he was taking his daughter to school that morning. "I was staring out the side window, tears rolling down my cheeks. She was dancing and singing in the seat next to me. She had no idea what was going on. I was thinking about how much I loved my wife and my daughter, and how much I was going to miss them . . . imagining their life without me, and how much better off they would be."

By this point, he was sobbing as he related the story to me.

"I kept my head turned to the side and wiped the tears with a napkin. I had made up my mind that today would be 'the' day. After a minute or two, I collected myself and put the tear-soaked napkin in the cupholder. My daughter was singing as loud as she could, but when my hand rested on the console, she stopped. She put her hand on top of mine and said, 'Daddy, I am so glad I have you.'"

When he told me that, a tear rolled down my cheek, and he, too, began to sob again. All I knew to do at that point was tell him I loved him, remind him that his daughter surely did, too, and so did God. "I know . . . I know," he cried. "She is a tower of hope for me . . . and she doesn't even know it."

We prayed together, and we have had plenty of conversations since then. My friend has certainly made great strides, and he occasionally says something like, "The 'tower' said to tell you hello." She doesn't know he calls her his 'tower,' but every time he makes the reference to me, it is his way of letting me know he is okay.

I looked ahead at the towers that illuminated the sky over Mobile. The creek was dark in this narrow canal. The reeds stood eight or ten feet tall on each side, and all I could see was what lay dead ahead . . . lit by the towers of Mobile and laying directly behind . . . slowly lost to the darkness of the Delta. I looked at the girls, Tyler, and Travis, and I realized how many towers surround us all. We all are . . . towers, that is. Lamps of light, cities on a hill, beacons . . . we are called to be towers, for life can be dark. We never know how our light might guide another to a place of hope . . . it is part of why I write.

Those steeped in depression look out on the horizon and see storm clouds on the southern horizon . . . "Thunderbolts and lightning, very, very frightening" . . . but the towers of light can be seen to the west and north . . . perhaps they will pursue hope and flee the storm. Darkness is a lonely place . . . it is up to us to illuminate the path.

"Badump!" The boat lurched to the side and then lifted in the stern. The girls sat up straight and looked around. "Was that an alligator?" one of them asked. I shook my head and said, "We went over the top of a log." While talking, I pressed the trim button to raise the motor, with the hope that we would simply slide right over the top and not get hung up on the log. I've had to walk through the Delta mud before to get a boat dislodged . . . but that was on a bright summer day . . . not a cold September night. A few tense seconds passed . . . the motor gurgled loudly, distorting the night's quiet, and I felt the boat release from the log. I breathed a sigh of relief and lowered the motor back down.

Tyler occasionally lit the creek up with a spotlight. By now, he and the girls had gotten pretty adept at identifying a "good gator." "There's a baby," he said, lighting up a patch of lily pads in front of us. An 18-inch-long, 1-year-old juvenile alligator sat atop the pads. Travis bumped the boat into neutral . . . having taken control of the helm so I could take a break. He eased the boat towards the gator's perch so the girls could have a closer look. The gator was frozen in the light, fearful of moving and revealing his 'thought to be camouflaged' hiding spot. Gators are naturally camouflaged . . . not quite as good as the PMC Outdoors camo that the girls wear, but it's still hard to see their patchwork green, brown, and black skin when it is hidden amongst the weeds and lilies of the water's edge. That's why we hunt them at night . . . their eyes betray them.

The boat drifted ever closer, gliding like a new fallen October leaf riding on the air of a gentle wind . . . the girls and Tyler stood on the bow of the boat like a flock of seagulls sitting on the stern of a shrimp boat . . . gawking at the shrimper and waiting for a prize.

"Fishing line! Dad! He's wrapped up in fishing line!" Tyler yelled. Before any of us could even get a glimpse, Tyler was flat on his belly on the bow of the boat— arms outstretched—and he scooped the young alligator up. Just in time, too, for the momentum of the forward motion carried the boat directly over where the gator was perched.

No doubt, the long, slender gator was engulfed by a nest of fishing line. His front left leg was pulled tight to his body, rendered immobile by the snaring effect of the nest. The line also pinched tight around his rib cage . . . I'm sure he had trouble taking deep breaths, as the line was clearly digging into his hide on his sides. The gator's back legs were free, but loops of line drug behind him, and long, severed lines drug even further. It was only a matter of time before one of these loops hooked a log or wrapped up on a lily pad. At that point, the gator would be doomed.

Travis pulled a long, straight-bladed Case hunter knife from its leather sheath and handed it to Tyler. Cape and Anna held the gator taut, while Tyler methodically worked the blade under and through the loops of line—careful not to hurt the young reptile—slicing away layers of depressing line as he went. For the most part, the gator cooperated. He kicked and squirmed a time or two, but it was almost as if he knew we were trying to free him. And, soon enough, he was.

I imagine the gator saw the light on the horizon and wasn't sure whether he should flee or not. Perhaps he remained motionless because it would have been a mighty struggle for him to crawl back on the comfort of the lily pad after we passed. Perhaps he sat still because he couldn't hold his breath for long enough to stay submerged. Perhaps . . . he just knew he needed to be rescued. No matter the circumstance, surely, he was desperate and afraid . . . it was only a matter of time before the darkness of the Delta consumed him.

Three towers stood in the light of the distance. Those towers ultimately rescued him . . . and I was so very proud that they did . . . and let him go as one happy alligator!

Towers loom large on the horizon. Ironically, though, sometimes the heroes that they are come in the smallest of packages.

Part Three

The tiny-mite gator splashed down into the water like an Olympic diver . . . the tip of his tail going through the same 'hole' that the tip of his nose made. He wagged his tail a time or two and briefly hid under a lily pad, but within just a few seconds re-emerged and held his head high. Swiveling like a periscope on a submarine, he didn't seem frightful in the bright lights . . . he seemed to smile and turn his head to the side, as if to say "Thank you" as we eased on up the creek. Cape, Anna, and Tyler all held on to the moment, retelling the events of just a few minutes ago, as if it were an ages-old story . . . it's not every day that someone gets to hold a living alligator. I was excited to hear their excitement . . . this is why we shepherd.

Travis and I have been in a lot of hairy places with our children. Anna and Cape are the same age, and, when it comes to fatherhood, he and I find it easier to learn from each other than to learn from our mistakes. Well . . . maybe it isn't easier . . . just less painful. Mistakes sometimes cause traumatic learning experiences. I much prefer a good suggestion or some gentle advice from Travis than I do a tornado of teen-raged crying and side effects from a mistake in parenting.

From this Delta to the Everglades and many rivers and campsites in between, we have lit many a campfire and stroked many a paddle. "I wonder how many miles we've paddled together," I pondered. "I don't know . . ." he offered, "Hundreds for sure. Maybe more." True enough . . . more miles than I can count. And we shepherded our kids the entire way . . . that's the point of it all.

Travis and I are two different men. He, the once rebellious son of a Baptist preacher, can fix anything with his hands. Me, the once rebellious son of a broken home, can fix most anything with my words. Travis has a calm, slow-to-act demeanor. Me . . . I am quick-tempered and more apt to respond in a flash. Travis' patience lends itself well to problem solving . . . me, I am more apt to "turn it on and off three times, and if that doesn't work, bang it on something." Point is . . . we have learned a lot about making better fatherhood decisions from being in each other's company. And, while I know a shepherd usually works alone, I don't think God intended for us to walk through the battles and struggles of fatherhood without the benefit of good advice from a friend.

Nobody should try to wade through the Deltas of fatherhood alone.

Cape and Anna worked the right creek bank with the spotlight, and Tyler worked the left. The water was now crystal clear. The marshes of the Delta provide a vital sponge-like cleansing to the water flowing through it. Here, the fast-flowing rivers usually stay muddy, but the back water marshes are typically much clearer and cleaner. The milfoils,

I wouldn't advise anyone to pick up anything that has long rows of sharp teeth. Alligators are meat eaters—even baby alligators—and they will eat your fingers, too! We only did this because of the situation we found ourselves in.

lily pads, cattails, and so much more all sift out the impurities that the water carries. Most of those impurities . . . hidden secrets, unseen by man . . . are, in fact, man-made.

I'm not a tree hugger, per se. I've never sent money to Greenpeace, and I've never protested a logging operation. In fact, I worked on diesel fuel burning tugboats pushing coal to power plants for years . . . I drive a diesel truck, and I'm sure I've done other things to create a carbon footprint. But even though I am not a political activist, my faith and beliefs compel me to be a good steward. God gave us dominion over all of the land in His first book. That dominion was not offered for us to lord over the land without regard for its well-being. In as much as conservatives might concern themselves with leaving the national debt to the next generation, we also must concern ourselves with leaving the next generation as pristine a landscape as we can . . . unmolested by unmitigated and unfettered dominion. Dominion does not suggest domination . . . instead, it suggests care and use . . . so, let us do so. Care, that is.

The water is crystal clear now.

We left the creek and ventured into Little Bateau Bay, but it's seemed hardly a bay that night. The tide was low—lower than I think I had ever seen it—and the water was still flushing out of the Delta. The bay is more of a pond . . . 50 acres, perhaps . . . on a normal day. But that night, the water retreated, leaving a series of canals that were woven through murky pads of vegetation, mud bars, and isolated puddles of water. Travis stood on the bow of the boat and offered navigational direction . . . we were snaking through the widest of the canals . . . maybe ten feet wide. At times, the reeds and sawgrass surrounded us and simply engulfed us. But for the lights from the boat, we would have been forever lost from the sight of man or beast.

Alligator eyes dotted the landscape on the other side of every opening in the reeds. "This is why we came," I thought to myself. In my younger days, I saw monsters lying in here . . . a place where few men know and fewer bother to come. This bay is a naturally safe environment for big gators . . . unmolested by men. The water is rarely more than a few feet deep on the best of days. That day, in the deep of the canal, it was maybe 18 inches deep. I could feel it . . . it was only a matter of time before we found a behemoth slumbering in the canal.

"There's one!" Cape yelled . . . clutching the spotlight with both hands so as to keep the gator within its beam. A nice four-footer lay flat on the bottom to the right side of the boat. He was in a bend, sleeping underwater on the upstream side of a batch of sawgrass . . . he was hidden pretty well under normal circumstances. He opened his eyes as we passed close enough to run an arm down into the water and grab him by the tail.

"He's way too small," Cape concluded. We agreed, but Travis and I had agreed early on to let the young folks make the decisions. We hoped they would experience catching the gator, from start to finish, so they could claim the thrill of the hunt for themselves. So . . . we kept pushing deeper into the intestinal bowels of the bay. At times, the motor drug the bottom. Other times, the sides caved in around us. "Travis, if the tide drops

much more, we are going to get stuck in here until morning." He nodded his head . . .
"Well, we are about in the middle. We can either keep pushing forward and push out
the other side, or we can turn around," he responded. As I surveyed the landscape, the
girls and Tyler all pretty well insisted we keep pushing forward.

And I'm glad they did. Around the next bend, at the end of a straight-a-way that was
maybe twenty yards long, Anna spotted a nice gator. He was to the right side of the boat
in about three feet of water.

The water was invisible . . . clear enough that you could tell that his yellowed eyes
were open. His squinted lenses tracked with the boat as it drew nearer. His head was
cocked towards the boat slightly, and his front feet were spread out wide, their claws sunk
into the sandy bottom. His biggest teeth shone through like daggers out from under his
upper jaw. His tail was thick and strong, and the spikes of armor tracked down both sides
of his tail and stood upright under the water. He was thick like a bull, broad shouldered,
and his muscles bulged from under his leathery hide. He was not scared of us—he
wasn't trapped in the creek with us. He knew we were trapped in the creek with him.

This was a big bull. "He is at least 12 feet, guys," Travis offered.

Tyler was already in motion. He had the rod in his hands and was moving into
position. Travis bumped the gear shift lever on the boat and shifted into neutral. The
boat slowed to a glide, flowing with the current. Tyler clicked the bail on the huge surf
casting rod . . . it was spooled with 1000-pound braided spider-wire that a Mack truck
couldn't break . . . a piece of lead the size of a golf ball swung heavy near the end of
the line. A few feet past that lead was a treble hook as big as the spread between your
thumb, index, and middle fingers.

In Alabama, to legally harvest an alligator, you can't bait him. You must hook, snag,
spear, or arrow him with a secured line. In other words, you can't just randomly shoot
alligators and risk losing the animals to the depths. Tyler swung the grouper-mouthed
hook past the big bruiser . . . dragging it through the sand and mud until the weight
crawled up over the gator's back . . . his head moved slightly as the hook bounced
across his armor . . . then the hook settled in, and the line drew tight as the boat
continued to drift.

"Get ready, T," Travis whispered a word of caution, and when it was precisely the
right moment, Travis pierced the still of the night . . . "Noooow!" In one fluid motion,
Tyler drew back as hard as he could on the rod, and all hell broke loose.

We've pulled gators from the deep. We've pulled them from the shallows. We've
never, until then, tried to pull one from three feet of water . . . and never sitting within
arms' reach of him. When the line drew tight, the Goliath gator arched his back and
bull-rushed towards the stern of the boat. His tail—easily seven feet and several
hundred pounds of pure muscle—swashed a spray of water that covered all of us . . . and
most of the boat. The rod bent ferociously . . . Tyler strained with all his might against
the power of the beast. The water exploded in a burst of mud and vegetation as the

Cape is my mini-me, and she hates it. She is so much like me that we often clash because of the similar stubborn traits that we share. It took me a long time to realize and learn that it is more important to let her be her than it is to assert myself so that I can be me. Know what I mean? We raised her to be strong, independent, and intelligent. She is all those things and more. Sometimes, those traits we raised her to be cause tension between us. So, without surrendering my parental obligations, sometimes I just let her be her and twiddle my thumbs. Even though we fuss sometimes, we also share a very special bond. One that is unlike the bond I have with Bay and Banks. Cape and I have paddled the Everglades, waded the swamps searching for deer, summited mountains, and all sorts of other things together. She knows that no one would walk through fire to save her like I would. And I know she'd do the same for me.

I love you, Cape Merrell.

gator grabbed hold of the bottom with his massive claws—tail and toes—and he surged so mightily that he swung the boat around. It rocked from side to side as he pulled the bow around and back to whence it came. Everyone held fast for a moment . . . for no one wanted to end up in the creek with the angry beast.

"Puuuullllllllll!" I hollered to Tyler, and he fought with the strength of 10 men. Veins bulged in his forehead and sweat and swamp water peppered his face. His teeth clenched, his biceps burned, and he groaned "Aaarrrrhhhhgggg!" against the brute strength of the 500-pound animal. Anna, ever the fighter, stood at Tyler's side, ready to lend a hand. Cape kept a light steady on the end of the line as it pierced the water's surface right next to the boat.

It was chaos.

And just as quickly as all hell broke loose, all went silent. The line went slack. The waters settled. The boat stopped moving and drifted back with the current. It was over. Tyler reeled the slack line up . . . two of the prongs of the treble hook bent straight . . . not strong enough to withstand the force that the beast mustered. Tyler breathed heavy to catch his breath. The rest of us sat silently . . . realizing the enormity of the giant that just destroyed our best hook in a few seconds. There was nothing left to do but move on . . . the beast won this round . . . slipped off into the darkness of the Delta, swallowed up in its invisibility. We wouldn't find him again that night.

Contrary to what some might think, most hunts don't end with the thrill of victory. Ours certainly didn't on this night, and many other nights have ended much the same. But that's not why we shepherd. The thrill of the hunt is part of it . . . but we come to mold and shape, culture and create. We come to talk about ecosystems and teamwork, God, and country. We come to inspire and challenge, encourage and teach. Alligators are fun for the night . . . shepherding is vital for a lifetime.

Take your kids shepherding outdoors. It doesn't matter where. It doesn't matter how. It doesn't even really matter what happens. It just matters.

POACHERS AND TRESPASSERS

Part One

I was the youngest cousin on my mom's side of the family. The next oldest guy cousin was Jim . . . he was four years older than I was. Past him was Jack, a few years older still. They were tough guys, and what prepubescent boy doesn't want to emulate the toughness of his older cousins? I spent a week or two every summer with them, and it always molded my personality for the next little while. Every kid wants to be like his older somebody . . . and these two guys were that somebody for those years of my life.

Jim's tough exterior hid the gentle giant within. He always looked after me . . . kind of like Benny looked after Smalls. He was quick to protect me and defend me whenever the older kids started in on me . . . once taking on one of the neighborhood boys in near fisticuffs when the bigger kid held me under the water too long. Jim and I did a lot together . . . from listening to rock and roll to playing pool to riding dirt bikes, I had a lot of firsts under Jim's guidance. In fact, he took me on my first camping trip. And you might say that it was that camping trip that started me on the path that would one day become Shepherding Outdoors.

Jim was at least 16 years old, so I would have been around 12 years old at the time. He and two other guys, whose names I can't recall, picked me up in his Toyota Hilux. A small-frame Toyota truck with bigger tires on the back than in the front, this two-seater, stick shift had an extended cab with some sort of flip-down seat behind the bench. Add on the addition of the camper shell on the back of Jim's truck, and we were about to set out on our first overlanding expedition. The truck was black, as I recall . . . and small . . . very small. Four teenage boys were not meant to fit in a Toyota Hilux. I have no idea how we piled up in the cab of that truck . . . surely some of us rode on the flip-down seat or in the bed of the truck, but I honestly can't recall. Recollecting back, though, I know only boys could master such a feat, for my knees and back would hardly let me sit in the front of that truck now . . . much less sardined in somewhere else.

It was cold. It was the December break from school . . . that meant hunting season, and we were striking out for some of our family land in Bay Minette, Alabama. It was the first time I would ever go deer hunting. It would also be the first time I would ever go camping.

We pulled into the long labyrinth of dirt roads leading to the family land. Winding past cut-over pines, clear-cuts, tall rows of plantation pines perfectly situated in very unnatural rows, and a few hardwood bottoms, we made our way to the field where Jim wanted to set up camp. It was a large field, full of sedgebrush and natural grasses. It spread out over 10 or so acres . . . browned by winter's grip, the grasses swayed gently in the breeze.

Turning into the field, Jim downshifted the standard transmission. It was a "four on the floor" as the old saying goes . . . that is, a four-speed transmission with the shifter coming up from the center floorboard. When he downshifted, the motor revved to get up the muddy incline at the field's edge. Topping the knob, the back tires spun just enough to feel the truck slip, and then surge forward, jolting all of us forwards . . . then backwards . . . we all looked like synchronized bobbleheads. Settling back down at the crest of the knob, we saw a truck and a group of men parked in the back of the field. These were big men, too . . . the tallest stood well over six feet . . . barrel-chested and hairy-faced, he spit a stream of tobacco out across his feet. The youngest of the three was still big . . . and antsy . . . almost dancing on the heels of his feet, he shuffled constantly as we rounded the field and made our way towards them. I couldn't decide if he was about to run or fight, but either way, his bulging eyes made me nervous. The last of the three was also the oldest. His hair was gray, as was his mustache. It curled at its ends, and the orange embers of a long cigarette rolled smoke up under the brim of his cowboy hat.

Tensions rose . . . poachers and trespassers are not welcome in South Alabama, nor are they predictable. "Good ole boys . . . never meanin' no harm" oftentimes find themselves in dire straits when confronted with the reality that they've been caught on someone else's land killing deer.

Jim was calm and cool and levelheaded, though—much more mature than I was at 16—as he approached these grown men. They shifted back and forth, exchanging glances with each other as he approached. "Wait here," he looked back over his shoulder and told me. He gestured the palm of his hand in a downward motion. One of the men mumbled something to another, as the third glanced at the guns all leaning against the back of the truck.

Realizing we were just three teenagers and a boy—Jim knew this was no time for testosterone-laced rants. With his gentle Southern smile and laid-back demeanor, he approached these full-grown men . . . it was tense for me. I was young enough to be nervous around any man with a gun . . . let alone, men who were caught doing something illegal. And, to make matters worse, there would be little room for compromise. Even I knew you couldn't "give in"—they were on the family land. Jim was not about to let them stay . . . nor could he retreat. For, to do so would surely be considered an open invitation to return at their leisure.

At 12 years old, even I could easily appreciate the danger of a situation. Worse though, because I was 12, I amplified the danger in my mind tenfold. Fear and anxiety crept up my pants leg . . . "Where is my gun? What if they shoot Jim? What if they shoot all of us? What if we shoot them?" Irrational thoughts—most likely spurred on by watching *Rambo* one too many times—consumed me. Jim left his gun leaning against his own truck. He eased over to them with his hands tucked into the pockets of his jacket . . . he presented himself in a sort of "Aw, shucks" disposition and gave them his big Caminas smile. Immediately, I could see the men's body language relax. Soon enough, with a few apologies, everyone was shaking hands, and the men loaded up into their 4x4 truck and left without any sort of hostilities or fanfare. As they pulled off, the oldest man leaned out the window and hollered, "Hope you boys kill a big one!" We all grinned and threw a hand up, each one of us nervously relieved that nothing dramatic had come of the meeting.

And, once again, my older cousin proved to be a hero of the meekest sort.

Part Two

We set out to walk a few trails that afternoon. We didn't see anything worth shooting at . . . an armadillo or two and a couple of squirrels. That afternoon, Jim taught me about hunter safety and what to do if I got lost in the woods. "This moss only grows on the north side of the tree," he showed me. "And the sun will set in the west, so if we get separated for some reason, you can hike out to the west to the dirt road we drove in on, or to the north to the main highway. I'll come find you." I appreciated him always taking a few extra minutes to make sure I appreciated the importance of it all, but I was not at all impressed with the thought that I might could get separated . . . and lost? "And, let me guess," I belted, "the three amigos who just left would no doubt be the first truck to pull up!" Everyone burst into laughter.

Still though, to this day, I remember those lessons . . . and while I now know that moss only generally grows on the north side of a tree, and the sun generally sets in the western sky . . . I often think back on Jim when I see moss on a tree. Striking, isn't it, that a simple conversation from 30 years ago could have such a lasting effect?

That is, after all . . . what Shepherding Outdoors is all about.

Not having much luck on the hunting front, we resorted to what most boys do at some point or another. We started shooting dead trees and logs.

But we couldn't simply shoot the logs as they lay. "Stand them up in a pyramid," one of the older boys suggested. "That way, when we shoot, the force of the blast will be spread out into three logs." Somehow, that seemed like pure genius at the time, so we obliged. The oak logs were heavy. Left over from a hurricane clean up a few years before, they were cut into about eight-foot sections. They had begun to rot, and the outer bands of wood were spongy . . . but the inner core still held its strength. We wrestled them into some sort of redneck teepee stand . . . and the engineer of the group lined up to take the first shot. "Kerplooowwwww!" The shotgun blast rang out and echoed through the woods. The slug hit the back log slightly right of center . . . the energy of the slug carried the log around to the left just enough . . . the log rolled, and the teepee came crashing down.

"Great…" I muttered.

The three older boys convened a meeting of the engineers to determine the best way to secure the teepee so that the structural failure wouldn't occur again. They argued back and forth . . .

"Hey, guys," I tried.

They never checked up, one talking over another . . . "We need to wrap a cord around it at the top."

"We need to dig holes and sit them in the ground."

"Hey, guys," I tried again.

They heard me not. I walked over to the fallen logs and rolled one out away from the others with my foot. No one paid me any attention. After I moved the log to a safe place just a few feet away, I loaded a slug into the Ithaca 20-gauge pump shotgun that my dad had given me, and, "KERPLOOOOOOWWWWW!"

The shot not only startled everyone, but it also silenced them . . . admittedly, it seemed significantly louder than the last. I looked back over my shoulder at the three engineers and said, "Or we could just shoot them on the ground." The other teenager quipped, "That's what I said!" A symphony of, "Aw, shut up!" and, "Yeah, whatever!" sprang forth as the engineers' meeting dispersed and everyone went to find their guns.

We all lined up like a firing squad and had our fill of killing the logs. Shots rang out in rhythmic fashion, each of us taking our own turn, in order . . . one after the other. Gun smoke hazed the air such that my eyes burned a little, and my ears rang from the percussions. The smell of burnt gun powder filled my nostrils, and empty shell hulls lay strown across the trampled sedgebrush. It was one element shy of a battlefield . . . "Where is the enemy?" I considered silently.

After shooting far too many slugs into the logs, we propped our guns up on the tailgate of the truck and pulled out our pocketknives. At this point, it was of little concern that every game animal within a mile had just listen to us lay siege to the beaches at Normandy. We wanted to dig out those slugs. And, though it only took a second to lodge the slug into the log, we spent 30 minutes or more dulling our best Case Sod Buster pocketknives digging for the slugs. All the while, we talked of making some sort of pendant on ever-so-fashionable '80s gold chains . . . though as I recall, we didn't have any of those either. The slugs sank deep into the heart of the logs. Deeper than our knives would pry . . . and deeper than our patience would allow us to pursue.

No pendants, no treasures . . . but good memories.

We built a good fire that night and ate Vienna sausages—not to be confused with some fine cuisine from Vienna, Austria, nor an even tastier morsel from Vienna, France. For those unfamiliar, Vienna (pronounced vy-aina) sausage is processed and formed logs of meat, made from all the pieces of a hog and chicken not fit to eat by themselves. The good news was that we also had potato chips to go along with them for our supper. I've never been a huge fan of Vienna sausages . . . those little log-shaped pieces of potted meat all stacked tightly together in a tiny can. They can't qualify as actual meat, but I suppose if you're hungry enough . . . so, I poured out the juice from the can and plucked the first log out with my finger.

"You shouldn't have poured that juice out! It's good stuff!" the youngest teenager said. He turned his can up and drank it. Everyone groaned in disgust . . . he pulled the can down from his mouth and burped as loud as any bear could have.

"There is no way I'm drinking that juice," I thought to myself. And I never did.

The fire smoked heavily from the half-rotten oak logs. We reasoned that we would burn the logs and sift through the coals and ashes in the morning, hoping to find the slugs. The air was still that night, so the smoke lay in on top of camp . . . hovering just a few feet above our heads.

We ate and talked and ate and talked . . . because that's what boys do around a campfire. That's where boys learn dirty jokes about horses falling in the mud . . . and where they talk of crushes . . . and rivalries, too. Campfires are good for boys. The conversation around a campfire is unique, nowhere else can these conversations occur . . . oftentimes, they become instructions into to rites of passage into manhood. Sitting across from these older "men," the amber glow of the fire flittering on their faces, I just fancied myself older and bigger and more mature . . . I soaked it all in. I knew I was experiencing manhood . . . and it meant something special to me.

After we had eaten 10 or 12 cans of Vienna sausages and a couple of bags of chips, Jim surprised us with some Little Debbie snacks. They were, of course, a hit. Oatmeal Creme Pies—which are about as American as baseball games and apple pies—do a remarkable job of erasing the residual taste of the processed meat. Even if one didn't like Oatmeal Creme Pies, surely, they'd be thankful for the residue removal.

Those three "men" dodged the smoke as it drifted from the fire. They talked about Sally Sue being a good kisser and other things that sufficiently embarrassed me . . . I suppose it was all designed to draw me in . . . and then they got me. "What about you, Walt? You ever kissed a guurrrrl?" My face turned red as I sat up straight and leaned back a little.

"Course I have!" I said emphatically. "Don't even know why you're asking." As I type this today, I don't remember if I had ever "really" kissed a girl . . . I know I pecked my first girlfriend in the third grade . . . but I sure wasn't going to let those guys know that.

"Who was she? Was she pretty? Was it a sloppy wet kiss or just a smooch?" They peppered me with questions, knowing the harder they pushed, the more embarrassed I got. "Shut up! I don't kiss and tell," I demanded, standing to my feet, and puffing my chest, as if I was to fight whoever challenged me again. "All right, all right, y'all leave him be," Jim, ever the protector, came to my rescue. The older boys laughed and changed the subject, but not before one of them made a few kissing noises and moaned about Sally Sue.

The fire dimmed, and Jim reminded us that we needed to be up before dawn.

Reluctantly, we all piled up in the bed of that pickup truck to sleep. I don't think any of us wanted to leave to warmth or the fellowship of the fire. But we did . . . four of us . . . into the back of the truck.

Did I mention it was a small Toyota pickup?

Think mini-truck. Think clowns at the circus. How we all fit, I have no idea. I do recall being head-to-foot in our sleeping bags, and we used backpacks as pillows, and hunting stuff was piled everywhere. Four smelly boys complete with foot stench, body odor, and Vienna sausage farts . . . I'm sure people would pay a premium for those accommodations. But for me, it was a truly awesome experience, as evidenced by the fact that I am writing about it some four decades later! What 12-year-old wouldn't want to compare the strength of each other's flatulence and sleep in a camper truck? We laughed and talked the night away . . . and dawn came early—for yet another round of tromping through the woods in search of the illusive white tail.

Part Three

We never had a chance at being successful hunters that day. A drunken and blind deer would have known we were in the woods . . . we were a single-file parade procession, four deep, through the dry leaves of the river bottom, and every animal within a half mile heard us coming. One would have thought we had wrapped our feet in brown grocery store paper bags . . . "Crunch, cratch, crunch, cratch." Adding to the noisemaker effect, we had little regard for the carry of our voices either. We laughed and teased and told stories of what we'd do if we shot a monster buck. Jim would occasionally "ssshhhhh" the rest of us . . . he apparently really came to hunt. And we'd hush for a few minutes, but we never stopped stumbling through the woods . . . all day, we marched around from pine forest to river bottom, from swamp to hilltop, and from can onward to can't.

We made our way through the bottomlands . . . towering and sprawling oak trees, naked of their leaves, all fallen to the floor below, until we came to the river's edge. It was flooded and impassable. The road that forded the river was sunk beneath several feet of water. The air coming off the river's water was cold . . . and dipping the tips of my fingers into the water . . . even colder.

"We aren't crossing the river today," Jim ordered.

"Thank goodness," I thought to myself . . . though, I would have waded it buck naked if the other "men" had done it. I understood the rites of passage implications, and those older boys wouldn't outdo me . . . but, thankfully, we didn't have to test my fortitude either. We turned back and hiked out of the river bottom towards an old family cemetery that was on the other side of the land.

I had never been to the cemetery. I heard Uncles Cordel and Anthony talk of it, and they talked of maintaining the grounds, but I'd never actually been there. Jim talked more in narration as we made our way up the one-lane pig trail. "This is where Granny Caminas' family is buried. She was a Locke by birth," he offered, as he pushed limbs out of the way. "People haven't used this cemetery in a long time." Turning directly to me he said, "Uncle Leon and Gramma Locke aren't buried here, but all of their people are." Turning back away from me to move up the trail, Jim released the limbs he was holding. I was not paying attention . . . the limbs were spring-loaded, and, "THWAP!"

After Jim let go, the tension in their grain constricted, and the limbs flew backwards at me at least a thousand miles per hour . . . if not more. My face was striped by the tiny branches at the end of the limb. My eyes watered just a little . . . "My bad," Jim sincerely gestured. "Are you okay?" Wiping my face—and my eyes—I raised my head and laughed off the pain . . . the embarrassment had a little longer sting. The guys all had a few good laughs and teases at my expense.

The pig trail opened up to a one-lane road, and Jim stopped. On the left side of the road, yaupon and privet bushes reached over the top of our heads . . . to our right, a clear-cut land of stumps and shrubs as far as the eye could stretch. "This is Uncle Babe's land," Jim said quietly, as he crouched over, almost squatting. I knew why he was whispering. I had never met Uncle Babe that I could remember . . . but I had heard stories. He served in "The War" . . . I don't know if that was World War II, or Korea, or Vietnam . . . my gut says one of the two earlier as opposed to the latter. The War had an effect on Babe, and I recalled Granny Caminas and others tell stories of how "out of sorts" Uncle Babe was.

A couple hundred yards from the property line in the middle of the clear-cut sat one lone live oak tree. Its branches reached at least 100 feet in every direction . . . stretching up to the sun and then rolling down and almost touching the shrubs at the ground. It was a massive tree. I stared intently at it . . .

"My dad says that tree is at least 200 years old."

Jim's words broke my gaze. Turning to him, I found him transfixed on the same tree. We all were fixated on it. It was majestic . . . and if ever one could deduce God's handiwork from nature, this was it. To this day, I've only seen two other trees like it . . . one in Geneva County, Alabama, and the other near Fish River outside of Foley, Alabama. The tree at Fish River is said to be the oldest live oak in Alabama. The tree in Geneva County is said to be the largest.

Beneath the towering canopy of the tree, nestled gently up next to the mountainous trunk, a peculiar straight line stood out to my eye. "Nature doesn't work in a straight line, Jim," I suggested. "What is that underneath?" Jim's gazed focused more intently. "A shooting house where Uncle Babe hunts. Let's hope he isn't in there right now. He's been known to shoot at people he thought were trespassing."

"Trespassers!" I retorted. "I thought we were on our property!" "Well," Jim offered, "we are. But from that shooting house a couple hundred yards away, it would be mighty easy to get confused about exactly where the line is."

"And he is crazy," I thought to myself.

I stared at the base of the tree, looking for any sign of movement or oddity in color. I became suddenly and eerily aware of just how exposed I was standing in the open road . . . I took three steps back to the mouth of the pig trail.

"Well, what are we doing here?" the oldest teenager wisely asked. "Come on . . . let's go."

Jim led the way the 100 yards or so down the open and exposed lane. We all followed single file, silently, leaning forward and holding our guns low, as if we were advancing beneath enemy fire. It seemed a half mile away . . . I focused on each passing tree, somehow imagining myself better protected by an intervening truck. One of the teenagers stepped on a pine limb that had fallen the year before. Brittle and dry, it snapped loudly under the pressure of his down trod. Every one of us shuddered at the snap and lowered our heads even more. Our pace quickened . . . and I could feel the crosshairs of Babe's rifle scope tracking me down the property line.

"He would surely shoot me last." I suspected silently. "I'm the smallest threat."

Our pace quickened even more, as did my heart rate. One of the teens breathed deep and quick behind me. None of us dare look back around to see what might be . . . perhaps, if we didn't see him, he wouldn't see us. With each step, I looked for my exit to the left and into the deep woods, away from "him" in case he did, in fact, start shooting. Finally . . . after what seemed like a country mile, Jim slipped back onto a pig trail and into the woods. Me? I was close enough behind Jim to read the label protruding from the back of his hunting jacket.

"If he gets me, he gets you, too," I reasoned.

Five yards back into the woods, Jim stood up . . . and started laughing. "That ain't funny, dad gummit," I said. "Did you make all that up?" Jim had a coy smile at times, letting you know he might be up to something . . . he let it show for a second, until the older teenagers started in on him. "I didn't make it up . . . now, come on, let's go." And, off he went down the trail.

"You made that up, didn't you?" I insisted. He wouldn't respond and kept silent until we emerged in a small field of tombstones.

Distracted by the danger that might have been, I lost sight of my surroundings and suddenly found myself standing in the midst of a very old cemetery of about 20 tombstones. Rattled by their presence and still adrenalized by the dash through open sniper country, I was too scared to read any of the epitaphs, but the chiseled rocks showed brilliant age. Many of them had moss growing across the top, and others were cracked and shifted. Some of the tombstones were the traditional round topped, sort; a few were crosses; others were simple rectangular markers laying on the ground. All of it was disheveled . . . none of the markers stood straight. Some of them were cracked and others worn.

"Did you know any of these people?" one of the teens asked. Jim quickly said, "No . . . they were dead long before I was born."

A song of questions followed . . . Where did they live? How old were they? . . . among others. Jim knew not any of the answers. We milled about for 10 minutes or so, careful not to step on any of the graves out of respect, "Because you don't want any haunts coming into our camp tonight."

"Great," I thought to myself. "First, a crazy uncle with a sniper rifle hell-bent on killing kids, and now ghosts angry because we disturbed their eternal sleep. We don't stand a chance."

"Jim?"

"Yeah, kiddo?"

"Can we go back a different way? I mean, away from Uncle Babe's land?" I wasn't up for any more *Fear Factor* games.

"Sure, we can…" as he chuckled. He led us deeper into the woods, away from Babe's land and through the back of the cemetery. I was not one to be spooked by the woods . . . lions and tigers and bears never much bothered me, but my nerves were shot. Crazy old men and ghosts hid behind every tree . . . every tuft of wind across the back of my neck surely was a ghost sneaking up behind me, and every twitch in the woods most certainly was Babe. Welcome to my nightmare . . . in broad daylight. My head swiveled, and I clutched the Ithaca shotgun like my life depended on it, for I was sure it just might.

I think the teens were scared, too, for everyone was deathly quiet for the next half mile of the walk. Eventually, though, we made our way out of the dark woods near the swamp and into the upland hills of the pine forest. Tall evergreens swayed gently above our heads as we weaved our way through the open forest floor below. Pine straw blanketed the floor and stamped the light out for everything beneath its layer. You could see for 100 yards or more as we made our way up and over a gentle knoll that spilled out into a hardwood bottom that flanked the field where we had camped the night before.

"I hear something," the youngest teenager exclaimed as he raised his gun to his shoulder. We all turned slightly to our left. I was second in line, he was third . . . now a few feet to my left and equally behind me. Jim brought up the rear of the parade. We all heard the same noise in the sea of our own silence . . . "Tuschk, tuschk, tuschk, tushck," the short-stroked shuffle of the dry leaves was the only sound that pierced the cool air. The source was close . . . behind a few privet bushes nearby.

Panic set in my mind . . . and probably the teens', too. I wasn't going to say anything, but I knew we were surely about to die. Babe . . . ghosts . . . Babe and ghosts . . . no matter . . . we didn't stand a chance. I stopped breathing and held my breath so I could hear better.

The pace of the shuffle continued until a small, unsuspecting, and apparently oblivious rabbit emerged from the right side of the hedgerow. Unbeknownst to me, the youngest teenager had tracked the sound with his raised shotgun, moving to his right until the rabbit revealed itself.

"KKKKEEEEERRRRRPLLLLOOOOOOOOOWWWWWWW!!!!!"

The percussion shock threw my head to the right and pushed my body with it. I could feel my hair part and furl around the curvature of my head. In the shock of it, I closed my eyes instinctively and turned away, ducking as I did. I wasn't exactly sure what had happened. My left ear went numb. I couldn't hear anything but an intense ringing on that side of my head. I stayed bent over and staggered for a few seconds. When I stood back erect, Jim was standing in front of my face talking to me and simultaneously scolding the youngest teenager. Jim grabbed my chin in one hand and forehead in the other, twisting my head to the side . . . back and forth . . . as he looked me over.

"Did he get the rabbit?" I asked. "No . . . but he pasted your face with gunpowder."

Jim still steadily admonished the younger teen, who was apologetic to say the least. "Man, I'm sorry. I didn't know it was that close."

"Close?" Jim asked. "He has a gunpowder ring across the side of his face! I'm surprised you didn't singe his hair with the muzzle blast."

Jim pulled his long-sleeve T-shirt down over his hand and wiped at my left cheek and forehead. He continued to paw at me like a mother cat dressing her kittens until I was sufficiently irritated.

"Are you okay?" he asked. I assured him I was. Slightly embarrassed by the attention, I turned everyone's attention back to the rabbit. "How could you miss him? He was only 15 feet away! You suck!" The youngest teen chuckled a bit, knowing there wasn't much he could say . . . the rest of the guys chimed in with their own ridicule and sarcasm as well.

"You didn't even know what you were shooting at! Bet you thought it was a ghost!" Jim exclaimed.

I knew then that I wasn't the only one scared in the moment, and that gave me some relief . . . At least the "men" were scared, too! No matter, we all eased our nerves with the humor of making fun of "Ole Two Shots" . . . "He can't hit you with either one of them!" We all howled. He didn't soon live down missing such an easy shot . . . or the ghost he was shooting at.

Sure . . . in hindsight, it could have been bad. But it wasn't. We all learned something that day about gun safety and line of fire and muzzle blasts. That's what helps boys grow into men . . . trial and error. The thrill of the hunter's instinct kicked in, and a mistake was made. That's not a reason to not let your boys go hunting. It's simply a reason to talk to them about awareness . . . and that's what we did an hour or so later when we got back to camp. Jim made sure we all understood the lessons to be learned. He was shepherding.

We never found that rabbit.

We never killed a deer, either. In fact, I don't think we ever saw one. But it was an expedition like no other. We were set to be men, and we were hunters. It was what Alabama boyhood was all about. This is where the red fern does grow. This is where the Alabama moon shines brightest.

Of course, we didn't kill anything at all. I suspect Elmer Fudd would have fared better. We did kill lots of time, and that was just fine with all of us, because the memories of the trip serve as better a trophy than any buck we might have mounted. I've carried those memories with me for all these years, and now, they have been memorialized forever.

Jim got saved a few years later. Word of his profession of faith made its way to me. It inspired me, and not too long afterwards, that memory, and knowing that my older cousin was led by Christ, I set my pride aside and made a few Spirit-led decisions of my own. We never talked about Jesus in the woods that weekend. Jim simply led me, and I followed. But because he invested that time in me in the woods of Bay Minette, Alabama—and so many other times, too—when it came to make important decisions, I looked to his lead again. Jim was always a good shepherd.

Jim's tough exterior hid the gentle giant within. He always looked after me . . . kind of like Benny looked after Smalls. He was quick to protect me and defend me whenever the older kids started in on me . . . once taking on one of the neighborhood boys in near fisticuffs when the bigger kid held me under the water too long. Jim and I did a lot together . . . from listening to rock and roll to playing pool to riding dirt bikes, I had a lot of firsts under Jim's guidance. In fact, he took me on my first camping trip. And you might say that it was that camping trip that started me on the path that would one day become Shepherding Outdoors.

WALKING HOME

Part One

It's always dusky dark when we climb out of the shooting house after hunting. Banks, my youngest daughter, is usually a bit timid as she backs down the ladder, glancing over her shoulder for the various woolly boogers she imagines to be nearby. Her concerns used to be much greater than they are now, but repetition and familiarity have eased them a bit. Still, she is only 11 years old, and I don't believe it unreasonable for her to have some apprehension of even the mildest mannered coyote or bobcat . . . or Sasquatch.

Years back, we would walk home with flashlights. As she has aged and matured, we gradually eliminated those mechanical illuminations. We now walk all the way home, mostly in the pitch of night, without realizing that we are no longer using a light. Where once she was frightened and apprehensive, she now finds peace and tranquility.

Such are the woods for me . . . Peaceful. Tranquil. God's gift to man for which we should all be grateful and good stewards.

As we walk the half-mile or so back home this night, she occasionally holds my hand. She's getting older now, transforming from a little girl to a young lady, and I know the days we call childhood are getting shorter. Soon enough, she won't hold my hand, save the direst of circumstances. I cherish this moment . . . there, in the pitch of night. I will cherish it again should there be another opportunity.

The air is crisp and still, yet the temperature is just warm enough to invite a few crickets to sing . . . and then fall back to the safety of their silence as we draw nearer. I've taught Banks about nature's silent alarm. A cricket will always stop chirping as something approaches . . . and then resume its melody once it grows comfortable again. We sometimes listen for crickets falling silent later in the evening on our hunts. Such is sometimes an indication that a deer or bear or raccoon or some other fur-bearing animal approaches.

An owl beckons in the distance as we walk down a slight knoll towards the back water of the old pond . . . we stop, like crickets, to listen. I contemplate "hooting" back to see if I might provoke a response, or at least claim one if the raptor responds by happenstance. Then, I reconsider, knowing that Banks would think my antics nothing but tomfoolery. The owl is silent anyway. I probably would have simply revealed how inept I was at calling. It's better this way.

We come out of the open fields and enter the narrows where the hardwoods grow. Crunchy, dried oak, hickory, and sweetgum leaves litter the ground. Our every step betrays our silence . . . Banks scolds me with a grin for walking too loudly. I look for color variations in the darkness on the ground, hoping to find the grass, the silence of which would satisfy her. I'm proud that she appreciates the value of the silence . . . not only because of the deer but also because she knows that silence is valuable in and of itself in life.

Coming out of the hardwood narrows, we near the pond and make our way across the dam. Our tradition has always allowed for whispering at this point in the trek. I think she contained herself for as long as she could . . . she unloads her thoughts about the evening hunt. It had not been a good one. We saw only a few deer and did not have had a good opportunity to shoot any of them.

"Daddy, don't be too hard on him," she whispered.

"I won't, baby." I responded.

Lincoln, our black-and-tan hound, trailed us to the shooting house. It sits over a ridge, so we didn't see him coming until he was nearly upon us. It was quite a motley scene, me trying to usher him away without yelling or exacerbating the situation . . . flailing my arms around at the dog like a drunk monkey, I hopped around in the field trying to "shoo" the dog . . . apparently, the drunk monkey in me morphed into an even drunker chicken. Banks later said that as I flapped my wings, I scratched with my feet . . . "I was just waiting for you to start pecking the ground!" she offered through a whispered laugh.

Lincoln, seeing my chicken impersonation, tilted his head slightly off-center and looked at me with bewilderment. I realized he was scared to come closer but too curious to retreat, so he began continually circling me to my left . . . and it was clear that I was not making any progress at convincing him to go home. Banks, watching from the perch of the shooting house, giggled into the bend of her elbow . . . this trip will never be remembered for the hunting experience.

Finally, I think out of boredom, Lincoln meandered away. Fear not, though . . . he stayed long enough that every deer within three moonshine stills of our house knew he was there, too. Banks has a soft heart for animals, and she knew I was frustrated that the dog had likely spoiled the hunt. She has seen me lose my patience with Lincoln a time or two before . . . those moments were not my best. Once, he gnawed the claws off of my bearskin rug. A second time, he found an open door into the house and pried open the refrigerator. Those were indeed dark days in my relationship with Lincoln.

Yet, he still follows me almost everywhere I let him.

Love truly does cover a multitude of sins.

Lincoln knows I love him. We spend time together every day . . . even on the days when he wallows in the raunchiest of roadkills. We walk; he works with me; he keeps guard . . . and though he has tracked many a wounded deer to its deathbed, he has never

It seems that deep in the nighttime winter woods, the stars are brighter, the air is crisper, and the woods are quieter. I can hear myself think . . . I can feel myself move and at times. I can see forever. I love the woods at night. There are fewer distractions. I can't see all the world is busying itself with. I can't hear all that bustles on the busy streets of nine-to-five. I am not distracted by the activity of man. That leaves me and God. And my girls. And that is alright by me.

joined us during the hunt . . . until that day. Banks and I spend a significant amount of time together, too. We hunt and fish; I take her to school every day; we laugh and joke and prank . . . and we even play beauty salon together. She and I share a unique bond . . . God is good.

Lincoln and Banks both love me unconditionally, and they love me despite my faults. I am thankful that love covers my shortcomings.

Banks and I cross the head of the pond, making the last bend in our journey. We can see the house from here, light emanating from the windows like embers in a warm coal bed. Just as those hot coals feel good to cold hands hovering above, the lights of a warm house feel good to the soul on a long walk home. The light from the house shines upon Banks' face ever so slightly, and for the first time since sunset, I can see her face. The radiance highlights her features . . . she is my light in the pitch of night. I stop her and snap a quick picture. Unimpressed by this moment, Banks resumes the march, and her pace quickens just a bit . . . eager to see her mama and hungry, too, I suspect.

Lincoln greets us halfway through the yard . . . wagging his tail sheepishly. He knew he shouldn't have followed us . . . I knew he couldn't help himself. That was enough. Banks hugs him and then, like synchronized swimmers, they both turn back to greet me. I kneel down and embrace them both.

Maybe it wasn't such a bad hunting trip after all.

Part Two

Sometimes, the best part of the coldest of winter days is walking home from the deer woods in the pitch of night. Frozen breath shimmers in the moonlight's glow. Leaves crisply rustle underfoot as I make my way. The cold night air laps against my cheeks, refreshing me with every glance.

The moon lights my way. Unimpeded by mechanical light, the light of the world reveals the path . . . making it straight. Deer stand at a distance, knowing I am there, but curious as to what I am. I keep straight and silent, so as to avoid concerning them.

A coyote breaks the silence of the distance. His brothers and sisters soon join in, sparking a response from a den much closer to me . . . a slight shiver runs down my spine. I remind myself that coyotes are basically harmless to people . . . but still.

The mile or so of my hike takes me over hills and through creeks and past ponds . . . the world is different at night, and the sky is always clearer and brighter in the winter. So is my head . . . clearer, that is . . . after an afternoon in the deer woods. And the cold December air is chilly and comforting at the same time. I rather enjoy it tonight . . . and think I shall visit again tomorrow.

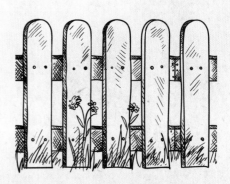

Chapter FIVE

ALWAYS A GOOD, GOOD FATHER

EVERY BRIDGE
HAS A VIEW

The bridge was strong and sturdy under my feet, yet my knees shook like jingle bells on a sleigh ride. I clutched the chest-high rail with both hands, consciously willing my next steps . . . one foot, then the next. Hannah might as well have been dancing in the ballet. She fluttered from one side of the bridge to the other without the slightest hesitation, as if she had wings and was certain nothing bad would befall either of us. I, on the other hand, was certain that at any moment, the bottom of the bridge would disintegrate, and we would surely plummet to our deaths.

"Come here," Hannah gestured, as she held out her hand. Releasing my "locked tight" grip on the rail, my hand felt some relief . . . especially taking her warm, soft fingers in my hand. "Stand up straight," she giggled. "If you fall from up here, being crouched over like the Hunchback of Notre Dame won't do you any good." I laughed at myself because she was right. I was crouched over in a crescent shape trying to stay lower to the ground . . . looking back on it now, I can only suppose that, subconsciously, I thought that the few inches that I crouched lower might somehow save my life when the trap door of gravity sucked me down the several hundred feet to the mountainous ground below. Standing up straight, I scoffed at myself for the absurdity of the notion.

Hannah gently tugged me away from the rail to the other side of the bridge. "Just relax," she suggested as she softly squeezed my hand.

I tried.

I took several deep breaths in a row, relaxed my shoulders, and tried to let the anxiety fall from my muscles. It worked, momentarily . . . until I looked down. And then the world started spinning again, and I was standing on the axis. My knees melted like wobbled-goop, and I grabbed hold of the rail again.

"Try sitting down," Hannah said, with a tad bit of sarcasm in her voice. "I'm not sitting down out here on this stupid bridge," I pridefully responded. Embarrassed now, I resolved to fight through the fear . . . I didn't know if Hannah intended to provoke this prideful response or not. No matter, she slipped her fingers into the fold of my elbow and took my arm.

Sometimes, the best picture of the view is the hardest picture to take. We were both staring straight into the sun, as we stood at the end of the Viaduct. We wanted the valley behind us to be in the backdrop, so with retina-burning tenacity, we smiled our best smile and tried to open our eyes at the instant that the camera clicked. No such luck. But that's okay . . . the picture still reminds me of how shaky my knees were and how quick Hannah was to take my hand and try to get me to relax. And that memory is what matters most.

There was a gentle fall breeze flowing through the Allegheny Mountains that afternoon. On a cloudy day, we might have found ourselves a bit chilled, but the sun burst forth from the mid-afternoon sky like fireworks on a hot summer night. What might have been chilled by the crisp Pennsylvania fall was otherwise warmed by the sun's dripping shower.

This viaduct, once the longest and tallest railroad structure in the nation—standing at 2,053 feet long and 301 feet high—offered a mystical gaze up and down the valley below . . . from our perch near the middle of this great expanse, we could see for nearly 100 miles to the north towards New York State and to the south, deep into the heart of the Keystone State. Fall had yet to fully announce its presence, but still, the palette of yellow and orange, lime green and olive, and brown and red were enough to make even Mona Lisa blush.

"God painted this," I said to Hannah. She didn't respond. We both just stared off into the hundred-mile oblivion of the expanse as the gentle fall breeze licked at our ears while the sun patted our cheeks. She didn't have to respond, though . . . I knew she agreed . . . "Thank you, Lord," I thought to myself. An eagle crossed the valley a few hundred yards from us . . . I imagined his intense gaze, staring back at us with skepticism and suspicion. "God made him, too," I said to myself.

And in that moment, I lost myself in the beauty of it all. The view. The expanse. The natural wonder. The red, the yellow, the orange . . . the rainbow of rustic fall colors. The majesty of the Lord of the sky. The majesty of the Lord of all. I closed my eyes and let the wind whisper to me . . . and chills crept up my back and neck.

Hannah tugged at my elbow. Pulled from the serenity of my senses, I opened my eyes to see her smiling back at me. "God made her, too," I thought to myself . . . and the chills crept even higher. "Come on, let's go out here to the end," she prodded. Internally, I didn't want to. But now, my prideful rebellion that suggested "I" was strong enough to overcome my fear of heights had transitioned into a grateful appreciation of what "He" had given me the opportunity to experience . . . and I didn't want to miss a thing.

I remember being a young father. I read *Strong Fathers, Strong Daughters*. I paid attention to other dads I respected. And I spent a lot of time demonstrating confidence in my decisions. But the truth was . . . I was scared to death. Not unlike the death grip of fear I once held the rail of the bridge with, I was scared to death because . . . I didn't know how to be a dad. My mom is not necessarily a domestic woman. She is strong and independent . . . not exactly Aunt Bee. I am one of three brothers. Both older, my brothers usually engaged in rituals designed to toughen me up. Point is, I had very little interaction with girls . . . yet God gifted me with three of my own. I usually held on to them with a death grip . . . scared to death to let go for fear they might . . . fall.

But as they grew out of toddler-ville and into middle-school age—Bay especially—I learned to trust Him. I realized that He would not have given me the gift of these beautiful girls without also giving me the ability to lead and guide and provide for their well-being. So . . . slowly, my fears gave way to trust . . . and I followed Him, not just in my relationship with Him, but also in my relationship with my girls. And before long . . . I was so busy taking in the view that was all the beauty they represented . . . that I forgot how scared I was.

This viaduct was no different. I had to let go of myself . . . to find Him in the details around me. And when I found Him, I found peace. "*All fear is gone, because I know He holds the future, and life is worth the living, just because He lives*." My own fear of heights had crippled me . . . and I think some men's fear of fatherhood or husbandry cripples them, too. But once we admit and accept that it is God who holds the future, "all fear is gone," and we can then see and feel and smell and hear and touch the beauty of it all.

But that wasn't the only lesson He would shepherd me into, standing atop that iron bridge of 100 years gone by. The second lesson, though . . . would not come until nearly 20 years later . . . as I reminisced with a new friend, Bernice Reed. Bernice, a Pennsylvania native, drove with her sister and her dear friend all the way from Pennsylvania to stay at the Cottle House Bed & Breakfast. We shared a visit in the kitchen one evening, and I shared the story of our visit to Kinzua Bridge State Park and the viaduct in rural Pennsylvania.

Bernice had never been to stand atop the bridge that overlooked the Keystone State . . . so I explained that it served as a functional railroad bridge, offering one of the few transits for railcars through the mountains . . . until 2003. In 2003, a tornado ripped through the valley and toppled 11 of the 20 iron pillars that were the bridge's legs and support. "The remaining legs still lay toppled and crumpled and ripped in the valley below," I explained. "It's quite humbling to see something that once stood so strong and proud laying in a twisted heap . . . seemingly forlorn for all of eternity . . . but were it not for that tornado—were it not for the chaos and the destruction—we would have never appreciated the beauty. You might say that out of the destruction came the beauty." As Bernice responded and offered a few additional thoughts, I realized the lesson that God had laid on my heart.

You see, Kinzua Bridge State Park is relatively new. Opened only after the tornado, what stood before was the mighty iron bridge, in service to the railroad and accessible only by the same. Hannah and I would have never ventured out onto a railroad bridge . . . and would have never had the opportunity to do so, but for the tornado. Out of the destruction came the most beautiful results . . . for only because the tornado destroyed half the bridge did the state create the park . . . and give us the opportunity to stand 600 feet out over the valley floor and take in all of the wide blue wonder . . . such beauty.

And isn't life much the same? My life was a wreck at one point . . . far from God, I sought comfort and solace in all things fleshly. And the more I fed the flesh, the more the pillars of my life toppled to the ground. But one day, as a grown man, I walked

The aftermath of a brutal storm is often obscure. A demolished house with dishes still on the table or hundreds of trees leveled except for one that still stands unscathed . . . and those tornadoes and hurricanes are not unlike the storms of life . . . mass destruction but a glimmer of hope that remains. That's because there is always hope . . . you just have to look for it. No matter how dark the storm grows, there is always beauty in the hope that remains. Just like the beauty Hannah and I found as we peered across the valley floor, there is hope in the storms of life too, you just have to look past all the chaos to find the serenity. And when you find it . . . the view is amazing!

down the aisle of Bethany Baptist Church in Andalusia, Alabama, and told Ronald Davis that Jesus was my Lord and Savior . . . and I wanted to escape the carnage and find Him. Out of the destruction of my life came something beautiful . . . and I needed God to open my eyes so I could see it.

If you are ever in Pennsylvania, say hello to my new friend, Bernice Reed. And stop by the Kinzua Bridge State Park. But most importantly, always remember that if you are scared to death . . . standing in a minefield of destruction . . . and convinced that chaos awaits your next move, just know that God holds your future, too. All you have to do is reach out and take His hand . . . and the beauty that will be revealed is unlike anything you can imagine.

God bless you today, friends.

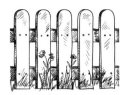

EVERY FENCE
HAS A PURPOSE

Some fences are designed to corral. Growing up, my dad had cattle and horses. He had more paddocks and corrals than I care to remember. We quarantined mares about to foal; we put the ornery Appaloosa stallion in a corral to get him acclimated, and we put horses in the stalls during winter storms to protect them.

All of those fences were designed to keep the animals safe from their own inability to discern or do for themselves. Usually, a pregnant mare doesn't need help delivering a baby, but occasionally, a foal is backwards or upside down. We put the mare in the fence so we could keep an eye on her in case she needed help. The Appaloosa I spoke of . . . he was new to our farm and wanted to leave. He could have easily pushed through a weak point in our four-strand fence, so we put him in the paddock. Better to stay and acclimate than run and get lost, or worse . . . Point is, those fences kept those animals safe. They were designed to keep the animals away from danger or harm.

Sometimes, though, fences are designed to keep danger out and not so much to keep the animal in. Chicken wire keeps the fox out of the henhouse. Hog wire keeps the goats safe from coyotes.

We have both types of fences in our lives, too. Usually, those fences are built by God. He goes before us and makes the path straight. We simply have to choose wisely to stay within the fences He has placed . . . there to protect us from our lack of judgment. The Ten Commandments are like a fence . . . sort of. Abiding by them corrals our behavior and steers us further away from sin. They keep us safe in our abidance.

Other times, though, He puts fences in our lives to keep danger out. Loving God first and loving our neighbors are good examples of fences designed to keep danger away. Loving God and staying focused on Him keeps us within His will. Being within His will is a surefire way to keep the enemy out. And though that doesn't mean there won't be trials and hardships, it does mean that life will be fuller and richer—in a spiritual and eternal sense. Staying in that fullness of God is like a fence that keeps the enemy at bay.

I am thankful for the fences in my life. Hannah sometimes refers to me as a donkey because I am too stubborn. She is right . . . and the fences that God places around me work well to keep me straight and protect me.

Even the fiercest donkey needs a little help every now and then.

I took this picture and wrote this devotional story while sitting under a tree at William Faulkner's homeplace, Rowan Oak, in Oxford, Mississippi. Faulkner is one of my favorite authors. He writes in a stream of consciousness style, and I often do the same thing. That is . . . we write exactly as we think the words into existence. "A Rose for Emily" is my favorite Faulkner work, though he is not my only favorite. Wilson Rawls, Ernest Hemingway, Mark Twain, Harper Lee, and many more are included on the list. Hannah and I always tried to make the girls keep travel journals when we went on vacation, and even to this day, we encourage them to read daily. I hope you do, too.

The view from my front porch whilst sitting in my most comfortable rocker. Of course, the rail is always in the wrong place.

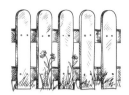

THE PORCH RAIL
IS ALWAYS IN THE
WRONG PLACE

Have you ever noticed that no matter where you sit on the porch, the rail always finds a way to block the view of what you want to look at? Seems that way to me . . . many days.

Today, too.

Tomorrow, we will load up the truck and begin the long road to Oxford, Mississippi . . . The Grove . . . Ole Miss . . . Bay's future. I can't see it. I can't see how to get there. I can't see what the campus looks like. I don't even want to try to look at her future today . . . for the porch rail is filled with memories of the past.

So, through the tears this morning, I force myself to crane my neck so I can see over the rail of the past. She deserves that from me . . . and, so, I do. I look forward . . . and let go. I trust that the Father has you . . . and that He knows what is on the other side of the porch rail.

The porch rail is in the wrong place this morning, but I know that just beyond it, there is something beautiful. Just like you.

God bless. I hope you all have a wonderful day.

F O G B A N K S

Ithink we all find ourselves in the fog from time to time.

Hannah and I sat on the water's edge listening to the almost motionless water lap at the sand every few seconds. The waves, such as they are, were almost imperceptible until they reached the sandy shore . . . and then, only because they pushed water up six inches or so into the sand, could one notice their presence. One after another, every few seconds . . . like the pendulum on a grandfather clock.

I pushed my toes down into the sand. She drew wet sand up with her fingers and drizzled it into a pile. It was a cold, spring morning . . . the sand was cold to the skin and sucked the heat from the cushions of our derrieres. The water was cold on my toes, but the sun, slowly finding its way through the trees, felt good. It warmed our faces and pushed away the thief that is the cold.

"Are you going fishing?" Hannah asked. "Yes, after we finish our coffee . . . but I am enjoying this right now," I responded. "Me, too," she said, as she scooted just a little closer to me. We talked of our trip and of the beauty of Apalachicola Bay . . . how the oystermen were already hard at work. We watched their boats scurry around, nearly at the horizon on the other side of the bay, seemingly jockeying for position and the best spots on the oyster beds. From our distance, we could barely make out the silhouette of the oysterman standing on top of the deck and working the tongs . . . but even though we couldn't see him clearly, we knew he was working.

The coffee was warm on my lips . . . I held the cup to my lips even after I swallowed the sip. The warm steam from the brew rose up and curled around my face. I could feel the sauna of steam on my right cheek, tickling my right eyelash as it rose up and around the brim of my hat. The bean juice was warm rolling down my throat . . . hot coffee on a cool morning soothes the soul.

Soon enough, though, both cups were empty . . . Hannah reluctantly stood up and shivered just a touch. She held out her hand and pretended to pull me up. On a warm day, I might pull us both back into the water. But this morning . . . a cool 60 degrees on St. George Island . . . she might protest. She walked back towards the retreat . . . I headed to my kayak.

The girls were all still sound asleep. Sometimes, the best peace is found in the comfort of the quiet. I paddled out towards the bridge . . . maybe 300 to 400 yards. I knew of an old oyster bar near an edge where blue water flowed deeper during tidal responses. This morning, I hoped to find big bull redfish huddled up in the deeper blue water, lying in wait for prey to tumble down off the old oyster bed. I paddled out into the channel . . . the tide was just starting to drop. I let out my small, makeshift anchor . . . a couple of bricks tied to some paracord . . . the anchor let out about 30 feet. "Fifteen feet deep," I suspected internally. With no real way to tell, I gauged the angle of the anchor line to be about 45 degrees, and I suspected that meant that the 30 feet, more or less, of paracord that I had let out, traveled about 15 feet out and 15 feet down. It was still a guess.

I cast live shrimp up on top of the oyster bed, "popped" them off the edge, and let them tumble into the deeper water. Three casts . . . then four . . . still no bites. My back turned towards the mainland, I'd throw each cast up into the bed some distance, give the shrimp a few seconds to orient itself in the water, and then slowly reel until the shrimp would be at the edge of the ledge . . . and then, whether it liked it or not, I'd pull it off the ledge with the hope that a 30-plus-inch redfish would be waiting . . . and then the fight would be on!

My first shrimp yielded nothing. Its last bit of life gone, I stripped it from the hook and cast it into the depths for the bottom dwellers to feast on. I retrieved another shrimp . . . this one a little larger . . . and hooked it through the horn. The first cast produced a bite! But I immediately knew this was no bull redfish. In fact, it only took a few revolutions of the reel to pull this young, juvenile speckled trout to the water's surface. A flip of the wrist, and the trout was released back to the wild to fight another day. Three more shrimp all produced the same results . . . juvenile fish with little to no fight . . . and even less meat.

The wind tickled my neck a bit . . . and it felt cold. I turned to look over my shoulder behind me, curious as to where such a cold wind could blow from, to see a fogbank looming large across the middle of the bay. It was rolling and roaring as it advanced, pushing higher and higher, faster and faster. Its silence was curious and counterintuitive . . . "Something moving that much ought to make noise," . . . "but it isn't." It tumbled upon itself like a down comforter rolling round and round in the dryer . . . fluffing outward with every turn.

I had never seen a fogbank like this one. I could see its advance . . . it was like a wall of cotton pushing towards me. I knew I would never make it back to shore before it overtook me, but I also didn't see any reason I couldn't keep fishing in the fog. I was catching fish . . . after all.

Five minutes later, and the leading edge of the fogbank was upon me. I had not caught another fish . . . and the ominous presence of the fog had spooked me a little. "What if a boat comes through? They won't be able to see me. What if I lose my bearing and get disoriented . . . will I be able to get back to shore?" Suddenly, in the immediacy of the peril, I felt the insecurity of my helplessness creep up my spine.

The wind rushed all at once, blowing my hat down over my eyes. The kayak lurched a bit and shifted in the wind, tugging at the anchor line as the wind pushed me out of the channel and into the shallow waters of the oyster bed. And just like that . . . 10 seconds later . . . the wind was gone, and all was still in the world again. Much like a thunderstorm, the fog pushed the air as it advanced . . . I found myself enveloped in the fog. It was thicker than I imagined . . . I couldn't see which way to go. I couldn't see the island, and I sure couldn't see the mainland. I knew the bridge was to my right, but I couldn't see it either. I lost sight of the poles that carry the electric and telephone cables across the bay . . . I couldn't see anything. And no one could see me.

I was alone.

I cast for another 10 minutes without even a hint of a bite. No doubt, the lack of sunlight turned the bite off. I tenuously marveled at the fog. It was so very thick . . . I estimated I could only really see about 100 feet in any direction. It was so thick that it even stifled the occasional early morning car crossing the bridge. Once a sharp noise bouncing across the still bay waters, now the motor noise was a drone growling from a distance. Water vapor collected on the brim of my hat and fell to a drip every 30 seconds or so, and the air was heavy in my lungs. Nothing but gray-white tufts as far as I could see in any direction . . . the isolation was disconcerting to me, and the rhythmic grumble of a diesel motor growing closer and closer was discomforting.

Shrimp boats were known to use this cut to get back into port . . . I didn't know what kind of boat that was . . . or even where it was . . . but I knew I needed to get out of this deeper water and find the safety of the shore. But which way? I knew the bridge was still to my right because I could hear the occasional car passing by. That was good . . . and that gave me hope. But still, I could hardly but estimate where I should "aim" to find the shore I'd left behind earlier.

I began to paddle . . . "Swish, swash . . . swish, swash . . . swish, swash…" Ten minutes passed. The bridge was still to my right, but the infrequency of traveling cars made it hard to get true bearings like sonar. Concerned I might be actually paddling parallel to the shore, I decided to call out . . . "Hannah?"

"Walt!" came the reply.

I could not see her. I could not even see land . . . but my instinct told me she would be worried about me, as she could not see me either. My gut suggested she would be out searching the fogbank, too, looking for me . . . because that is the depth of her love.

Her voice rang like a fog bell on a buoy . . . guiding me home and safely to her. She met me on the shore with a smile . . . we talked the last 50 yards or so until I found her standing at water's edge, like a siren beckoning to passing sailors . . . her call bringing the irresistibility of safety and warmth. Her smile is what I remember most . . . how comforting it was to see her and to know that she found joy in seeing me, too.

Sometimes, life seems foggy . . . but there is always a way home.

"I cry out to God Most High, to God who fulfills His purpose for me," Psalm 57:2, ESV

No matter how alone you feel today . . . no matter how lost you think you are . . . cry out. An answer will come, for He is faithful. He sees through every fog of life . . . and

Apalachicola, Florida, St. George Island, and Dog Island hold a special place in the heart of our family. Not only is it a fishing mecca but the solitude of the Forgotten Coast is what we want from a vacation or getaway. When so many run to the crowd for the bright lights and hustle and bustle of tourist traps and vacationlands, we retreat to the quiet sanctuary of the isolated and the remote. We want family time with each other, not entertainments sitting next to each other.

Only a few minutes after I took this picture, the massive fogbank had completely consumed the bridge out to St. George Island. A few minutes more and it had completely consumed me, too.

He is always there, waiting by the shore . . . even when we can't see Him . . . waiting to guide us Home. And when you find Him, He will smile because all He wants is to see you safe and warm in His presence.

God is good.

HYSTERIA IN THE WISTERIA

It's Sunday morning.

You know I don't write or work on Sundays, and . . . we are about to leave Oxford, Mississippi, and bid farewell—for a time—to Bay . . . she begins her journey through college now.

But I wanted you to ponder something today . . . there is hysteria in the wisteria.

Life is complicated. We are busy. We distract ourselves from the busyness of life with more things that consume our time and consciousness. If we are not careful, life becomes hysterical. And, like the twisting branches of a wisteria vine, it becomes chaos.

Grandchildren intersect with work; work crosses over into suppertime; children encroach into marriage; volunteering crawls over lawn care; fishing trips creep over the top of mentoring.

And before we know it, our busyness has created a tangled web of vines that only resemble chaos . . . hysteria.

And then we cry.

Stress, anxiety, depression, and so much more are, oftentimes, wrapped up in those vines.

And when it all becomes too much . . . we stop crying and simply cry out.

And God is faithful to answer . . . in fact, He is much better at answering than we are at listening. I've found many times in my life where He answered me amidst the chaos with a simple response: "Be still, and know that I am God" Psalm 46:10, NIV.

Feeling overwhelmed today? Just be still . . . He will show you how to untangle the chaos of the vines.

"For God is not a God of confusion but of peace."
1 Corinthians 14:33, ESV

—I CAN ONLY IMAGINE—

"Heeeyyy, Laawwd!"

My late father-in-law, George Gantt, had a bunch of distinctly "him" expressions . . . maybe one day, I will detail them all, but one that I was particularly fond of was a very long and exaggerated, "Hey, Lawd!" . . . though sometimes, he would convert it to, "Hey, Lawdy!"

He didn't say it all the time . . . only when something was both funny and surprising. As I would finish telling him a funny tale from work, he'd exclaim, "Hey, Lawdy!" when he didn't see the twist coming at the end of the story . . . and then he'd laugh, as only he could laugh, with the biggest smile you ever did see covering his face.

His voice would boom across the room as he dragged each syllable well beyond its intended stretching point . . . a simple three-letter "h-e-y" turned into half a paragraph. Only to be outdone by the stretched-nearly-in-two and contorted Lord-y . . . turned "Laaaawwwwddyyy!"

But he reserved these expressions for only the most momentous of occasions . . . these expressions were not to be wasted on the routine or mundane occurrences of daily life. It was almost a compliment if you could tell a story that invoked a, "Heeeyy, Laaawwwddyyy!" from George. It was a badge of honor that he pinned only to the worthy.

Ted Watson and his daughter, Susie, sang a beautiful hymn in church one Sunday. Seeing the two on the stage together reminded me of one of those times when George put the icing on the cake that was my story . . . by exclaiming, "Heeey, Laaaawwwwddyyy!"

It seems particularly fitting that I share that story with you, too.

Ted Watson is a big man. He is from the small community of Bermuda—the 'r' is silent for local folks—which is just outside the booming metropolis of Repton, Alabama. At last count, the census takers knocked on some doors twice just so Repton could keep its official status as a town. Ted is the biggest thing to come out of Bermuda . . . "big" in the sense that he is quite accomplished . . . former Alabama Superintendent of the Year, Ted retired from his long-standing tenure as chief of the Andalusia City Schools. He is certainly a "big" credit to his profession . . . and he is also "big" in the sense that he was, perhaps, one of the best football players to ever cross the field at Jacksonville State University . . . or at least, that's the way I heard it.

Some years back, Ted was one of the go-to singers in the church for what we call "special music." That is, music that someone from the congregation sings to the glorification of the Lord and to the delight of the rest of the congregation. Ted has a "big" booming voice and, certainly, God has gifted him in his abilities. Usually, our special music is always sung by women, and while I always enjoy the melodies of the higher ranges, I particularly enjoy anytime Ted sings . . . because his deeper ranges are soothing to the soul. Whenever I see Ted stand at the "special music" time of our service, I get a little giddy . . . because I know that what is to come next will be powerfully beautiful. This day would be no different.

Ted stood confidently, yet unassumingly, and made his way to the pulpit. For a big man, Ted has a great sense of humor . . . he uses it well to disarm people so that his size or deep voice doesn't intimidate them. Ted always does a good job of mixing humor into his introductions before he starts singing . . . and usually, the humor is self-deprecating, such that the audience relates to Ted well . . . he is not above us or below us . . . he is simply one of us.

He stood at the pulpit that morning making a few remarks about why this song is so special to him, why the lyrics speak to him, and how much he has practiced working out the lyrics so that the song is perfect. And then he began to sing . . . it was the first time I had ever heard the song . . . the powerfully visual lyrics conjured images in my mind's eye of standing before Christ . . . awestruck at His majesty. Couple the imagery with Ted's booming baritone voice, I was blown away. The words to the song "took me there," if you know what I mean . . . standing at the foot of the Father, I could only imagine how I might respond . . . in awe and amazement, surrounded by His glory. By the time Ted got through singing, tears rolled down my cheeks . . . just as they do right now.

I left church that day overwhelmed by the presence of the Holy Spirit and by the conviction that God is truly so good. I left even more impressed and astounded that Ted Watson wrote and sang such a powerful song. I still am overwhelmed by the goodness of God . . . as for Ted's song . . . well, that is the best part of the story.

A couple of weeks went by . . . I remarked several times to Hannah about how fantastically Ted could sing and how powerful the lyrics to the song were. I even cornered Ted up at church the following Sunday and begged him to sing it again soon. He was both humble and gracious. One particular afternoon, I was driving home from work when the recorded version of "I Can Only Imagine" came on the radio. I had to pull over on the side of the road . . . speakers blaring . . . just to take in the full experience of hearing the song on the radio for the first time. To say I was moved would be an understatement. Not only were the lyrics so visual as to tell a great and passionate story, but my dear friend Ted Watson wrote them! Now . . . I'm sure Ted attributed his rendition to the band MercyMe, but somehow, I missed that . . . you see, I left church that day thinking Ted wrote the song, and, for weeks afterwards, I went around telling folks that they just had to hear Ted Watson's new song on the radio.

Every time it played, I'd nudge whoever was in the car with me and tell them how I went to church with the guy who sings this song.

"Hey, have you heard that song, 'I Can only Imagine?'"

"Yes, I have. Isn't it wonderful?"

"It is so vivid and mesmerizing! Did you know Ted Watson wrote that song?"

The conversation oft times repeated itself . . . I was so proud of Ted, and I knew he was too humble to brag on himself, so I did it for him . . . to anyone and everyone who would listen. No doubt, friends tolerated me, and others listened to my assertions with curious oddity as I repeated that same story more times that I can count. And through it all, somehow, the Lord saw fit to make sure I never heard the radio DJ attribute the song to MercyMe . . . for I even thought that, through the magic of technology, Ted sang the radio version also. The true singer, Bart Millard, lead vocalist of MercyMe, bears a striking resemblance to Ted's boisterous baritones.

Soon enough, all good things come to an end, and it was with great embarrassment that I learned that I had made a complete fool of myself . . . repeatedly.

One Sunday afternoon, not long after I realized my blunder, George and I sat in the living room chatting after lunch. I started out . . . "Hey, remember that song that Ted sang in church that I told you he recorded and got on the radio?" He nodded his head, and I proceeded to tell him of my blunder and the embarrassment of the entire town thinking I was either a comedian or an idiot. By the time I told George the whole story, he and I were both in stitches, and he complemented my laughter by bellowing, "Heeeyyy, Laaawwwdy!"

"I can only imagine what it will be like
when I walk by Your side.
I can only imagine what my eyes will see
when Your face is before me.
I can only imagine.
Surrounded by Your glory,
what will my heart feel?
Will I dance for you, Jesus,
or in awe of You be still?
Will I stand in Your presence,
or to my knees will I fall?
Will I sing, Hallelujah?
Will I be able to speak at all?
I can only imagine.
I can only imagine.
I can only imagine when that day comes
when I find myself standing in the Son.

I can only imagine when all I will do
Is forever, forever worship You.
I can only imagine.
I can only imagine."

I can only imagine how awesome it must be, and I have no doubt that the overwhelming joy and surprise of it all prompted a big, "Heeeyy, Laawwdy!" and a whole lot more on the day George Gantt walked through those pearly gates.

Chapter
SIX

BY THE CAMPFIRE

CRABBY ALLIGATORS

Rumors of a big alligator had circled the neighborhood for a week or so. Some had seen it sunning on the sandy beaches at midday. Others had seen it cruising the piers at dusk. One or two claimed it had stolen their redfish or speckled trout while they were fishing. Universally, though, the sentiment was consistent . . . it was big.

Us kids . . . we had all seen it, too.

"I was swimming with a few of my buddies when I leaned back and bumped a log. I turned around, and it was a huge alligator!" someone would claim. Another boy from the neighborhood said, "I saw it eat somebody's cat." And another would claim, "It's as big as our boat . . . it came swimming up next to us the other day."

With a neighborhood full of elementary-school-age boys swapping tales of giant alligators eating whole boats, it became difficult to discern fact from fiction . . . trouble was, though, we engulfed every bit of it as fact and then added our own fiction to it and then regurgitated it. Because that's what little boys—and some adults—do when they are a little unnerved and also a little excited . . . we make the alligators of life bigger than they really are.

All of the talk made for a troublesome few weeks. My friend Danny lived closest to the Goliath. "My mom said I can't go swimming anymore," he lamented.

"Ever?" I asked.

"Ever . . ." Danny sank his chin down into the palms of his hands with fret.

"At least we can still fish," I offered. But that didn't seem to help resolve his heartburn . . . "Old Man Smitherman said it took a redfish clean off his line. Scared him so bad his wife said she had to get him some nitroglycerine."

Puzzled, I was. "Nitrogl . . . what? What's that?"

Danny considered the matter for a moment before responding. "It's medicine that you take to help you sleep. You take it at night," he explained. I was 10 . . . maybe 11 years old.

"Well, bet he had nightmares," I responded.

"Shoot yea!" Danny agreed.

Danny's dad was a kind man, always quick to offer a joke and a great suggestion for "the ladies." Of course, at our age, he knew we had no interest in "the ladies," and his advice was more of a ribbing than anything. He was also cautious by nature. He was an engineer, and his skeptical approach to construction—always looking for the weakest link—bled over into life as well. He always had a few last-minute queries before we ventured out . . . "Do you have extra hooks? Did you remember to get extra gas for the boat? Do you have a raincoat?" . . . always looking for the weakest point with hopes of strengthening it . . . and us, too.

"You boys be careful down at the water today. Maybe you should take a shovel or a long stick . . . just in case," Mr. Deese offered.

"Sure, Dad," Danny obliged, and grabbed a shovel as we set off for the afternoon's adventure. We had a few crab nets and some chicken legs. Crab nets are not complicated or strong. They will catch a blue crab . . . they most likely would not catch an alligator. Nevertheless, our plan was to bait up that ole gator and see just how big it really was . . . "We'll get some pictures of him, too," I said, holding up my Kodak. The plan was simple enough . . . tie the chicken legs to the crab nets, lower the nets down into the water, and tie them to the pier. When we saw the nets moving, we'd pull the line in and hopefully get a glimpse of the behemoth before he retreated.

Crab nets, if you are unfamiliar, are simple contraptions. Imagine a wire ring about two feet in diameter, with woven cotton twine intersecting all throughout the midsection so as to make a bowl-type net. In the middle, two extra pieces of twine lay seemingly purposeless . . . you use those to tie the meat to the center of the net. In our case, we'd tied our chicken legs with this twine. The entire ring was slung by three lines, all intersecting to one long rope about three feet above the net itself. We'd tied the end of the rope to the pier.

Mobile Bay is famous for blue crabs. In fact, there was a time when blue crabs throughout the Southeast came from Mobile Bay. Crabbers worked trap lines further out from the piers, catching the bigger adults by the dozens and selling them to the local fish houses.

We crabbed more for entertainment most days . . . if we caught one or two, we'd grab them behind their back legs and hold them in our hands like a weapon. The crabs, frustrated by being manipulated by obnoxious boys, would flare their claws, ever ready to pinch the first thing they came into contact with. We'd always start by enticing them to pinch each other. But that grew boring, as the crab's hard exoskeleton made it obvious—to even us—that one crab pinching another crab was almost pointless. They would lock up their claws into each other and hold on . . . forever, it felt. We'd usually tire of the perpetual death grip and figure out how to separate them. It was only fun it they jousted . . . we wanted to see action, not long hugs from two adversarial crabs.

Bored of the hug fest, we'd separate them, and then things progressed to the next level of gamesmanship. "Snap, snap, snap" . . . the claws would click as the crab sensed something close by. I was trying to catch my crab . . . its claws flared up toward my hand, as it circled to keep me in front of itself. Like a cobra, you have to distract a crab with one hand and then reach behind it with the other. I distracted it with my left hand, and just as I was about to reach around with my right hand and grab its hind legs . . .

"Snap!" You can't actually hear the claws snap together . . . but when someone sneaks up behind you and latches an angry and disgruntled crab to the little fat rolls on the side of your torso . . . well, let's just say, I can't type the sound I made, for it wouldn't be appropriate.

It is an intense feeling of pain as you writhe to get away from the crab, fearing when you escape its first clamp, because then the crab will simply clamp its other claw to another part of your body . . . and then back to the little fat roll with the other claw, and there you'll be, stuck in some twisted game of crab twister where it has your hand and your side and won't let go of either. Dancing and jumping . . . the seconds seem like hours . . . all you hope is that the lurch downwards with each jump will cause the crap to let go or lose its grip. I was nearly in tears as all of my buddies laughed and giggled... and I even laughed through the pain, for I know they got me good.

Finally, with a thud, the crab let go and fell to the wooden decking of the pier. Still bent in pain, I found the nearest deck chair and sat down to examine the damage.

"He drew blood! Stupid crab!"

Everyone was still laughing and cackling at the mastery of their shenanigans. Now bent on revenge, I maneuvered to pick up the same crab . . . "I'll show you guys," I said, reaching around behind the crab so as to make a weapon out of it. Blood trickled down my side and into the elastic waistband of my swimming trunks.

"Guys . . ." a voice muttered in the distance, while the rest of us jockeyed for position on the solitary crab that we now had in our possession. "Guys . . ." but no one checked up. Slapping at each other's hands and pushing the next friend's arm with hopes that a finger may jostle a little too close to the ornery crab . . . "GUYS!!!"

The night went silent.

Lost in all of this crabbery, we forgot about our actual mission . . . the alligator.

Terrance stood hovering over where the crab net was tied off. He was holding the rope in his hands . . . the end of the rope dangled, unattached to any crab net. The chicken leg was gone . . . the rope was frazzled and tattered.

"I went to see if there was another crab in the net . . . this is what I found." Terrance was baby-faced . . . still is. His face always begot sincerity, but we had also all been the victim of his pranks before . . . thus began a five-minute duet twixt him and Danny . . .

"You're lyin'."

"Am not."

"Are, too." It was quite the intellectual debate.

And finally, an alibi stepped forward . . . "He ain't lyin'," Robbie volunteered. "I saw him pull it up. He didn't cut the rope."

And thus began an enthusiastic discussion about how big the gator must have been to rip through that rope . . . such as it was.

"I felt the pier shake one time," another of our brethren offered.

"I heard it death roll, but I thought it was a school of mullet."

I grew up on Mobile Bay and in the Mobile Delta. We fished, caught crab, harvested oysters, and drug shrimp nets as a way of passing the time. And I am allergic to shellfish! I can touch them . . . just can't eat them. But I get great joy from watching Hannah and the girls devour a plate of crab claws or a bowl full of West Indies Salad.

And still another suggested, "I saw its wake from where it swam by, but thought it was probably from a boat."

No doubt . . . this gator grew more and more ferocious by the minute, and with each passing tale, we grew more and more scared . . .

We dispatched search parties, two "men" to the north and two "men" to the south, to look for the submarined beast. Scanning the water's edge with small plastic Eveready flashlights, we dared not travel far enough away from each other that we lose sight, for fear that one of our groups may need to come to the aid and rescue of the other. By now, fear was setting in . . . and we were starting to believe our own lies about near misses, sightings, and apparitions.

Soon enough, though, we abandoned our search, reasoning that the "Mighty A" had likely circled back to see if more chicken was to be found near the community pier where our adventure first began. We spent the rest of the night—or at least until our adrenaline gave way to sleep deprivation—circled up on the end of the pier swapping war stories. An Eveready flashlight stood on its end, beam shining straight up to the night's sky from the middle of our circle of brotherhood, casting a gentle glow upon our faces. We talked a bit more about alligators, but soon enough, the conversation moved to the cute girls at school.

It seems to be a rite of passage . . . elementary-school-age boys beginning to explore their curiosity about an attraction to the opposite sex. Circled up, we talked about how pretty this one was and how "fine" that one was. We were too young to understand sexuality. We certainly didn't understand sex. We just knew they were cute, and we wanted to puff our chests out a bit . . . because that's what men need to do from time to time . . . puff their chests out.

A mosquito buzzed my ear . . . the high-pitched whine sounded like an airplane propellor spinning way too fast. I swatted at the noise, only to have it resound a few seconds later. I swatted again, and the cycle repeated itself, until, finally, the blood sucking vampire found my neck and drank until it was so fat that it could barely lift off. Of course, I didn't realize the mosquito had bitten me until it was done. I clapped my hands together as I caught its silhouette from the corner of my eye . . . the flashlight's beam backlit it. "Clap!" I opened my palms to find blood splattered in them. "He was full," I said to the group as I showed them my hands.

"That's what that alligator is going to do to you if he gets a hold of you," Terrance responded. "Slap his jaws shut and bust your guts!"

Exhausted, out of chicken, and blood-let, we started back up the pier to walk back to Danny's house. The moon, once high overhead, now lay low on the horizon . . . "Anybody know what time it is?" Danny inquired.

Terrance, always at the ready, offered that it was "about 3 in the morning." He didn't have a watch . . . he was looking at the moon, holding his thumb up, as if he was measuring knuckle joints between the horizon and the moon's position in the sky. He insisted it was an accurate way to tell time.

"Shut up . . ." I told him.

"No really, my dad taught me this. It works . . . I'm not lying. I promise." We all shook our heads and started again, walking down the pier back to dry land.

Piers on Mobile Bay are typically 50 to 75 yards long . . . a requirement that is necessary to get to water deep enough to drive a small bay boat. Generally, at mid-tide, the water at the end of any pier is about chest deep to an 11-year-old boy. A super high tide likely requires that same prepubescent boy to do what we called the "tippy-toe dance" to keep his head above water. That is . . . hopping on the tips of your toes to keep your mouth and nose high enough out of the water that the next passing wave didn't flood your lungs. Low tide was somewhere around waist deep . . . maybe less.

From the end of the pier, the land appeared murky in the low-hanging moonlight. By then, our Eveready flashlights were pretty well run down . . . more appropriately they were "Barelyreadys," as the batteries were nearly dead. Robbie stopped dead in the middle of the pier.

"What's that?" he whispered.

Like the Three Stooges plus a few, we bumped one into the other . . . none of us were prepared for Robbie's sudden stop. The surging collision nearly forced him off the edge of the pier and into the water.

"What the . . . What are y'all doing?" came a demand from the rear of the once single-file line.

"Ssshhh! Robbie sees something." Pointing at a long dark object lying in the grass just off to the right of the end of the pier, we all soon realized the object of his ocular affection was very real and very big. Some 20 yards away, we couldn't tell for certain what it was . . . but our minds and our mouths soon started speculating in grand fashion. Danny tried to reassure us . . . "It's a log that washed up."

Robbie quipped back, "You ever seen a log move?" That was all it took for the motors of our imagination to rev into high gear . . . "He must be 15 feet long!" "Look, he has his mouth open . . . he is waiting on us." "He is! He is trying to ambush us!" Soon enough, we realized our peril . . . "There is no way off the pier. We all have to get by him."

Danny elbowed his way through the crowd huddled across the gangway of the pier . . . "You are all idiots . . . It's a log." With that, he started walking towards the mighty beast . . . being the good friends that we are, we followed . . . "I want to see this!"

Ten steps toward the ambushing agent of doom made its silhouette much clearer . . . it was becoming obvious it was a log, but it was still just dark enough to leave a tinge of uncertainty. Danny, five steps ahead of the rest of us, stopped even with the beast and turned to face us. With some measure of coordination, we all stopped, as if General Patton was about to address his troops upon returning to the shores of the Philippines. "You see, losers? I told you it was just a . . . . OOOOHHHHHHhhhhhh. Mmyyyyyy. GGGAAAAWWWDDDDD . . . IT MOVED! RUUUUUNNNNNN!!!"

Like Forrest Gump . . . we ran. And, like school-age girls . . . we screamed the entire way. No doubt, the neighborhood was growing weary of our antics by now. I saw a light come on in the upstairs window of a nearby house. Back at the end of the pier, catching our breath, we took stock and roll.

"Everyone here?" "One, two, three, four . . . where's Danny? Danny? DAAANNNNNNYYY?"

"I'm right here, you dorks," came his reply.

I could make out his silhouette . . . standing on top of the log.

"Geeezzz . . . you scared the crap out of us!" one of our number remarked.

"I know!" Danny celebrated. "Y'all ran like a bunch of scared ninnies!" And he was right . . . there was no dignity in our retreat. "I guess y'all would have left me for dead," he observed.

"Yep . . . " came a sarcastic and unamused response from somewhere at the back of the line.

The next morning, Danny's dad woke us for breakfast. We were exhausted . . . turns out, Terrance wasn't too far off with his lunar thumb clock. The clock on the wall said it was 2:30 a.m. when we came back inside the night before. It didn't take long to fall asleep, though . . . that was a blessing. Too tired to tell booger tales and too sleepy to argue, we relented.

During breakfast, Mr. Deese asked all about the night's events. Eager to tell every detail, each one of us took turns inserting important tidbits into the story . . . at times, the truth was secondary to the fear factor . . . but what did I know? Maybe the gator really was "20 feet long." He laughed and "oohed" and "aahd" with each morsel of information, careful to never dampen our enthusiasm, and he assured us that, today, we'd find our prey.

"After breakfast, y'all should head back down to the beach," he suggested. "I've got some more crab nets in the garage. Take a few. And I bought y'all some more chicken legs last night, too."

"Gee, thanks, Mr. Deese . . . you're the greatest." And he was.

Mr. Deese knew how to shepherd us. Always quick to challenge us to do the right thing for the right reasons, he never fell prey to the temptation to demonstrate worldly masculinity . . . for he was biblically masculine. He was what most of us needed in our lives . . . we trusted him . . . we took in every word of advice, even about "the ladies," and I still remember much of it today. He was a good shepherd.

"Y'all take a couple of shovels with you," he suggested, as we left the table to assemble our gear for the expedition. "Shovels? Again, Dad?" Danny asked.

Always looking for the weakest link in the plan, Mr. Deese suggested, "You might need to keep him away from you . . . you can use the shovels to push off." He gestured with his arms as he talked . . . it seemed reasonable enough to us. Ten minutes later, we were headed back to the community pier . . . shovels, crab nets, chicken legs, Kodak, and a few other pieces of meaningless gear in our packs.

The hike to the pier was only about 10 minutes. No doubt, the neighborhood was abuzz with the mighty gator hunting expedition . . . Mrs. Johnson even wished us "Good luck!" as we crossed her yard. "Thank you, ma'am! We are going to get him." "I know you will," she said, "but be careful!" Rounding the curve at the end of the street, the trail to the pier forked to the left and cut down through the woods and a shrub line of the adjoining property owners. Crepe myrtles draped over the path at times, and large, thick azaleas flanked each side . . . "He could be laying in here waiting on us, and we wouldn't see him until it was too late."

"True enough," Terrance said, but ever the vat of wisdom, he opined that "gators don't like the way azaleas smell." None of us knew otherwise, so we accepted his statement as fact. The myth was repeated for fact several times over in those next few minutes.

Emerging into an open space near the beach, we rambled and moseyed without much care . . . not being very astute hunters . . . as any good hunter knows you approach feeding grounds with stealth. We approached more like the clown car at the circus . . . overloaded and boisterous! Ten steps from the beach, Danny, who was at the lead of the pack, once again stopped dead still and shushed us all.

"Oh, shut up!" someone clamored in response. None of us were going to fall for the same gag twice in the same place.

"I'm serious!" Danny insisted. "There he is!" You could almost tell from the tone in his voice that this was no prank. I leaned around his left shoulder for a better view, and sure enough, there he was . . . Goliath.

He was massive. "He is at least 10 feet!"

"More like 12."

"I bet he weighs 500 pounds."

The clamor and speculation spread like germs at a kindergarten birthday party. We stared in awe . . . and then the sinking, unsettled reality began to set in. "We came to slay this beast . . . and it is huge." Danny pulled his buck knife from his pocket and opened the blade. Terrance choked up on one of the shovels. I put a lasso loop in the end of the rope I was carrying.

"What's the plan, boys?" I asked.

A few minutes of conversing, then arguing, then conversing again . . . all amounted to time wasted. "Walt, you go around behind him and put the lasso around his neck," Danny suggested. I, in turn, thought a better approach was for Terrance to take the shovel and whack it on the top of the gator's head, knocking it unconscious. Terrence, however, thought Danny should jump on it and stab it in the brain. Curiously, we all thought the best plan was for someone else to make the first move . . . all that talk the day before had dwindled down to whimpers of machismo at this point.

"Whatever . . . let's just go put the lasso on his head, and we can all drag him up the

*Hunting alligators was a lot easier 20 years ago.
Seems the bigger they are the harder they fall . . .
but the older I get the harder it is! We killed this
10-footer about five or six years ago. Tender white
meat and full bellies make all the struggle worthwhile!*

beach and tie him to a log." Everyone agreed with Wade's compromise. Plan in place, we spread out through the Johnsons' yard like attack fighter jets falling into formation . . . two to the left, two to the right . . . we wanted to corral the gator so it didn't flee and thwart our efforts. Each one of us spent as much time watching each other as we did the gator.

"Don't you chicken out and let him get by you," someone chided.

"Shut your face," came the response. We didn't take kindly to man card challenges . . . even at that age.

I twirled what was to be the lasso over my head from time to time . . . crouched over, trying to keep a low profile. My rope—a near salvage-quality rope rescued from the inner depths of Mr. Deese's old bass boat—lay limp, half-rotten, and wet. We were too young and dumb to know that this rope would barely hold air in its loop . . . much less a thousand pounds of angry gator meat. The rope had oil stains on it from the bilge muck in the hull of the boat. Its braids were beyond frayed at some places, and the notion that the loop I had tied in the end would ever work as a lasso was absurd. We were about to attack a full-grown, adult male alligator of at least 12 feet . . . with an oversize spaghetti noodle.

The shortcomings of our plan became more and more recognizable with each crouching step that we took . . . slowly circling the beast. The alligator lay motionless on the beach. The gentle surf lapped at its tail and hind legs. Its front legs, torso, and head all lay prominently on the white sand.

"He either has no idea we are here, or couldn't give a crap that we are here," I mumbled to Danny. We each took another step closer . . . Danny agreed with my contention with a head nod, but then regained his focus . . . "Get ready to lasso him."

I started twirling the rope. There I was . . . ducking low, some 20 feet in front of the largest alligator I had ever seen, twirling a rope over my head like a helicopter . . . and somehow, I had convinced myself not only that this plan was going to work but that the alligator had no idea of our presence. You see, the Johnsons had a few shrubs in their yard, right at the beach's edge . . . I positioned myself behind a nice yucca plant, convinced that the helicoptering rope above the yucca would do nothing to draw the suspicion of such a mighty beast. "Swirrrlll, swirrllll, swirrlll . . ." the rope whistled each time it rotated above my head.

"Throw it noooowwww!" Terrance yelled. With that, I summoned my deepest strength and let loose the mightiest lasso throw I had ever mustered. The rope sailed majestically through the air, and the loop of the lasso opened wider than the mouth of the Mississippi . . . I tracked its motion in astonishment . . . it was a thing of beauty, and it landed perfectly over the top of the tallest stalk of the yucca plant.

"You idiot," came the first acknowledgment.

"Oh, my gawwwd," came the next.

My machismo moment of grandeur . . . that moment every boy dreams of . . . the one where he becomes the hero who saves the world . . . just came to rest in the spiked throngs of a yucca plant. There I stood, shoulders sunk, head down . . . deflated.

"Get the rope!" Danny yelled. I lifted my head quickly, noting that the gator was still sunbathing on the beach. "A chance for redemption," I thought to myself. Hope for redemption can make a man think he is invincible . . . I pushed the sharp, pointed yucca spears to the side as if they were cotton tufts and pulled the lasso back up over the top of the stalks. The dried and discarded stalks of yesteryear lay all around the base of the plant . . . they crackled and popped under my bare feet . . . and the plant shook like a runaway rocking horse, back and forth, as the rope unleashed the spring-loaded tension when I finally pulled the lasso off the last tip of the plant.

Perched amidst the yucca stalks, I spied my prey. Much closer because of my advanced position, there was nothing to interfere with my throw now. "Swirlll, swirllll, swrilll . . ." And with visions of John Wayne in my head, I let that lasso sail once again. It was, again, a thing of beauty, and surely, any rodeo expert would agree . . . it was absolute pure mastery . . . landing squarely on the great beast's broad back, nearly perfectly oriented towards his head. "Yes!" I exclaimed, clenching the fist of my free hand.

The alligator was unfazed . . . not even acknowledging the rope landed across his back.

"Pull it tight over his neck," Terrance urged . . . as if I didn't already understand the complexity of the lasso.

"Perhaps he doesn't know I made that near perfect throw," I boasted to myself, now fully redeemed from my yucca plant debacle . . . pride coursed my veins. I gently pulled on the rope . . . it slipped down in between the ridged armor of the alligator's back . . . and slowly, but surely . . . the lasso closed to a nearly perfect straight line . . . without even the slightest consideration of snaring the gator.

The alligator was still completely unimpressed by our efforts.

"Pull it in and try again," Terrance urged. I started frantically pulling the rope back and looping it in my hand.

The sun glistened off the gator's back. It had been out of the water long enough that only its tail and back feet showed any moisture . . . the rest of its leathered hide was dry and sun-soaked. In various shades of green, the gator's hide drew the eye upward to the armor on its big, broad back. Ridged points protruded from its skin—an ancient protection designed to keep its backside safe from attack—and the armor looked hard and imposing. The gator's back was broad and wide . . . as kids, we could have likely ridden it like a horse. The gator's belly was swollen out around its girth as if it had recently gorged itself on a neighborhood dog. It back feet were massive... large enough to cover a dinner plate.

It was huge.

"Are y'all sure he is alive?" Danny asked.

His question was met with a barrage of responses about how stupid he was . . . how we had all seen him move . . . "I just saw him blink!" But the more we talked, the less certain we became, so convinced of our fear that none of us were actually sure if his question was legitimate.

"Terrance, go poke him with the shovel."

By now, we were all within 10 paces of the beast, standing in the wide open. The gator had not budged.

"His eyes look hazy to me. They look like a dead deer's eyes." Danny opined.

Terrance took three steps closer . . . more towards the gator's hind legs. He held the shovel by the shoveled end and eased the handle end out towards the mighty beast. "Thwap!" The shovel handle rapped against the armor plates on top of the gator's tail.

Nothing moved.

"Do it again," someone urged. Terrance obliged . . . stepping one step closer. "Thwap, thwap!"

Nothing.

"He's dead," Danny assessed. We all began stepping closer . . . somewhat in agreement that the beast we had all been so scared of over the last 30 minutes was, in fact, harmlessly dead. Terrance was poking the gator in the side with no response . . . and soon enough, we were all standing right on top of it gawking and teasing each other for being scared of a dead gator. We considered skinning it for its hide, though that was certainly just talk, as none of us had the skills necessary for such a complicated task. We talked of cutting its feet off for trophies but decided that Danny's knife wasn't up to the task. Then, we finally agreed we would cut some of its teeth out and make necklaces . . . all of us wearing one, like some sort of Alligator Hunters' Secret Society.

I squatted down at the gator's mouth. Its jaw was slightly agape . . . I could smell the hint of foulness coming from its mouth . . . "Talk about bad breath!" Danny said with a laughed. "Don't make fun of ole Albert." And he tapped Albert the Alligator in the side of the belly with the toe of his shoe. At that moment, Albert let out a massive growling groan, summoned from the deepest part of his bowels. He sounded like a demon-possessed carnivore determined to eat little boys.

"Rrrrruuuunnnnnnn!!!!!!" And run we did . . . screaming like little girls until we were safe.

"Surely he is right behind me," I thought to myself as I whimpered with each high step . . . lifting my feet higher and higher to keep the chomping gator from grabbing one of my ankles. I panted as I ran, near hyperventilation . . . only stopping because the others had, too. Assembling together some 50 feet away, we turned to find Albert had not moved an inch, and no one had been eaten.

It took a few minutes for us to collect our wits and reapproach Albert. He had not moved, but his belly was noticeably deflated . . . "That's a lot of hot air," Terrance chimed. And he was right. The air trapped in Albert's belly became dislodged when Danny jostled his side . . . and rushing out of his mouth . . . he growled... even though he was dead.

Turns out... someone had shot and killed Albert sometime during the early morning hours. The neighborhood was safe once again.

Seems "hot air" was plentiful throughout . . . neighborhood talk of a mythical giant had everyone in an uproar. And though the beast had been slain, we later realized that none of the neighbors had actually lost a dog to the gator's appetite. We also soon discovered that only a few of the neighbors had even seen the gator. As for us, we were just as full of hot air, too . . . we let our imaginations overtake our tongues, and we had spouted all sorts of tomfoolery in the bravado of the hunt. Even our talk of girls on the pier was "hot air." The hunt itself was "hot air" foolishness, too . . . a rope, a shovel, and a pocketknife. It's a wonder we didn't get eaten alive.

So, with that thought, I think the only conclusion left to recognize is to thank the Good Lord that ole Albert was full of hot air, too.

The American alligator is a freshwater animal that ranges from Texas to North Carolina. Once endangered, now they are prolific in the backwaters and brackish coastal waters that flow into the Gulf of Mexico. I remember in the early '80s spending all day in the Mobile Delta and seeing one or two alligators. Now, one can hardly look a few hundred yards in the Delta without coming across a gator. Once, in college, Hannah and I were visiting with my mother in Fairhope, Alabama. We went for a swim in the salty brackish waters of Mobile Bay. After a few minutes, some folks further down the beach waived their arms to catch our attention, and then pointed out into the water to warn us of an approaching alligator. Our retreat cut off, so we simply bided our time as the behemoth passed us by. In my experience, alligators prefer to avoid humans. That is unless they have been fed by humans and then they become very dangerous, for they lose their fear of human contact.

FROM THE
NEXT ROOM

"Tick, tick, tick." The egg cracked against the side of the clay pottery bowl. And then another. And then another. "Swiiiizzzzzle, swiiiizzzzle . . ." Her hand swirled round and round above the bowl as she beat the eggs into a yellow, murky mess. "Shooka, shooka, shooka," first the salt and then the pepper adorned the golden swirl of eggs in the bowl in the middle of the chopping block.

The cast-iron skillet slammed down hard on the eye of the stove, raking across the bars as it slid to a stop. With a few "clicks" of the knob on the back of the stove, the eye came to life, and the heat from below started to penetrate the skillet. She silently peeled each strip of bacon back away from the slab and laid them in the skillet, side by side, until the skillet's belly was full, from one end to the other. A slight hint of sizzle came from the last piece that she laid down as the skillet got hotter.

The biscuit pan and bowl sat silently next to the bowl of eggs. She turned her attention there . . . like she has done a thousand times before, she made a nest in the flour with the backs of her fingers and poured in a little buttermilk. I could hear the milk and flour "squish" together as she worked the mixture with her fingers. After fifteen or twenty seconds, she "plopped" the wad of dough down onto the chopping block . . . it reminded me of my childhood . . . the sound mud clods make as they crash to the ground . . . us boys hurling them at one another at the creeks edge. Wet . . . thick . . . "kerplop." Then, I heard her twist the can as it scratched against the wood chopping block . . . not a grind, but a scratch, as the metal can slid over the wooden surface . . . cutting each circle of dough precisely the same size. Occasionally, she tapped the can against the side of her dough bowl, and I knew she had just dunked the can in flour . . . a lubricant that would keep the dough from sticking to the can as she cut. Soon enough, the oven door creaked and urked as the old hinges worked—no doubt coated with years of baked-in smoke and infused with layer upon layer of heat-treated coatings of 20-plus years of use—and the cast-iron biscuit pan slid into place on the oven rack. The noise made by the grating of the two pieces of metal is surely a close cousin to fingernails on a chalkboard. The oven door then slammed shut as the springs in the hinges pulled it tight.

As the door shut with a "slamp," I tuned in to the bacon sizzling on the stove. An orchestra of tiny gurgles was accompanied by an occasional "pop" solo that prevailed over the undertone of the sizzle. I could see in my mind's eye the grease "pop" out of

Brenda's biscuits . . . they are near heaven on earth. Add some pear preserves and just leave me be . . .

We often provoke conversation as we linger around the table by asking questions like "If you were stranded on a deserted island and could only have one type of food for the rest of your life, what would it be?" It never fails that somebody at the table says "bacon!"

the pan and onto the nearby stove . . . or counter . . . or maybe even her arm, though she never uttered a complaint. No doubt, her arms are immune to the hot sting of bacon grease, having felt its burn a thousand times over. The "gurgles" and "pops" rose to a fever pitch occasionally, and with the new pitch, I heard the faint sound of a fork dragging its tongs over the bottom of the blackened skillet . . . followed by a quick "tap, tap, tap" from the fork banging down on the side of the skillet.

The bacon was almost ready.

I heard her stir the eggs again, for good measure, and then the carafe from the coffeepot rattled a bit. It's a distinctive sound of glass and coated metal colliding . . . followed by the plastic of the top part of the maker. A second or two later, the pot "clanged" against the rim of a cup . . . And, even over the bacon sizzle, I heard the cup fill to the brim. The coffeepot collided hazardously back into its spot as I heard her "sluuuuurrrrpppp" at the top of the nearly overflowing coffee cup. I couldn't hear how hot the coffee was . . . but I knew it was scalding hot . . . because we only "sluuuurrrrp" when it is too hot to actually sip, much less drink.

The cup "rapped" against the Formica countertop, and the fork scratched across the bacon skillet again . . . and again . . . and again. With each drag, the sizzle grew quieter . . . and quieter . . . and quieter . . . until, soon enough, all that could be heard was a pop here or there.

She "swirled" the eggs again, and I heard the skillet come to life again. But not the same as before . . . no doubt, she had poured much of the bacon grease off before she poured the eggs in . . . and so their response to the hot skillet was audibly different than the bacon. Muffled and muted, the eggs danced in the pan, but not with nearly the same pizzazz the bacon had. I heard the grain of a wooden spoon stir around against the bottom of the skillet as the eggs tumbled end over end . . . each side finding the transformative heat of the bottom of the skillet.

Dishes rattled and clanked against each other momentarily . . . and then the systematic "thump" of each plate could be heard as it found its place on the old wooden breakfast table. Glasses and cups soon followed . . . and then the familiar sound of the "clinks and clanks" of silverware settling to rest next to the plates.

"Breakfast is ready!" she hollered . . . and I knew it was. I heard Banks "thump, thump, thumping" from the back as she ran to the kitchen. My mother-in-law, Brenda, pulled the biscuits from the oven just as Banks turned the corner.

"I get the middle biscuit!" she yelled, with the jubilation that only comes from beating your older sisters to the middle biscuit.

And such is the sound . . . from the next room . . . as Brenda cooked breakfast this morning.

Too bad you can't smell it through my words . . . or, maybe you can. And I regret to inform you . . . there isn't enough for all of you.

Sometimes, you just have to listen . . . from the next room.

GOD SAVED A FARMER

Part One

In his song "Simple As Dirt," Chris LeDoux once sung about the complicated life of a farmer:

"I love my wife and kids, just like my daddy did,
And my daddy's dad before.
And their philosophy was handed down to me.
Life is as easy as a hard day's work.
Simple as dirt."

Paul Harvey wrote of the farmer, too: "*And on the eighth day, God looked down on his planned paradise and said, 'I need a caretaker.' So God made a farmer.*"

A few mornings back, a Bibb County, Alabama, farmer woke before daybreak. It's planting season, and he had a full 18-hour workday ahead of him. "Simple as dirt," right? His wife woke with him . . . they don't even use an alarm clock anymore. They've done this same morning routine for 25 years, and their bodies' internal clocks work better than any Casio. She slipped on her robe, headed to the kitchen, and put on a pot of coffee. She watched Brenda Gantt's latest cooking video as the brew sputtered through the filter and into the brown-stained-glass pot. The coffee was strong and filled the air throughout the house. Smelling it from their bedroom, the farmer pulled both his boots on and made his way to the kitchen table. He winked at her as he came through the kitchen door and patted her on the tail as he passed . . . sitting down to the table, he stared out the window into the darkness of the predawn night.

She poured him a cup of black coffee . . . steam rolled and danced above the cup as she sat it on the table in front of him. The light bulb inside the schoolhouse globe flickered a bit as thunder rolled in the distance. She gave a worrisome look out the window . . . he smiled . . . hoping to ease her concerns. As he did, he was overcome with a sense of gratitude . . . always thankful that God had brought them together. He knew he never could have overcome all of the storms of life had it not been for her.

Grinning, she pulled the brim of his hat down over the top of his eyes and shook it from side to side a few times . . . then she turned to start breakfast.

They didn't need to talk . . . they knew each other's thoughts.

The eggs crackled and popped in the grease of the iron skillet. The grits gurgled and bubbled in the pot next to the eggs. A half-dozen slices of bacon were ready at the side of the stove, wrapped in paper towels. The eggs cooked in the bacon grease, sizzling to the perfect degree. He poured them both another cup of coffee as she 'helped' their plates. An egg for each of them . . . smothered under a veil of grits and topped with a thick slice of butter. She arranged a few slices of bacon on the side and slid the plate in front of him.

He reached his hand up and took hers in his . . . "Lord, we thank you for this day. We ask you to keep us safe in every storm, and we are so very thankful for the bounty of your harvest. Father, bless this food, this family, and this home. Amen." "Amen," she affirmed, taking her plate and sitting down next to him.

"Think you'll get much done today?" she asked. "Looks like it's going to rain most of the day." "Oh, yes, ma'am," he said confidently. "Tommy is coming over, and he is going to help me change out the fuel injectors on the big tractor. We can do that, rain or shine. After that, I'm going to take the other tractor and try to turn that lowest field . . . if it's dry enough. Then, I'll feed the cows and get a few odds and ends done."

She nodded her head in understanding as she sipped the coffee.

Tommy is their son, the oldest of three boys. He turned 28 years old last year. He and their middle son both have their own farms nearby. The youngest son is at college at the University of Montevallo. He is studying business and hopes to come back and help with that aspect of the families' farming businesses.

"That sure was good, Mama," he said. "That might have been the best grits and eggs I've ever had." She grinned and chuckled and shook her head. He said that about everything she cooked . . . a tribute to her grandfather, who always gave her grandmother the same compliment. It made her smile every time he said it . . . because she knew he meant it. He leaned over and kissed her on the cheek and told her he loved her, stood from the table, and turned the coffee cup so as to pull the last swig, and then disappeared out the kitchen door and into the morning's night air.

The light bulb in the schoolhouse globe hanging over the table flickered again as the thunder rolled . . . a little closer this time. She finished her coffee, staring out the window into the black of night. In the distance, she saw the barn lights turn on and heard him rumble about, digging for tools and whatnot. The rooster crowed a few times, and a few of the old cows said, "Good morning," . . . and she started to sing . . . "*Working nine to five . . . what a way to make a living*." And then she laughed to herself. She loved Dolly Parton, but as a farmer's wife, she had never had the luxury of working nine to five. She leaned into the living room and looked at the old grandfather clock that her parents left to her. It was 4:58 a.m. "More like five to nine," she thought to herself . . . without a bit of resentment. She made her way to the bedroom to freshen up for the day.

Outside, the farmer slipped his leather gloves on. Each had a hole in the end of the index finger, worn through from months of hard work. The farmer goes through two or three pair a year, "But I got all my fingers still," he thought to himself. He climbed up into the cab of the big green tractor and turned the key one click. The fuel pump spun up for a few seconds, and with a second click of the key, the old green giant rumbled to life. The diesel growled as it came to idle . . . the farmer eased his foot down on the pedal, and the engine growled even louder . . . but the rhythmic "clap, clap, clap" and a strain once the engine revved high reaffirmed for the farmer what he already knew . . . one of the fuel injectors is bad, and the others are almost gone.

The groan of the engine rattled against the steel frame of the barn . . . sheets of metal lined its walls and captured all of the noise from the green giant . . . "I should have opened those doors," he thought to himself, as the deafening sound and the black soot—both from the engine—filled the red iron metal-sided barn. He turned the key back two clicks, and the beast came to rest . . . but the building rattled on . . . as the thunder rolled ever closer. He went back into the shop room and grabbed his tools and struggled to remember where he put the new injectors . . . he bought them yesterday at the parts house. He suspected he left them in his truck and made a trip back out for naught . . . later finding them under the seat of the tractor. "Best place to hide something is to put it where you'll never think to look," he laughed at his own antics.

He raised the big roll-up door, pulling the chain downward as the door went upwards . . . a light sprinkle littered his boots as the door went higher. The sun—if you could see it—surely hovered just on the horizon. The sky was dreary, though, and the sun's only revelation was that it was no longer pitch-black. The farmer could see some of his herd huddled up under a few live oaks down near the creek. "Lord, don't let lightning hit that tree," he prayed, as a bolt flickered far off on the horizon. He pulled his hat down tight and made his way back across the yard to the house. Tommy should be there soon . . . another cup of coffee would do nice in the meantime.

She met him at the door . . . "Get in here," she insisted. "Don't you have sense enough to come in out of the rain?" she scolded. "Yes, ma'am," he agreed. She sat him down at the kitchen table and brushed the drizzle from his shoulders. She already had the coffee on the table. He pulled his gloves off and laid them on the floor . . . "You never lay work gloves on Mama's kitchen table," he silently reminded himself.

"James Spann is saying the tornados may come more our way," she offered. He raised his eyebrows slightly . . . his weathered forehead wrinkled as he turned to look out the window. The clouds rolled low over the treetops.

Spann, a Birmingham news station weatherman, gained the trust and respect of most Alabamians back in 1998 when he made what could have been a career-ending gamble . . . he talked the general manager at ABC 33/40 into letting him interrupt programming to cover a tornadic event . . . until the threat was over. The custom of the day was to interrupt programming for 30 seconds . . . maybe a minute. Spann's desire was to save people . . . he didn't care about tradition. During that broadcast, Spann pleaded with viewers, "Take cover immediately! This is a dangerous tornado."

People listened, and lives were saved. The gamble worked . . . the next day, in a live, on-air interview, a long-haired Oak Grove man broke down crying . . . "James Spann, you saved my life." Spann was visibly shaken by the gratitude.

"If James Spann is saying it," the farmer acknowledged, "we'd better pay attention." "Well, he is saying it looks like the worst storms are going to shift to the east towards us instead of staying over in Mississippi," she responded. He grunted a little, shook his head, and walked over to the television. Spann was already on the air . . . ever so cautious to raise awareness without creating panic. The farmer sipped his coffee and listened to Spann for a minute or two . . . his concentration was broken when he heard the grumble of the motor from his son's truck pulling in the driveway.

Part Two

Tommy's truck grumbled to a stop . . . sputtering and skipping, grasping for life even after he turned it off. He slammed the door shut and flipped the collar up on his Carhartt jacket . . . the drizzling rain was cold on the back of his neck. "I forgot my hat," he thought to himself as he trotted over to the barn. His dad was right behind him in the yard. They went straight to work on the old green beast.

The sun eased up over the horizon, and dawn turned into late morning.

"Y'all get it fixed?" the farmer's wife asked, as the two men came in the kitchen door.

"Runnin' like a top," the farmer responded, with a slight grin on his face.

"Thank the Lord," she said . . . "We can't afford another mechanic bill like the last one we had."

He nodded his head in agreement, "I know, Mama."

Tommy eased over to the old cast-iron sink. The porcelain around the rim of the sink had suffered a few dents and dings and chips . . . Tommy rubbed his finger over one particular chip, recalling the day well. He was 16 years old, and his middle brother was 14. They had just gotten home from school when the phone rang. It was Betsy, Tommy's sweetheart. The cord stretched across the room from the wall. The boys weren't allowed to have cell phones. Tommy stood at the kitchen window talking to Betsy about the day. She went to a neighboring school, so this was an afternoon ritual in the farmer's house. Tommy would normally talk until the farmer summoned the boys to the barn or to the field. There was always work to be done.

"Paw said to come on," came a voice from the porch. It was Tommy's little brother. "Besides, I gotta use the phone, too. Hurry up." After what surely must have been an agonizingly long three or four seconds . . . "Get off the phone; I gotta use it!" Tommy looked over his shoulder, still talking in stride to Betsy, and rolled his eyes at his brother . . . staring intently through the screened door, then he turned back and looked back out the kitchen window.

"Anyway, sorry 'bout that. My brother won't shut up. What were you saying?" Silence.

"Hello? Betsy? Hello?"

Tommy turned to find his little brother standing at the other end of the looped and tangled phone cord . . . having pulled it from the phone's base. His other hand clasped downward on the base where the phone hung on the wall . . . he had hung up on Betsy.

"Told you I needed to use the phone. It's important. Give me that!"

In one instantaneous motion, Tommy said, "Okay," while raring back and hurling the phone's handset at his little brother. The throw looked like that of a major leaguer who never warmed up . . . raring back and knocking two pots hanging from nails on the side of the cabinets . . . they both fell, one of them catching the edge of the sink and sending shards of porcelain flying. The phone fared worse, flying past its intended target and knocking a picture of Mama's parents off the wall. Amidst the chaos, the boys collided in the middle of the kitchen, and quite a tussle ensued.

Like John Wayne emerging from the mist in an old Western, the farmer stepped from the porch and collared each of the boys, one in his left hand, the other in the right. He dragged them outside by their shirt collars and the nape of their necks . . . the boys found themselves helpless in his powerful hands. He dragged them across the yard . . . "Okay, Daddy, we'll stop. Let go!"

The farmer clenched down even tighter on the boys' necks . . . "Oww, Daddy!"

On the far side of the yard, the farmer pinned the oldest boy up against the fence with his hip. Reaching over with his free hand, he opened the pen's gate . . . "What are you doing, Daddy?" came a desperate plea. The farmer finally broke his silence. "Putting you where you belong." He then took the younger boy and hurled him into the pen. Tommy protested, "Daddy, don't!" But it was too late. Tommy couldn't even brace himself before the farmer hurled him into the pen, too.

Both boys landed flat on the ground, one on his stomach, the other on his back. The pigs rooted around at the other side of the pen. The boys both stood to find themselves covered in mud and pig slop. The farmer shut the pen and glared at them in frustration. "The only reason I'm not beating you both is because that's not who we are. You want to act like pigs? Well . . . here you go." The boys hung their heads and slung the mud from the tips of their fingers.

Inside, the farmer's wife began to cry as she picked up the shattered glass from the picture frame. The farmer walked back in the door to find her there . . . kneeling on the kitchen floor. He bent down and lifted her shoulders. She stood, and he held her tight in his arms . . . she loved being in his arms. They felt safe and powerful, like they could

"And God said, 'Let there be lights in the expanse of the heavens to separate the day from the night. And let them be for signs and for seasons, and for days and years, and let them be lights in the expanse of the heavens to give light upon the earth.' And so, it was." Genesis 1:14-15, ESV fix anything that troubled her . . . and most of the time, they could. She pressed her forehead against his chest and sobbed. All he could do was hold her.

The boys stripped down to their underwear on the porch and stood at the screened door silently. The farmer looked over at them . . . their faces pressed to the screen. "We are sorry we broke the picture, Mama." She lifted her head from her husband's chest, looked at them, and said "I don't care about that glass, boys. Most things in life can be fixed or replaced . . . some things can't be. It's not the glass being broken that troubles me." Then, she turned and went back to the bedroom.

The farmer walked over to the door. The boys took a few steps backwards as he pushed open the screened door. He stood a step higher as he was inside the threshold of the kitchen door, so his presence loomed even larger over them.

"Boys, that may be your mama, but she is my wife, and she is my wife first. I only have a few God-given jobs, and one of them is to love that woman like Christ loved the church . . . and I do. You understand?"

They both nodded their heads up and down.

"Answer me, boys," the farmer demanded. "Yes, sir," they sounded off in unison.

"Don't you ever hurt her like this again. You were raised better than this, and we expect more . . . now go on and get cleaned up. We've got work to do."

The boys stepped towards the door, but the farmer didn't move from the threshold.

"You're not coming in this house covered in that filth for your mama to have to clean up behind you. There's a water hose right there in the yard. Get to it."

The boys hung their heads and turned towards the yard. The hose was in the middle of the yard at the base of a grand pecan tree . . . every passerby on the dirt road would soon see them in the yard in their tighty-whities, and to make matters worse, the water would be freezing cold as it pumped up through the well from 400 feet down into the earth.

"This is all your fault," the oldest said.

"Shut up and turn the water on," came the response.

The farmer turned and finished cleaning up the glass and porcelain. While he picked up the pieces of the shattered glass, the image of her parents lay beneath the glass appearing fractured . . . he couldn't help but consider how the cold water would wash those boys clean. With each piece of glass he picked up, the image beneath became clearer, and with each splash of water, the boys became cleaner. Soon enough, all of the pieces were picked up, and the picture of her parents was safe and sound, undistorted by the fractures of life. The boys stood at the door, waiting to be told they could come in . . . washed clean from head to toe.

The farmer looked up at them and nodded . . . they came in the door and stood in the kitchen. "You boys understand what forgiveness is?" he asked. "Yes sir," the oldest responded. "When you are forgiven, the water of grace washes you clean . . . and takes away the shattered pieces of life and restores you whole . . . just like this picture." The younger of the two boys spoke first . . . "I'm sorry, Daddy. It's my fault. I was being selfish and wanted Tommy to get off the phone. I know I did wrong."

"Don't tell me," the farmer answered. "Tell your brother." A minute or two later, the boys had made up. They went to their mama and apologized to her again. Of course, she hugged them and told them how much she loved them and sent them to dry off and put on some clean clothes.

Tommy's trance of memories about the chipped sink was broken by thunder rolling across the ever-darkening sky . . . "Y'all been watching the weather, Mama?"

"James Spann is on there now," came the reply.

Tommy finished washing the thick grease and soot from his hands . . . the stains of life swirled around the sink and were carried down the drain by the cleansing water. Tommy shook his head as he remembered what his daddy told him all those years ago . . . "Thank you, Jesus," he said, as he grabbed the dishrag and dried his hands off.

Thunder rattled the windows again . . . as it settled to quiet, Spann's voice came clear again . . . "You folks in Bibb County need to be watchful. This is a pretty serious thunderstorm developing and headed your way. Let's keep a close eye on that storm as it tracks to the north and east."

Part Three

Tommy walked over to the kitchen window and looked across the 40-acre pasture to the south. The sky was gray, but he could see the lightning popping in the distance. Every few seconds, the sky would ignite . . . mostly from the same point on the horizon, more or less.

"One one-thousand, two one-thousand, three one-thousand . . ." Tommy counted to himself until the thunder cracked. "Dad, that storm is only about a few miles away. Maybe you should come take a look?"

The farmer walked into the kitchen and peered out the window. What seemed to be a thousand years of wisdom flowed from his squinty eyes . . . he had seen plenty of storms before. He lived through the Brent, Alabama, tornado in 1973. Taking five lives and leveling the town, that F5 tornado touched down 139 miles through Alabama. It was the longest track tornado in the history of the state. He still didn't like to talk about it . . . hiding in the basement at church as the tornado ripped the church apart, board by board . . . but everyone in the family knew he always paid attention when Mother Nature spoke. One man died in the church that morning. Thankfully, he and his parents, brothers, and sister were all safe. He respected weather because of that tornado.

"I've seen that look before," his wife said. "What do you see?"

The farmer shook his head just a little, but never broke his gaze to the south. He watched intently as the wall cloud formed beneath the thunderstorm that pushed northeast.

"Daddy?" Tommy prodded.

"Call you brother, and tell him they need to be paying attention," came the simple response . . . but Tommy understood the full message that was conveyed. Tommy was single and had no children. His two dogs would be fine, but his middle brother was married and had three kids. He picked up the phone and dialed the number.

"Hey, bro. Dad said to be paying attention . . . Yeah, from the south . . . Turn on the TV. Spann is on it. But look, it ain't far away. Pay attention . . . I don't know if it's a tornado or not! I'm just telling you Dad said to pay attention . . . alright . . . love you, too." And with that, he hung up.

Turning around, Tommy found his dad still staring out the window. He joined him at the edge of the sink, his fingertips subconsciously traced the outline of the porcelain chips missing from its edge. They both stared intently. Tommy alternated his gaze between the storm to the south and his father's eyes.

The storm raced north. The lightning now only allowed for two or three one-thousands before the thunder followed. In the moment, Tommy recalled his daddy teaching him the importance of the relationship between lightning and thunder.

They were fishing on the Alabama River, and a stormed loomed on the horizon to the south. "Don't we need to go, Daddy?" the younger 12-year-old Tommy asked. "Well, son, we probably have a few more minutes. That storm is still 20 miles away or so."

"How do you know?" Tommy asked.

"Good question. You see, thunder comes from an explosion that happens when lightning flashes," the farmer explained. Tommy had a puzzled look on his face. The farmer chuckled . . . "You see, when the explosion occurs, you see the lightning almost immediately, but you don't hear the sound of the explosion until a few seconds later. That's because light travels much faster than sound. So, you see it first, and then hear it."

Tommy nodded his head as if he was catching on, and then asked, "How do you know it's still 20 miles away?"

"Math," the farmer said. "See, sound travels about 1,100 feet per second. There are 5,280 feet in a mile. So, it takes sound about five seconds to travel a mile . . . more or less. When you see lightning, start counting . . . one one-thousand, two one-thousand . . . and so on. For every five counts you make before you hear thunder, you know that lightning is a mile way. If you count 10 seconds . . . two miles, 15 seconds . . . three miles. A few minutes ago, I counted . . . and I figure that storm is still 20 miles away."

Tommy never forgot that lesson from his childhood. He counted the seconds again . . . this storm is a mile away.

From the living room, Tommy heard his mother causing a commotion . . . "Let's go! Let's go!" she screamed. Turning the corner into the living room, Tommy saw the big red polygon on the television screen . . . James Spann sounded a cautious alarm . . . "You folks south of Centreville, y'all need to get to your safe place now."

Tommy turned to his daddy . . . "Come on, Daddy. It's time."

The farmer's wife led the way to the hall where Tommy grabbed a hook hanging from the wall and slipped it into a hole in the floor. Pulling upward, a door rose from the wooden planks, hinged and spring-loaded, almost like an upside-down set of attic steps. The farmer's wife went first, calling her house dog down the steps, too . . . the dog hesitated, and the farmer scooped it up as he made his way down the steps behind his wife. Tommy came last, pulling the door back down behind him.

"Make sure you bolt it shut," his mama reminded him.

He did as he was told. It was eerily silent in the storm shelter. Made of reinforced, triple-layered, cinder block walls all filled with concrete, the farmer built that room when he built the house. One solitary light bulb hung from the ceiling. The concrete floor was hard and cold. The ceiling in the room was steel, insulated with foam and wood . . . the farmer traded a local scrap dealer for the sheets of blued steel.

The room echoed . . . every tap or scratch was intensified . . . and any outside sounds were dulled. The three of them, each one to themselves, strained against the deafening silence, trying to hear anything. The farmer clicked on the radio he kept in the room, but he had not checked the batteries in probably a decade . . . it was useless.

"Quit fumbling with that thing," his wife chided. "I can't hear."

Seconds turned into a minute or more. Nothing. They heard nothing. They felt nothing.

"You reckon it passed?" Tommy asked.

The farmer's face remained steadfast and stern. He held his hand up slightly, as if to say, "Wait."

Tommy stood up and stepped towards the stairs. As he raised his hand to push open the door, the ground began to shake, and the penetrating sound of chaos pierced the room. The light bulb went out, and the room went dark . . . the wire feeding into the light bulb stripped from the fixture and vanished out of sight. The sound of fury was all around . . . tearing and cracking . . . crunching and breaking . . . like two ships colliding at full speed . . . Tommy covered his ears and ducked down. The farmer grabbed his wife and held her tight. The steel roof shuddered and vibrated, as if something strained to wrap its tentacles around the edge . . . trying to pull it away. In the pitch-black, the farmer felt dirt or dust or soot fall on his face and into his right eye. He looked down to try to keep it from penetrating further . . . his wife prayed out loud . . . he prayed silently.

Tommy just yelled, "Hoooollllddddd oooonnnnn!!!!"

Water. Water. The farmer felt water running down his back . . . pouring in from somewhere . . . he leaned forward to get out from its cold clutches as the house seemingly shook to pieces all around him. He felt his wife begin to sob in his arms . . . he pulled her tighter and spoke for the first time into her ear, "It's going to be okay. The storm will pass any second now." He felt her nod her head in acknowledgement as she tried to control her breathing. And he was right. In an instant, it was over, and the farmer opened his eyes for the first time since the dirt fell. He could see light around

Sunrise . . . whenever you see a setting sun, just take comfort that the Son always rises.

one side of the steel roof of the sheltered room. He fumbled around in the semi-darkness and made his way to the stairs. Pushing upwards, he couldn't open the door.

"Tommy, give me a hand." Together, they pushed open the door, and all three of them climbed the stairs.

They stood atop the storm shelter and looked around their yard . . . their yard. The farmer's wife began to cry. So did the farmer.

"Don't cry, Mama . . . We can rebuild. It'll be okay." Tommy tried to console his mother.

The farmer turned his face up to the sky and closed his eyes. The rain that fell washed his face clean. He took his hands and collected a little water and pulled it up over his eyes.

"James Spann saved our lives," the farmer's wife sobbed in gratitude.

"No," Tommy said. "Daddy . . . you saved our lives. This shelter . . . we'd be dead if it wasn't for you."

"No . . . you're both wrong," the farmer said graciously. "God saved us. He is the shelter . . . and don't you ever forget it."

God saved a farmer.

LAST MANGO
IN PARADISE

Hannah and I waded through the palm fronds and other underbrush as the trail snaked its way up the mountainside. The jungle canopy above was a dense, multilayered awning that held the sunlight at bay . . . and we were thankful for that, as it was reaching the mid-90s. A tropical depression was brewing southwest of our tiny island getaway off the Caribbean coast of Honduras, and it was drumming up the temperatures and the humidity. Our journey would lead us to an ancient Mayan burial ground some three or four miles to the other side of the almost uninhabited island.

We were younger then and in better shape . . . but the heat and the climb were still obstacles that worked against us. Pushing off with each step up the hillside, my knees ached as sweat poured from my scalp. Ahead on the right, we could see an opening in the canopy that caught our attention. Drawing closer, the canopy opened and revealed a mango tree, as beautiful as it was massive . . . and dripping with fruit, red and yellow and orange . . . deliciously tempting, low-hanging fruit.

Excited at the refreshing oasis, we needed a respite. Perched on a root under the tree, the wind found its way to us through the opening above . . . this mango tree was free from competition from other trees . . . imagine, if you will, a doughnut of no trees, and this mango served as the doughnut hole. I learned later that natives kept the area around the tree free from competing interests so the tree would thrive and its fruit would be easier to harvest.

Sitting on the massive root leg under the shade of the mango's enormous umbrella canopy as the wind tickled my face, I pulled out my handy Case knife and began slicing out mouthwatering pieces of the deliciously sweet, juicy mango. The fruit dripped as I cut, and it quenched the thirst of even the most dry-mouthed hiker. And, sweet? It was sweet like the kiss of my wife on a romantic Friday night . . . raw, unadulterated, pure, passionate mango . . . handpicked right from the tree. One piece of the fruit nearly "hit the spot" . . . a second piece would be just right, I thought to myself. Hannah, too, indulged . . . but only a few bites for her.

Another 10 minutes passed under the shade of the big leaves, and I felt fully recharged . . . no doubt, the natural sugars were already doing their best to rejuvenate my body! Our spirits and our energy renewed by the brief respite, we charged the hillside with a renewed vigor. The well-worn trail was easy to follow. Though the occasional fallen tree crossed our path, it was otherwise as clear as the path swept clean by the native leaf-cutter ants.

Known for their ferocious bites, these ants literally use their awesome mandibles to cut leaves, carrying them back to the colony to be used as forage material. They sweep the forest floor clear of all debris along the path where they travel to and fro, presumably to make the journey less tedious. It's quite an awesome spectacle to see firsthand . . . at 1½ inch wide, their highway thru the jungle is an unmistakable spectacle that snakes through the fallen debris at the feet of the giant trees looming overhead.

We ventured deeper into the jungle . . . the scurry of iguanas would occasionally unnerve us, as they always waited until we were relatively close to alert us to their presence, running off to the nearest tree to seek refuge. Large red parrots dotted the trees, and their warning calls to all around of our presence could be deafening at times. It was late fall, and they had young in their nests . . . we were a potential threat.

We took longer and harder steps as the hillside steepened a bit, and that was when the first sign of trouble appeared. It was a rumble of sorts . . . a deep, low growl. It almost sounded like distant, rolling thunder . . . and I could feel the deep bass vibrating in my core. Hannah heard it and stopped dead in her tracks. Her facial expression let me know she was alarmed . . . I studied her eyes as they intently focused on dense jungle . . . searching for the source.

A moment or two later, we heard another slow, drawn growl from the jungle floor . . . this time, more easily discernible as to its origin . . . Hannah turned back to me, searching over my shoulder into the midst of the canopy when, for a third time, the beast made its presence known. . . .

"Is that your stomach?" she confusedly asked, with a hint of trouble in her eyes. Sheepishly, I said, "Yes." We hadn't been married very long, and we had yet to cross the threshold of digestive destruction . . . and I had never intended to cross it in the depths of the Honduran rain forest. I knew I was in trouble, though . . . no amount of clinching or waddling would ever get me back to the safety of a modern-day bathroom. I was about to lose my modesty, my decency, and my lunch, all in one clean swoop.

I urged Hannah to move on up the trail, hoping she would get clear and out of sight, for I knew, given the massive amount of internal pressure I felt, that I was about to make Mount St. Helens look like a fire ant hill. Time was not my ally . . . she needed to walk faster . . . and quit laughing.

Thankfully, we had just passed a downed tree, perched parallel to the trail about 20 yards back. One end still resting on the stump, the other end made its way to the ground, and it was the perfect height. I looked up the trail and back again . . . content no one could see me, I pulled my britches down and eased down . . . shimmying back, finally relaxing. Just as I was about to unleash . . . I heard a crack and a pop. Panic set in, as I felt a slight drop in the log below me. It was too late, though . . . even the momentary pause in the momentum shift didn't give me enough time to react. Things were already set in motion that could not be undone.

Before I could shift my weight, the older-than-I-realized deadwood snapped under the pressure and back . . . and down . . . I went. Did I mention we were making our way up a mountain? This deadwood was perched alongside the trail . . . and a deep ravine . . . and I found myself tumbling backwards, end over end, shorts around my ankles, down into the depths of the ravine. I must have scored at least a 9.9 on the gymnastics floor dance routine because, when I finally came to a stop, every creature in the jungle was silent and staring at me . . . no doubt they were in pure awe.

I lay on the flat of my back, mentally taking stock . . . what hurt? Was anything broken? I still had to use the bathroom . . . my mind raced as I heard Hannah's voice, as if it faded into view. She started out asking if I was okay . . . then digressed to laughter. True love, no doubt. As I sat up, trying to orient myself to the steep slope, I felt the most intense and piercing pain I've ever felt on my buttocks near my hip. Surely, I've been stabbed, I thought. In an instant, the same measure of pain struck me on my opposite hip. I writhed away, trying to see over my shoulder what cactus-like plant was stuck in me. It was excruciating . . . and relentless. Now, a third probe jabbed me as I tried to squirm away, this time in my right thigh. It was agonizing, and the pain was radiating down both of my legs. As I writhed, I let out a blood curdling and involuntary scream that vibrated down the jungle ravine. Desperate, I contorted more than a circus act and finally found my attacker . . . leaf-cutter ants . . . and they were cutting me apart. By this point, I was dusting and brushing myself like a half-naked hummingbird just learning to fly, and these flesh-eating vampires were firing on all cylinders . . . communicating with their secret walkie talkie antennas, saying, "Bite him now!"
You know how ants do. Subconsciously, I started making all sorts of deals with God about what I'd do if I could just get away from these ravenous infantrymen, and I was charging up that hill faster than Teddy Roosevelt and the Rough Riders.

Somewhere at the bottom of the ravine were my pack, my shorts, and my underwear.

Free from the ants, I stood mid-trail wearing only a T-shirt and my tennis shoes . . . Ping-Pong-ball-size swollen nodules formed across my midsection as I gasped for air, still suffering tremendously from "gastric necessititus." Hannah surveyed me up and down with a devilish smirk on her face.

"Guess those mangos weren't quite ripe yet, huh?" she asked.

I quipped back, "Well, let's just say that you can bet your sweet behind that those were my 'last mangoes in paradise!'"

To this day, I don't know that I've ever eaten another one.

And that was all that was ever said about the whole fiasco. To this day, I still get the cold chills just thinking about it.

Someone once asked me what I thought hell would be like. I simply said, "An ant-infested hill in Honduras, covered with mango trees."

If you can't laugh at yourself, then you are missing out on a lot of the joy of life. Lord knows, I laugh at myself all of the time, and this day, Hannah surely did too!

— R E M E M B E R   T H A T   T I M E —
I   G O T   B I T   B Y   A   S N A K E ?

Every man has a morning routine. Some drink two cups of coffee while smoking three Marlboro Lights, then they head off to the throne, followed by a quick shower . . . mine used to be something like that. Still, other men rise early, run a mile or two, shower, and eat a bowl full of cereal before making their way to the throne. Others might read a devotional, have some prayer time, then go to the throne. And still, others might do any combination of these things . . . one being the throne.

Point is . . . every man's morning routine will always take him to a throne . . . and I don't mean the kind that's made out of gold.

And these routines are sacred. Ask any man.

Hannah knew my routine. She knew it was predictable . . . and sacred . . . and she knows not to interfere with my routine. Back then, my routine was to make a pot of coffee and drink a few cups of coffee before she got up, have some quiet time for prayer or reflection, then I'd fix her a cup, and we'd visit for a while . . . then I would go to the throne.

I don't know about you, but I like to read some. I like to read more when my other options are narrowed by my circumstances. I don't have a computer in my bathroom . . . fact is, I don't know anyone who does. And I suspect a laptop would be extremely cumbersome on the throne, so I read hunting and fishing magazines. I'll throw in an occasional gun magazine, and sometimes, the Bass Pro Shops Master Catalog. Those are all throne room essentials. When they come in the mail, Hannah will simply take them straight to the throne room. She knows that to place them anywhere else is a waste of time and space. And, truth be told, I rarely read any of those things outside of my morning routine. Fact is, those periodicals are part of my sacrosanct routine.

Every spring, several of the hunting magazines that I receive publish articles about snakes. Usually, the article includes amazingly detailed pictures that are always a great refresher course on the cues to look for in identifying poisonous snakes. I always have a little trouble distinguishing the various vipers that prefer the water, and since Hannah and I have lived on a lake or creek or pond for as long as we've been married, I always intensely study these springtime snake refreshers. Water moccasins are not my friend. I have no quarrel with most other water snakes—or even most snakes in general—but I aim to trample every moccasin under the heel of my boot.

There I sat on the throne, excited that, just a few days before, a new hunting magazine came in with what looked to be a great article about snake identification. Hannah thoughtfully put it in the bathroom for me. I was 300-words deep into rereading a vividly detailed article about all of the identifiers of a moccasin—complete with what had to be some of the most brilliant photography work ever—and I was intently interested in the subject matter of the article . . . namely, moccasins, copperheads, and banded water snakes. This was, in fact, the second or third time I'd read the article, as it had been in the bathroom a few days now . . . and each time, I'd exit the bathroom to seek out Hannah so as to impress her with my newfound knowledge of the treasonous vipers.

That day, I was more in tune with the photographs . . . studying each one intently, recalling the verbal descriptions from the article's text.

"You will notice that it has dark bands where its eyes are. It sort of looks like it's wearing a mask. Sometimes, the dark bands can go completely over and past their eyes starting from the tip of their nose. The dark bands can also start from the back of their eyes going towards the back of their heads."

I studied the pictures, surveying the dark eye bands so as to familiarize and remind myself. In some of the pictures, the moccasins have a raccoon-like appearance.

My study was disturbed by a stampede coming down the hallway. The thunder of feet pounded on the hardwood floors of the hallway and grew nearer and louder. I could tell that the herd turned into my bedroom and came to a rushing halt at the bathroom door. Cries of "Daddy! Daddy!" echoed in the bathroom. And, before I could even react, Hannah burst through the bathroom door, and the girls, some of them or all of them—I am not sure who was standing behind the door—panted furiously because of the excitement of whatever calamity troubled them.

"Come quick, Daddy!" a shrilled voice exclaimed. "It's the biggest moccasin I've ever seen, and it's about to bite Lincoln!"

Well, no red-blooded American male would not run to the aid of his best friend. So, without need of another ounce of encouragement, I sprang from my throne, tossed my magazine to the side—as I was now an expert on water moccasin identification— and bolted down the hall towards the back door of the house. My bravado and my underwear were all that I needed, and that was all I had.

I keep a loaded shotgun in a secret hiding place near the back door for occasions just such as this, and so, almost without missing a step or breaking stride, I retrieved that scattergun with a proficiency that even Wyatt Earp might envy. Running down the hall, I heard Hannah say in the faint distance behind me, "He's behind the truck!" I burst through the back door, gun in hand, and immediately saw my faithful dog, Lincoln, laying behind my truck.

"I'm too late . . . he's already been bitten," I thought to myself as I ran through the yard and up the hill to my dog. Lincoln was lying on his side, legs outstretched right behind my truck. I was out of breath by now, and my heart raced as I lowered that 12-gauge and furiously searched for the murderous crook that had slain my dog. "That's the best dog I ever had!" I vented to myself, already writing his eulogy. I paced all the way around the truck, looked in the yard on the edge of the driveway, and finally concluded that there could only be one place left for the slithering serpent to hide . . . he must be under my truck.

I would avenge Lincoln's death.

I backed up a step or two from the truck—to not lay down belly to belly with the heathen—and prone myself to the ground, shotgun in hand . . . and did I forget to mention that I was in my boxer shorts? The cold concrete sent a chill around my belly as the two connected, and the chalk dust from the driveway attached itself to me like a dust storm to a wet rag. My eyes scanned like military radar, my heart raced, and my nerves tinged.

Lying flat on the ground, I stretched out my arms so as to project the shotgun. My back ached in the unpropped arch of sweeping the gun under the truck to look for my foe. In that moment, simultaneously, three things happened:

First, my dog raised his head and made that questioning sound dogs will make, as if he asked, "What in the Sam Hill are you doing?"

Second, Hannah let out a belly laugh, the likes of which I've never heard from any woman who wasn't demon possessed.

Third, my neighbor hollered across the way, "Walt? Everything okay?"

Then, Hannah yelled something from the back door about April Fools' Day.

So, I stood up, shotgun in hand, picked my dignity up off the driveway, and strolled back into the house as if my boxer shorts were made of gold. I kindly returned the shotgun back to its residency and received cheers and was heckled from all the villainous women of my household as I returned back to my throne . . . and to my routine.

An old friend once told me to never take myself too seriously. He added that there is always something to be learned from laughing at yourself. It was advice well intentioned and well received. It has served me well through the years and works well to keep me grounded. In that moment, I couldn't help but laugh . . . even if Hannah was the snake. She got me . . . that she-devil! She got me good, and soon enough, the whole neighborhood would share great stories across the dinner table at my expense.

But my old friend is right . . . humility is a virtue. And there are few better ways to find humility than being the victim of a pretty good April Fools' Day prank.

I hope you, too, can find a way to laugh at yourself today. It's good for the soul. "A joyful heart," after all . . . "is good medicine." Proverbs 17:22, ESV.

And, in case you are wondering . . . yes, I think Lincoln was in on it, too. And even the best snake identification articles can't help you see the "snake that would of bit ya" if you're not looking in the right place.

— THE CATTLE DRIVE —

The dust rolled up off the dirt road like steam boiling up off a hot pot of coffee. It was thick, too . . . it choked at my throat as my red bandana did its best to keep the red dirt from finding its way to my lungs. I pulled that same bandana loose to wipe the stucco concoction of dirt and sweat from my forehead. The bandana had left a perfect crescent-shape tattoo . . . made from filtering the red clay dirt from my breaths inward. My cheeks were rosy from the red, and around my eyes, I wore a raccoon's mask of red clay, too. I beat the bandana against my knee and tied it taut back around my nose and mouth.

The clip-clop of metallic horseshoes rang against the hard clay bottom of the red dirt road. It was hypnotic. "Clip-clop. Clip-clop. Clip-clop." I stared into the herd of steers not too far ahead . . . their tails swishing and swatting back and forth, to and fro . . . their rumps sashaying along without a care in the world. Occasionally, one would lift his tail up and to one side. Instinctively, the herd that followed near behind the raised tail parted like the Red Sea . . . allowing the gestational deposit to drop and fall to the ground. Of course, cows probably give no second thought to their flatulence and such . . . I wish my nose could avoid it at times . . . but then again, the smell of red dirt, cows, horse sweat, and flatulence . . . well, there is only one place I've ever found that curiously intoxicating aroma—that is on Booger Brown's Annual Roundup Cattle Drive & Rodeo.

And it never fails that in those moments I'm blowing red dirt from my nose or arching my back to try to find some measure of comfort for my saddle-rotten butt . . . in those moments, I wish I was somewhere else. But any other time . . . like right now . . . I wish I was back in that saddle, riding around that herd, with my old friend, Booger, and some of those other cowboys.

I'm not a cowboy. Let's make that clear. Right now, I have on a suit and tie . . . and I am sitting in the lobby of the St. Clair County, Alabama, courthouse waiting on a capital murder case. But right now . . . my buddy Booger is in the saddle, pushing that herd. And I wish I was there with them.

Booger pulled the reins back on his milky brown gelding. The horse's white feet stopped and turned back towards me. Ten seconds later, my horse advanced its pace up next to Booger's horse. Booger always wears a smile as big as Kentucky . . . and he generally is a pretty happy fellow—although, like all of the rest of us, he wrestles steers

Booger Brown and I met many years ago at the Iron Works Men's Ministry, Old School Men's Meeting. He found his niche, just like I found mine . . . and occasionally, we meet again on the trail of life. Happy trails, old friend. Be sure to follow Booger on Facebook at BoogerBrown.

in life, too. His real name is . . . well, wait a minute . . . that might get me in trouble. I know his real name, and occasionally, I call him by his real name just to get under his skin. "Real name," I called out. He grinned and answered, "What's up, cowboy?"

"You know I ain't no dang cowboy. I never met a horse that didn't try to kill me. This one will, too," I said, gesturing down towards my steed. "Just give him time."

"That's a mare," Booger said laughingly. I leaned over in my saddle and strained my neck trying to look between the horse's legs. Honestly, I didn't know . . . hadn't paid attention . . . but I wouldn't have put it past Booger to have a little fun at my expense. And he almost did, for I leaned just far enough that I nearly fell off that horse and flat on my face.

"Easy there, partner," he said as he grabbed my shoulder. Pulling me back up, he admitted, "I was just kidding. It's a boy." Looking up at his ear-to-ear grin, I couldn't help but shake my head and laugh.

"Dang, if you ever get a ticket in Covington County, you are toast!"

He protested my humorous retort, "Come on now, that ain't fair!"

"You know what ain't fair?" I asked, not really concerning myself with whether he knew the answer. He leaned forward in the saddle and said, "What?"

"That you always stick me at the back of this herd. All I do is smell cow farts and eat red dirt. Last time I did this, I had a sinus infection for a week when we got home." I smiled broadly to let him know I wasn't really all that upset, but for good measure, I yelled out, "Don't you smell that!?!?"

Booger doubled over laughing at me. "Come on, Sasquatch," . . . a sarcastic reference to my outdoor adventures . . . "You have done far worse than this!" And he was right, but complaining about it and giving him a hard time were good distractions from the toil of the labor.

"You can go up front and lead or ride out on the edge and corral. But, what you gonna do if one of these steers cuts out? You may be a shepherd, but these ain't lost sheep," Booger said. He knew I couldn't rope at all. There was no way I could ever lasso a steer and bring him back to the herd. And, though I can ride better than most novice riders, I also wasn't eager to chase a steer down and try to cut him back to the herd. He knew he had me. I knew he did, too.

"What am I gonna do?" I asked with an air of defiance in my voice.

"That's right," he quipped.

"I'll tell you what I am gonna do," I smarted back at him.

"Alright then, tell me," he urged, elevating the octaves of his voice above mine.

"These are your cows, right?"

"That's right. Un-huh. So, what you gonna do?"

"Well, seein' as how they're your cows . . . I'm gonna watch that steer run off and not do a dadgum thing about it. If it was someone else's cow, I'd go get it. But not yours!" I howled with laughter, and he did, too. He shifted back in his saddle, tipped the brim of his hat back so his face was exposed, and then he played his ace of spades . . . "And that's why you're always gonna be in the back!"

What could I say? Not much . . . but I didn't come to be a cowboy. He knew that. Lord knows, Booger wouldn't have invited me because of my skills. I came for the fellowship and the brotherhood. And times like that are times I will never forget.

"Gitty-up, horse!" I nudged my steed in his ribs, and he picked up his pace slightly. The "clip-clop" hypnotics rang louder in my ears. I blew a dust blob from my nose, hocked up some dirt from the back up my throat, and spit out across the road. Looking over at Booger, I said, "It's been a good day, hasn't it, brother?"

"It sure has, old friend. It sure has."

Right now, as I type this story, I'm in between court at the courthouse in St. Clair County on a capital murder case. And, as I type this, Booger is out there on the trail, somewhere in Geneva County, Alabama, pushing that herd of steers. I know he is hot and sweaty and tired . . . his back hurts, and his hands are dried . . . his voice is raspy, and his sinuses are draining . . . and man, I sure do wish I was with him.

Maybe you know Booger from his television shows. Maybe you know him from some other way. I know him because, just like me, he is a regular guy trying to figure out when he is supposed to be in front of the herd, leading, and when he should be at the back . . . just following.

THE EXCHANGE

I walked out of the courthouse about 6:30 that evening. There was a bustle of familiar faces in the parking lot . . . our office manager, Erin Wilson, could not get her vehicle to start, and she had captured the help of Chief Nickey Carnley. Little Emma, Erin's daughter, scurried about in the parking lot kicking rocks as Erin's husband, Matt, pulled into the parking lot at about the same time I walked outside.

It was dusky dark, and the air was pleasant. But the heat of the midday sun still radiated from the black asphalt . . . the intense heat wafted across my face intermittently as I ventured across the parking lot. I could tell that Erin was having mechanical problems with her vehicle . . . the hood was up. I could also tell that Matt and Chief Carnley were already well underway to diagnosing and correcting the problem. I wanted to offer assistance . . . but not be in the way, for too many chiefs almost always lead to chaos.

Besides . . . I'm no mechanic. I couldn't offer much to the effort. I made small talk and generally stayed out of the way—offering moral support more than anything else. I was compelled to stay, though, until the other men sorted out the problem. I wasn't immediately sure why I was staying . . . they didn't need my help. I'm sure Erin appreciated the gesture, but probably would have agreed that it was altogether unnecessary. Even I, standing there watching the other two men wrestle with battery cables, thought to myself that my presence contributed nothing. Yet, I could not bring myself to leave. I was, in fact, compelled to stay for reasons I did not discern in that moment . . . though, they came to me as I began to type this story.

As Matt and Nickey unscrewed this widget and tinkered with that gadget, a solitary Chevrolet Suburban pulled into the other end of the dimly lit "Courthouse Employee" parking lot. No one stirred from the vehicle . . . it just sat idling. "Odd," I thought to myself with puzzled curiosity. I turned my attention back to the widgets for a minute. Little Emma was talking about ice cream. I was glad she was . . . cravings for ice cream are definitely contagious, and I had it in my mind to stop on the way home and buy a menagerie of ice cream flavors for Banks and me to feast on later that evening!

"Definitely some chocolate," I thought to myself. "And her favorite is cookies and cream . . . and I'll get some mint chocolate chip, too!" The vision of ice cream cones dancing in my head was interrupted by another vehicle entering the now empty courthouse parking lot. Empty that is, except for that lone Suburban . . . still idling. Now, this smaller sedan—a tannish brown Ford, I think—pulled in next to the Suburban. They both idled, as if they were lined up for the start of a drag race.

My naturally curious mind began searching itself for a rational explanation.

The movie theatre is adjacent to the courthouse, so I considered that possibility . . . but reasoned it away, for if they were going to the movies, they would have gotten out by now.

Ah, drug deal? Seemed a perfectly logical explanation. I considered calling one of the guys I knew that was on patrol that night. But my mind went back to exploring other possibilities.

Perhaps it's teenaged Romeo and Juliet secreting themselves away from friends . . . no, can't be that. Were it so, the boy would have been to the other car like Flash Gordon.

My mind searched. The widgeting continued. Emma tinkered in her school backpack . . . the rocks of the parking lot no longer gathered her attention. (You know a child is beyond bored when they resort to school obligations for entertainment.) Erin did what every good wife does while us men spread our peacock tail feathers and strut for our wives . . . she attentively held the flashlight. I chuckled a bit to myself, thinking of all the times I worked so hard to impress Hannah with my ability to fix or do or build or whatever . . . and with tail feathers spread proudly for the strut, I would require her to participate in some mundane manner . . . holding the flashlight, for example. I had to laugh at myself, because she was rarely as impressed with my feathers as I was. And I am certain, as I take this glimpse into the rearview mirror of life, that it was my perspective that was flawed . . . not hers.

As for me . . . I was trying to watch the two cars without being obvious.

"Don't mind me, I'm just kicking rocks," I thought as I ambled about in the parking lot trying not to act too interested in the two vehicles.

"Oh look, I'm just looking at my phone . . . not paying any attention to you people in the car," I thought as I tried to navigate into position to get a picture of one of the car tags.

"I really appreciate the architecture of the O'Neal Building," I thought as I pretended to crane my neck upwards toward the rooftop of a nearby building as the male occupant of one of the vehicles looked up and our eyes met.

I had made my way halfway across the parking lot, kicking rocks and ambling, when the passenger door to the Suburban opened. A little boy, no more than 10 years old, stepped down out of the truck. He, too, had a backpack and an overnight bag and what appeared to be some sort of toy truck. He waddled around behind the truck, labored by his load . . . and I don't mean the bags he carried.

He was met at the rear of the truck by an adult man. "Daddy!" I could hear him shout with excitement. The boy's dad glanced my way as he stooped down and scooped his son up, embracing him with what could only be the long hug of reunion.

The boy's mom now stepped from between the two vehicles . . . the boy turned back to her, twisting from his dad's arms . . . toy truck still in hand. "Bye, Mommy. I love you!" the boy said. That was his labored load. He didn't want to leave, but he wanted to go with his daddy, too. His mom reached out and gave him a big hug. I couldn't see them, but I know there were tears in her eyes.

The boy's mom and dad spoke courtesies, but that was all. Soon enough, everyone got back into their vehicles, and the procession receded back into the darkness of the night.

Dad and son will no doubt have an awesome weekend together. I hoped their time was to be filled with wigglers and fishing poles; watching wrestling on TV, followed by debates about whether the blood on the wrestler's head was real; building roads in the yard for that toy truck; and eating pork and beans straight from the can . . . because that's what dads and sons ought to do . . . and so much more.

The boy's mom is probably going back to an empty house. There was no indication that she or the boy's dad had remarried. She might fall into a Lifetime movie and a glass of red wine . . . she might cry a little . . . she will blame it on the movie, but it's really because she misses her little one . . . and probably because life didn't turn out the way the little girl she once was had planned.

That little boy is her world now. He is all she has, and she struggles to share him, even though "he" is the father.

Worst part, though . . . is that "little man" didn't choose this. He is just trying to get through the highs and lows of it all. Sure, he is excited to see his dad, and he can't wait for the big adventures of tomorrow, but tonight won't be the same because he is so used to sleeping with his mom nearby. He will, no doubt, be excited to see mama again on Sunday afternoon, but he will miss "coming off the top rope" and crashing into his dad's stomach while yelling things about "Macho Man" Randy Savage . . . or whoever the famous wrestlers are today.

Divorce sucks from a kid's perspective. Don't ever underestimate that.

The day before, I'd spent two hours with a 20-year-old kid who was in jail for trafficking in drugs. He was a drug addict. A bad drug addict. He started smoking marijuana when he was 13 years old and progressed from there to other things. Ask him why . . . he'll start talking about his parents' divorce and his relationship with each of them.

Divorce hurts from a kid's perspective. I'm 48 years old now. Trust me, I know. It still hurts.

I usually try to end every story with a positive morale . . . but sometimes, the emotion of it all can overtake me. As I dwell on those exchanges between my own parents and my heart aches for the pain that I know waits for that little boy . . . here is the best I can muster.

Matt and Nickey finally got Erin's truck running . . . and Banks and I ate a lot of ice cream that night before Hannah got home.

Hug your spouse, and make sure they know how much you love them. Then, hug your children and make sure they know how much you love them. If you're divorced, make sure they also know that you understand how hard their struggle is . . . because it is.

"What therefore God has joined together, let not man put asunder" Mark 10:9 KJV.

It's fitting that we come to the end of Volume 2 with this story. A story of rescue interlaced with a story of children heartbroken by divorce. I hope this book inspires someone to rescue a child . . . perhaps their own. I pray it stirs sparks in marriages, such that there is never a meeting in a dimly lit parking lot to make an exchange. It is my wish that this book leaves a positive mark on families far and wide . . . because after all, we are called to be the light.

CLOSING THOUGHT

And here we are . . . the last few pages of what I hope you have found to be a "good book." I remember when I finished *Where the Red Fern Grows*. I felt as though I lived those Ozark adventures and endured the sleepless nights of coon hunting right alongside Old Dan and Little Anne. And after the finale, I felt like a boy who had been dragged headfirst into manhood . . . and my two best companions were left behind. I also cried with joy when Scout looked up at the fellow hiding behind the door and said, "Hey, Boo." Boo Radley, the misunderstood recluse turned hero of *To Kill a Mockingbird* saved Scout's life. For the first time, she understood he was a friend. Her revelation changed me and my observations of the people around me.

As a lawyer, I've long aspired to hold some measure of the respect Atticus Finch held in the fictional town of Maycomb. I didn't fully appreciate the scene Harper Lee described at the end of Tom Johnson's trial until I was in my twenties. Johnson was wrongfully convicted of a crime he did not commit, and Atticus lingered in the courtroom after the jury pronounced their verdict. The white members of the segregated galley had retreated out the back doors of the courtroom, but the black galley, upstairs in the balcony, waited patiently. As Atticus started down the aisle of the courtroom, all the balcony galley stood. They stood out of respect, for though the outcome of the trial was not what they had hoped, they respected that Atticus did what was right. Reverend Sykes scolded Scout. "Miss Jean Louise, stand up," he said. "Your father's passin'."

John Grisham's *A Time to Kill* was another "good book." So was Harry Homewood's *Run Silent, Run Deep*, Fred Gipson's *Old Yeller*, Mark Twain's *Huckleberry Finn*, and Jean Craighead George's *My Side of the Mountain*. These books left me with feeling. Some made me laugh. Others made me cry. But every "good book" I've ever read made me feel something.

But there is truly only one "Good Book." That book is the Holy Bible. It tells the story of the greatest protagonist ever written about. So great was this protagonist that as I read Acts Chapter 4, I feel as though I am standing in court with Peter and John as Peter declares that it is "better to be judged right in the eyes of God than in the eyes of man." Knowing Peter and John were so bold in their faith as to defy the threat of imprisonment should they ever preach the name of Jesus I feel "something." That "something" changed my life because I carry it with me every day.

So, as you turn the page on this, the last page of this book, I hope you feel something. I hope you feel love and joy; heartache and sorrow; peace and tranquility; urgency and intensity; but most of all . . . I hope you feel as though you were there with us . . . every step of every adventure.

"As iron sharpens iron, so a man sharpens the countenance of his friend." Proverbs 27:17, NKJV. God bless.